NEXT STOP ON GRANDPA'S ROAD
HISTORY & ARCHITECTURE OF
NC&ST.L RAILWAY DEPOTS & TERMINALS

BY
TERRY L. COATS

GRANDPA'S ROAD PUBLISHING,
GOODLETTSVILLE, TENNESSEE

© 2009 by Terry L. Coats

All Rights Reserved

No portion of this book may be reproduced in any fashion, either mechanically or electronically, without the express written permission of the author. Short excerpts may be used with the permission of the author or the publisher for the purposes of media reviews.

Second Edition, December 2013
Second Printing, September 2014
Third Printing, March 2015
Fourth Printing, March 2016
Fifth Printing, December 2017
Sixth Printing, April 2019

Printed in the United States of America on acid-free paper

ISBN 978-0-578-48832-5

LCCN 2010921557

Edited by Bob Allen

Cover design and interior layout by Joyce Dierschke

Photographs and illustrations provided by the author

Published by and available from:

Grandpa's Road Publishing
226 Swift Drive
Goodlettsville, Tennessee 37072
www.ncstldepots.com

TO GRANDDADDY AND GRANDMAMMA
WHO TAUGHT ME TO LOVE TRAINS.

ALPHEUS FINCH BRADBERRY
1902–1983

VIRGIE LEE (SANDERFER)
BRADBERRY
1908–1990

Nashville, Chattanooga & St. Louis Railway
~ Grandpa's Road ~

The Nashville, Chattanooga & St. Louis Railway was an extraordinary railroad. The Nashville & Chattanooga, the forerunner of the NC&St.L, was the pioneer railroad in the State of Tennessee. The road had a long and glorious history from the time of its chartering in 1845 through the time of its merger into the Louisville & Nashville Railroad in 1957.

Emerging from the disastrous years of the War Between the States, the company set upon a path of becoming one of the most prominent railroads in the South. A hostile stock buy out by the L&N would curtail those efforts. But even the controlling reigns of the L&N would not stop the NC&St.L from its mission of becoming one of the most progressive rail systems of all times.

A railroad is made of iron and steel but its real strength comes from a human element. The NC&St.L was special because of its people. Their esprit de corps and devotion to the railroad itself set it apart from any number of other railroads. They loved Grandpa's Road … and it showed.

It was not that its locomotives were built out of stronger steel than other roads' or that its depots were constructed with wood superior to other structures … it was just that the railroad was built well and maintained well. All of its physical plant was well treated, not just because of company policy, but because of personal pride in a job well done.

This was further borne out by the people touched by the railroad; its shippers and passengers. Most of the NC&St.L depots and stations are but a memory now, the shippers moved on to other companies for the transportation of their goods, the automobile and the airplane displaced the lure of the passenger train, much of the rails and ties have long since been abandoned, those of us who remember the railroad first-hand and those of us who have studied the history of the line are saddened at the loss.

It is hoped that through pictures and the written history, that the love of this railroad will remain alive. As you enjoy this history, and travel Tennessee, Kentucky, Alabama, and Georgia remember the times and the romance of the train. You might take a little time to stop and visit some of the still remaining stations along the way.

Dain L. Schult
Nashville Chattanooga & St. Louis Preservation Society

Foreword

Author Terry Coats recounts memories of yesteryear ... the allure and the hustle and bustle of the hometown depots and stations along the Nashville, Chattanooga & St. Louis Railway, known to many as *Grandpa's Road*. Whether it was a depot or station in a *whistle stop* town or union station in a major city, people from all walks of life and most of the products and goods we consumed came through the depots and stations.

Parents sent their children to college on the train, mothers and wives sent their sons and husbands to war, men left for business trips, relatives came to visit ... all by train. America moved by the railroad.

If you were a farmer, it would be through the freight depot the product of your labors would go to market. If you operated the local gin, mill, or small manufacturing plant, the depot would be the portal through which you shipped your goods ... so that in another depot they could ultimately make their way to the consumer.

The local station served a multitude of functions in addition to being an area for passengers to wait for their trains ... offices for the railroad company to conduct its business, the agent in charge to control the movement of the trains, the local telegraph, and the Railway Express Agent. They also served as a freight house or livestock yards, and in most towns became the local gathering place as well.

How many precious memories surrounding the depots and stations can you recall? While most are gone today, we remember them fondly. The reader will laugh, cry, and feel proud remembering the *good ole days* and a living a romance with history lost.

Terry Coats takes you back in time with his well researched history of the Nashville, Chattanooga & St. Louis Railway and its depots and stations and includes many interesting and lesser known historical facts. Do you know the only depot in Tennessee that you can only get to from Alabama, or the only battle in U. S. history where the cavalry defeated the navy, or how the *Panic of 1837* was ghostly similar to our economy and government response of today. With numerous photographs and floor plan illustrations of nearly every depot and station along the road, you will be able to see and point out to your children and grandchildren where you were when you fell in love with the railroad and your hometown depots and stations.

Bob Allen
Editor

Acknowledgements and Credits

This volume would have been impossible to produce without the gracious and substantial contribution of photographs, drawings, and guidance from many persons.

I am indebted to several persons and institutions for allowing me access to their railroad photographic collections. Without their help, this volume would have been a large collection of words with no visual aids.

I have drawn heavily on the photo collections of the following:

- National Archives, College Park, Maryland
- Tennessee State Library and Archives
- Marietta Museum of History
- H. C. Hill, III, collection of his Grandfather H. C. Hill official photographer for the NC&St.L Railway
- Charlie Castner, The L&N collection at the University of Louisville
- Terry Bebout
- Allen Hicks
- Mark Perry
- Dr. William O. Greene, III
- Dain L. Schult
- Dennis Lambert
- Tom R. Knowles
- Beth Arnold Lee, collection of her father William Arnold Photography Studios
- The late Bob Bell, who graciously shared his photo collection with those who loved railroading

We all owe a large round of appreciation to those who over the last fifty-five years worked so diligently to save the marvelous old depots, section houses, and other the structures of the Nashville, Chattanooga & St. Louis Railway. I especially want to thank the people and municipalities who purchased and preserved these old NC&St.L stations. These buildings were refurbished as homes, businesses, museums, offices, and storage buildings. In my four years of researching these structures, without exception, the current owners opened their homes and offices to me and helped in any way they could in my efforts to document the depots. Thank you all.

I want to thank those who encouraged and advised me in the writing of this book.

And to my wife, Jane, who I have seen too little of over the last four years as I spent time on this project and who accompanied me on more than her share of explorations to remote parts of four states to locate and document these remaining depots. I love you.

Terry L. Coats

Contents

Introduction 1

Coming of the Railroad 4
    Impact of Railroads on the American South 5
    Railroads Come to Tennessee 7

History of the Nashville Chattanooga & St. Louis Railway 12
    Before the Coming of the Railroads 12
    Railroading In Its Infancy 15
    Birth of the Nashville & Chattanooga Railroad 17
    Prelude to War 20
    Nashville & Chattanooga Railroad: The War Years 20
    1870s to 1890s: The NC&St.L Comes of Age 24
    Tennessee 1897 Centennial and International Exposition 31
    The 1890s 33
    United States Rail Administration 37
    Dutchman's Curve: Worst Passenger Train Wreck in American History 38
    Boom or Bust 39
    1941 to 1950: Decade of Re-growth 40
    Chattanooga's Attempt to Evict the Railroad 45
    Passenger Train Travel after World War II 46
    End of a Dynasty 53

Down at the Depot 56

Gone But Not Forgotten 59

Train Management and The Agent-Operator 62
    The Telegraph 64
    Timetable and Train Orders 65
    Semaphore Signal 68
    CTC on the NC&St.L 68

Segregation on the Railroad 71

Standardization 75
    Gothic Revival or Carpenter Gothic Architecture 81
    Inherited Depots from Other Lines 82
    Queen Anne Architecture 84
    Non-Traditional 85

Terminals 87
    Nashville 88
        First Railroad Stations in Nashville 88
        Nashville & Chattanooga Railroad 1854 Union Depot 90
        Union Station 93
        1897 Tennessee Centennial and International Exposition 95
        Construction Begins on the New Terminal 98
        Bats and Ghosts in the Belfry 109
    Chattanooga 110
        First Combination Depot 110
        1859 Union Station 111
        1882 Victorian Passenger Depot 112
    Atlanta 114
        1853 Train Shed 115
        1871 Union Station 117
        1930 Union Station 120
    Memphis 121
        Early NC&St.L Terminals 121

Chattanooga Division 129
    Cumberland Mountain 130
    Shelbyville Branch 133
    Cowan and Pusher District 133
    Tracy City Branch; "The Mountain Goat" 134
    University of the South 137
    NC&St.L Motor Transit Company 137
    Sequatchie Valley Branch 139
    Orme Branch 140
    Lebanon Branch 141
    Train Depots in Lebanon 143
    Old Hickory Powder Plant Branch 144

Nashville Division: "The Windy" 165
    Nashville & Northwestern Railroad 165
    Centerville Branch 173

Huntsville Division 188
    Winchester & Alabama Railroad.. 189
    Huntsville & Elora Railroad 190
    Tennessee & Coosa Railroad 190
    Huntsville to Hobbs Island 191
    Hobbs Island to Guntersville Barge Transfers: "The NC&St.L Navy" 192
    Sparta Branch 193
    Columbia Branch: Duck River Valley Railroad 194
    Middle Tennessee & Alabama Railway... 197

Paducah & Memphis Division 208
    Tennessee Midland Railway Company 208
    Paducah, Tennessee & Alabama Railroad 209
    World's Longest Single Truss Bridge.. 209
    Hollow Rock and the Bruceton Yards... 210

Western & Atlantic Division 225
    Western & Atlantic during the Civil War 229
    Georgia Politics and the Railroads.. 234
    Rome Railroad 233

Adaptive Uses 241

Appendices ....
    Railroad Abbreviations and Names 254
    Railroad Terms and Definitions 260
    Constructions, Acquisitions, and Leases of the N&C and NC&St.L
    Railway 1850-1957... 264
    Historical Timeline.. 267
    Station Locations, Mile Markers, and Facilities 274

Index 307

INTRODUCTION

In the late 1970s, I had personal business cards printed. Atop the cards I chose to affix the Nashville, Chattanooga & St. Louis Railway logo. On more than one occasion after I presented my card to someone they would remark, "Oh, do you work for the railroad?" I would have to politely answer, "No, I did not work for the NC&St.L and then go on to explain that the railway had gone out of business in 1957 when I was only seven years of age." The fact is that neither I nor anyone else in my family ever worked for the NC&St.L. When we lived in Memphis, my father for a short time in the early 1950s painted boxcars for the Illinois Central Railroad. That is as close as I have come to having any railroad connection.

This was not the case in so many other families. It seemed that when just one person in these families worked for the NC&St.L, almost everyone in that family worked for the NC&St.L. For as long as can be remembered, the Nashville, Chattanooga & St. Louis Railway had been referred to by the endearing term, *"Grandpa's Road"* or the shortened *"Grandpa."* Throughout the history of the *road* you would have found a great proportion of sons, brothers, uncles, fathers, and grandfathers all working for the NC (NC&St.L) In some cases there were even daughters who followed their fathers in service to the NC.

In the 1990s the merged L&N and Seaboard Railroads referred to itself as the *"Family Lines,"* a moniker someone in the public relations department of the L&N and Seaboard Railroad gave the combined lines. But, long before the 1990s merger, it was the NC&St.L that could claim to be a true family line in a blood and fraternal relationship.

Because I have no direct connection to the NC&St.L, it might seem strange that I now find myself writing a book on the subject of the Nashville, Chattanooga & St. Louis Railway. How did I come to this point? The answer is fairly simple. Between the ages of six and ten I lived in Dresden, Tennessee. Our house was within seventy-five yards of the Dresden, NC&St.L depot. Many evenings of my youth were spent lying in bed listening to the passing of a NC&St.L freight train … no more than a short train's length from my bedroom window. Additionally, many of my days were spent at the Dresden train station in the company of Mr. Samuel A. Butts, agent-operator in Dresden.

Dresden, Tennessee Mile Marker 132.0, built 1891.
-*L&N Collection, University of Louisville*

Samuel Arthur Butts was born and reared near Kingston Springs, Tennessee. He hired onto the NC&St.L on November 16, 1907 when he was in his early twenties. He became the protégé of Mr. W. C. West, the station agent at Kingston Springs. At the tutelage of Mr. West, Sam learned telegraphy, completing the course in

less than eleven months. His date of employment was November 16, 1907, with his first assignment being a telegraph operator in a boxcar station at Mays Trestle. Mr. Butts worked at Kingston Springs until its closing on May 31, 1938. Seeking a different assignment, Sam bid for the station agent's job at Dresden, a position held at that time by his brother Joseph Butts. Because Sam had more seniority, Joseph was rolled from his job in Dresden and transferred to the station at McKenzie, Tennessee, where he took the position as freight agent. On June 12, 1938, Mr. Sam took over the agent's position at Dresden and worked at that station through the 1957 L&N merger, and finally retired as an L&N employee in 1965.[1]

Samuel Butts, Agent, Dresden, Tennessee, ca. 1955. -*Samuel Butts, Jr. Collection*

In a 1957 interview with the Dresden Enterprise newspaper, Mr. Butts stated that, "He enjoyed his job very much and that the people of Dresden were the finest people he knew to work with… it has been a pleasure to serve them." Of course this type of comment is just the type of statement you would expect from an employee of the NC, an employee of Grandpa's Road.

To date there have been three definitive books written on the history of the NC&St.L Railway. The 'bible' of all NC&St.L histories is the 1967 book by Richard E. Prince, *Nashville, Chattanooga & St. Louis Railway: History and Steam Locomotives.* Next in this series was the 1995, *Nashville, Chattanooga & St. Louis Railway: The Dixie Line,* by Charles Castner. In 2001, my friend and Nashville, Chattanooga Preservation Society President, Dain Schult, undertook writing a third history of this marvelous line when he completed his, *Nashville, Chattanooga & St. Louis: A History of "The Dixie Line."* For a diverse look at the history of the NC&St.L and as a reference to the steam locomotives of the road may I suggest you read these books?

The subject of this book is the depots and other structures of the Nashville, Chattanooga & St. Louis Railway. It was my intent to limit the scope of this book to that topic without writing yet another history. The history of the railroad was covered quite adequately in the three earlier works. As my work on this book progressed, I soon realized that in order to tell my readers about the depots, many of which were inherited through mergers, I would have to at least write a cursory account of the railroads past and about the mergers. You will find an abbreviated account of these facts later in this book.

Though the NC&St.L has been gone for over fifty years, there are many of us who remember those yellow striped boxcars and the blue and Confederate gray diesels that once

---

1   The Dresden Enterprise and Sharon Tribune. March 15, 1957.

passed the depots of our small towns and called at the terminals of our cities.

I wrote this book in remembrance of my youthful days spent at a NC&St.L depot in Dresden, in remembrance of Samuel A. Butts who introduced me to the NC, in remembrance of one of the most progressive and innovative railroads to traverse the rails, and to honor the memory of those men and women who dedicated their careers to the Nashville, Chattanooga & St. Louis Railway and *Grandpa's Road*.

Terry L. Coats
February 2010

Engineer and Fireman. -*Mark Womack Collection*

Coming of the Railroad

It is hard to imagine a rural United States before the coming of the first railroads. We must turn to contemporary documentation from that time to give us a glimpse of an era when transportation from place to place and the cartage of materials was done either on foot, by horse and wagon, or by flatboat and steamboat.

Up until the late 1700s, ninety percent of all inhabitants in this country lived within five miles of a navigable stream or an ocean. Slowly these people who had called the delta regions of the east coast their homes began to forge inroads through the gaps in the passes of the Appalachian Mountains. As they ventured overland, the first white traders used natural paths made by Native Americans and the bison before them to find their way into the wilderness or they traversed rivers and streams using canoes and small watercrafts.

In 1775, Daniel Boone opened the Wilderness Road from North Carolina into Kentucky and then into the Tennessee Valley. By the early 1800s, the Cherokee, Creek, and Choctaw allowed the Federal Government to cross their territories with mail routes, but the Native Americans kept control of the area by owning and operating all inns and ferries on the turnpikes and rivers in the area.[2]

As statehood took hold in the expanding areas of Tennessee County, North Carolina, courts were allowed to build the first primitive roads in the state. Around 1811, the federal government built the first turnpikes on a national scale.

Even with the improvements of the infrastructure prior to 1850, there was little connection between the Great Lakes, the Mississippi Valley, and the seacoast on the Atlantic Ocean. The only connection between these areas was by river, lakes, canals, or a link of very primitive dirt and macadamized roads. In the late 1840s, this condition would slowly begin to change as railroads began operations. America's first railroad companies did not form in an attempt to bridge this transportation gap all at once. Small incremental steps were taken to slowly reach out from one area to another. The money to build the first railroads came from the private sector. Investors were solicited from those whose land was in proximity to the proposed right of way and from businessmen in terminal cities where the railroads would locate. To these investors, the railroads would bring prosperity, profits, and commerce. Even with the new interest by financier, the building of railroads in America got off to a slow start. As late as 1850, there was no more than 7,500 miles of rails in the entire country.

The coming of the railroads also meant expansion. A city of any size relied on a daily

---

2   *Tennessee: A Guide to the State*, Complied by the Federal Writers' Project of the WPA for the State of Tennessee, Transportation Chapter. December 1939.

supply of fresh food. Without modern preservation, food would have to come from no farther away than it could be carried in one to two days travel; a factor that had limited the growth of cities from ancient times. The establishment of a faster moving rail system allowed food to be shipped from a great distance away and still retain its freshness. Up until this time, growth of inland towns had been retarded because trade from those towns was restricted to local markets only. The coming of the railroads would for the first time in recorded history allow cities and towns to grow at an unrestricted rate.

As America pushed west, settlements were made at riversides because the towns relied on the water for commerce and transportation. The first railroads built in the United States were as connectors between these waterways cities. Raw materials would be brought by the railroads to towns like Memphis, Nashville, and Chattanooga so those materials could be loaded onto boats for movement by water. Later, these railroads would go into head-to-head competition against the flatboats and paddle wheelers to link inter-waterway cities to the seaports.

Impact of Railroads on the American South

Early American Homestead in the South

The American South of the early 1800s was an agrarian society. The farms of this period were self-sustaining enterprises on which the farmer would raise a diversity of crops, mostly for the consumption at his own family table. True to his Celtic ancestry, he also raised his own livestock. On most farms, you would have found hogs, cattle, sheep, and some poultry. He was a jack of all trades. He plowed his fields, cut his own firewood and made much of the articles he would use in his daily life. Using the flax and cotton from their fields and the wool sheared from their sheep the family produced homespun clothing. Many, but not all, of the consumer goods used by the family would be produced on the homestead as well. Rustic furniture, soap, candles, and some of the farm tools were among the items produced. When an item could not be produced on the farm, it would have to be purchased.

The typical farm family was generally able to barter certain items, such as eggs, milk, tobacco, or any increase in livestock, for the commercially produced items needed. In the 1830s there was not a great deal of profit in farm-raised products. Eggs were selling for no more than four or five cents a dozen, butter might bring eight to ten cents a pound, and other

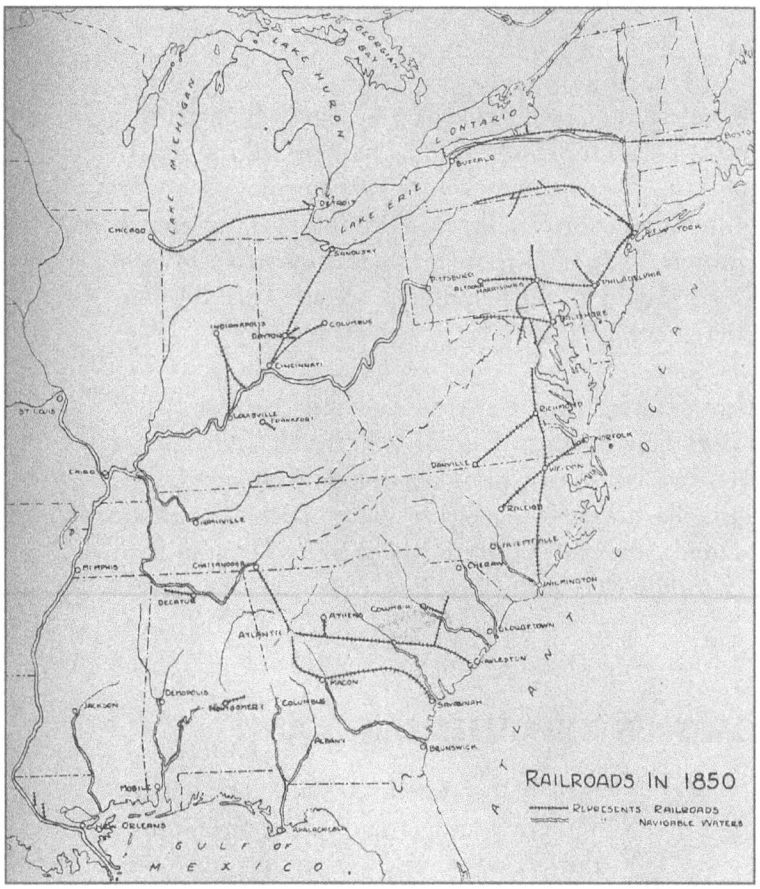

Railroad Map from 1850

farm products only brought a proportional price. These items could be exchanged for needed items such as plows, cloth, shoes, and sugar; items that could not be produced on the home front. These finished products usually brought premium prices in comparison to what the farm products brought. It was a meager existence at best.

As communities grew, the inhabitants developed a trading network with their neighbors as well as with the general store at the crossroads. This system worked well for local trading, but more was needed for trading on a commercial scale. When the farmer harvested his annual crop, when the local tannery, gin or lumber mill needed to bulk ship to large town such as Nashville, shipment would have to be carried by the wagonload to a river port and then barged down the waterway to its destination. In some cases, the shipment would be carried overland by wagon to its destination. These overland trips however were very time consuming and costly endeavors. A two-hundred mile roundtrip over the terrible roads of the day could take as long as ten days to complete. Shipping down the river by packet boat was not much better. Shipments were sporadic at best and when the rivers were frozen or the water level was low, traffic stopped completely.

It must have been welcome news in Tennessee and Georgia when the first talk of building of railroads was announced. A fast moving train using a direct route to the city would surely expedite the movement of materials from these rural areas. An additional benefit to the farmers would be that for the first time they would be able to import and export through the same channel. Up until that time, inhabitants in rural areas would usually ship raw materials to one port and receive finished goods from another. The industrialization of southern cities helped by the coming of the railroads decentralized much of the manufacturing monopolies held by northern cities. No longer would the planter send flax and tobacco to New Orleans to purchase farm equipment or other finished products from New England.

RAILROADS COME TO TENNESSEE

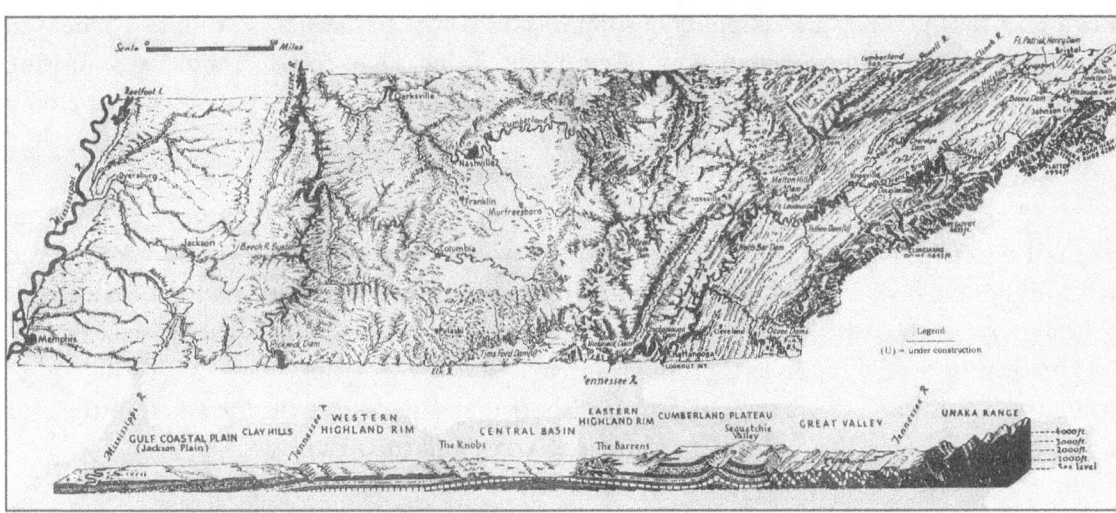

State of Tennessee topographical map. -*Terry L. Coats Collection*

Before the introduction of the railroad to Tennessee, transportation was limited to the speed a man could walk or, at best, how fast a horse could pull a wagon or a stagecoach … a three day journey to the east coast and ten days to Philadelphia or New York. It is hard to believe, but the first president of the United States traveled no faster nor in any more comfort than did the pharaohs of Egypt or the Caesars of Rome. The introduction of the railroad would dramatically reduce that travel time.

In 1804, there was such a limited amount of roads in the state of Tennessee; the state let bids to local county governments encouraging them to build roads and bridges and to establish ferries. Progress moved slowly. It would not be until 1831 that the first macadamized road would be built in the state.[3]

Though northeast Tennessee was the first section of the state to be settled; the first years of the nineteenth century saw the frontier push further west into the middle and western parts of the state. A shift in population was affected as frontiersmen migrated to the waterways of the Cumberland basin in middle Tennessee, and the Tennessee and Mississippi Rivers in the western part of the state.

Interest in railroads in the state developed as early as the latter part of the 1820s but this interest did not sweep the state as a huge wave. The Tennessee General Assembly granted six charters for railroad construction in 1831, but when none of the companies granted a charter could raise additional financial backing, the efforts withered. There was a reason for

---

[3] *Tennessee: A Guide to the State*, Complied by the Federal Writers' Project of the WPA for the State of Tennessee, Transportation Chapter. December 1939.

the lack of enthusiasm. The four largest cities of Tennessee … Knoxville, Nashville, Memphis, and Chattanooga … all developed along the banks of a major river. Each relied heavily on the steamboat for the influx and shipping of supplies and at first city leaders saw no real benefit in expending large amounts of money to develop railroading when the steamboat was meeting their needs.[4] This mentality would change; the railroads would come, but it would be on a retarded timetable.

East Tennesseans would be the first to endorse the railroads; they saw the building of a rail system as a way to counteract the shift of power that was ebbing away to central and west Tennessee. It was thought that a rail link to the ports in Charleston and Savannah would counterbalance the natural river routes afforded the other two sections.[5] The same basic idea was not lost on west Tennesseans. Though situated on the Mississippi River with a myriad of tributary streams and rivers on which to transport materials, astute businessmen in the area were anxious to develop a rail system to the east coast and the Atlantic.

One of the earliest railroads to charter in the United States and the first in Tennessee was the Nashville & Chattanooga Railroad. The chartering of the N&C by the state of Tennessee on December 11, 1845 set in motion a history of a very progressive and innovative company. From its chartering until its closing in 1957, the NC&St.L, as it would be named later, would have a profound effect on the social, economic, and political life of all the communities through which its tracks passed.

In January 1847, Colonel Vernon K. Stevenson, the future president of the Nashville & Chattanooga Railroad, addressed the legislature of the state of Tennessee. He petitioned the legislature to loan the N&C funds to build his railroad. Always the shrewd businessman, Stevenson gave a convincing report to the assembled body concerning the advantage his railroad would be to the economy of the state. He traveled to Charleston, South Carolina to obtain the latest costs of corn, bacon, tobacco, and other products. The reason for his visit to Charleston was to do a cost analysis of products being shipped to New Orleans versus shipping the same product to South Carolina. Up through the 1840s, most raw and manufactured products from the Mississippi Valley had been shipped by river to the port of New Orleans. Stevenson wanted to make sure that the business venture he was entering into would be a viable one; in his opinion it was.

---

4   The city of Nashville was so enamored with the steamboat it almost refused to back the building of the Nashville & Chattanooga Railroad. It took the realization that if Memphis connected to the east coast via the building of the Memphis & Charleston Railroad the M&C would take a considerable amount of trade away from the Middle Tennessee area. The backing of the N&C by the city was almost a self-defense reaction.
5   Knoxville and East Tennessee did have the Tennessee River on which to ship, but this river did not have a natural outlet to any major port. To get to another major city, materials on the Tennessee River had to travel hundreds of miles southwest into Alabama then back north through middle Tennessee before it finally reached the Ohio and Mississippi Rivers in western Kentucky. At that point a boat would still be 500 miles up river from New Orleans or 300 miles down river from Cincinnati.

Stevenson's presentation must have been convincing. The state endorsed the bonds he was seeking in excess of $1.5 million dollars. With the appropriation of the monies, Stevenson started construction of the railroad in August 1848. Trains were running on the line within three years.

To the people along the route of the Nashville & Chattanooga the coming of the railroads was almost a quantum leap from the days when all raw materials had been carried to market by wagon or flatboat. To those who witnessed the transition from slow road and water transports to the new rail system, the speed, convenience, and efficiency of the iron horse was nothing less than astounding.

Prosperity and change followed the rails. Very early in its history the N&C was instrumental in transporting cash crops, livestock, coal, minerals, lumber, and other raw materials to manufacturing centers. They would complete a circle by transporting flour, meal, textiles, lumber, shoes, wood ties, and other finished products to the market place. The railroad served faithfully as the transportation supplier for industries in all the cities and hamlets it served. The railroad was vital to the growth of the economy of these emerging locations. On the back of the nineteenth century railroad rode the expansion of technology and commerce. The Nashville & Chattanooga was a critical part of the transition of the South from an underdeveloped region to a mature industrial society.

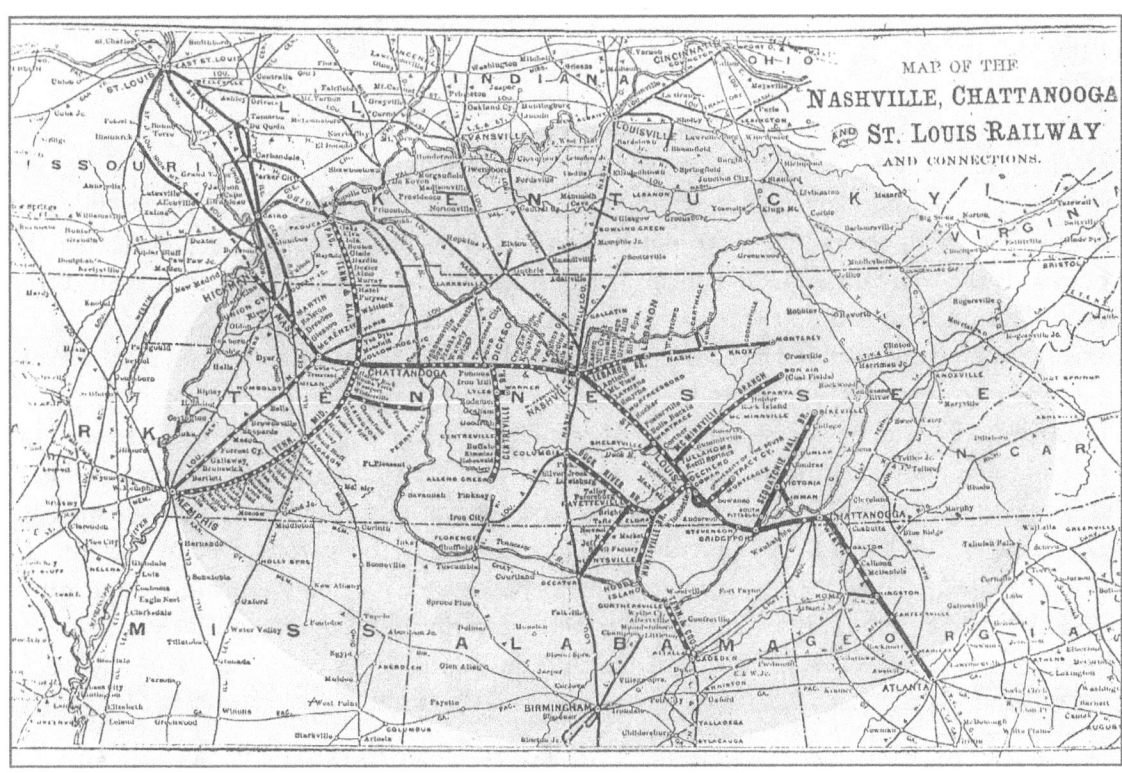

NC&St.L Railway system wide map. -*Nashville Chattanooga & St. Louis Railway*

The railroad allowed untapped sources of raw materials to be garnered from the areas served by the rails. Stands of timber were cut and the logs sent to mills, cotton and other crops could be moved to processing mills and plants. Tennessee, Alabama and Georgia each held vast stores of minerals and raw materials. Clay, limestone, coal, rock, and phosphates were among the commodities moved by the railroad. Several branches of the N&C were built specifically to tap into these reserves. The NC&St.L Railway extended their line to Sparta in 1884 to connect to the line already in place to the Bon Air coal fields. Later, this line was extended an additional 16 miles to Ravenscroft, Eastland, and Clifty, Tennessee when the coal mines were developed in the early 1900s.[6]

Likewise, when the phosphate mines in Allens Creek, Tennessee were expanded, the tracks of the Hohenwald Branch were extended south from Kimmins to serve the facilities. The extension of the railroad into these deposits of natural resources was a winning proposition for both the NC&St.L and the mining companies. The railroad looked to increase revenues by hauling carloads of materials and because of the availability of economical railroad transportation, a less expensive extraction of these natural resources became a reality for the mining companies.

As industry and commerce developed across the system, the NC&St.L developed its business prospects. The NC lay in a strategic location between Memphis and Chattanooga and Louisville and Atlanta. The former cities were a link west to east, the latter north to south. This left the company in an enviable position of being a bridge railroad to a great deal of the country.

To most, the coming of the railroad was a technological miracle, and in most cases communities clamored to attract the railroad to pass though their towns. That is not to say that the train did not have its detractors. Just as the coming of the personal automobile and truck in the 1920s severely hurt rail passenger and freight business, seventy years earlier the coming of the railroads severely gouged the business of the teamsters and river men of the 1840s. Within a short time the heavy loads of goods were being transported on rail and no longer over land and river in the conventional way. The first railroad freight rates substantially undercut the rates of the boat and wagon haulers with whom they were competing. The Nashville & Chattanooga displaced not only many of these long distance haulers, but also much of the supporting infrastructure in the industries. The need for wagon and boat builders, harness, saddle, and bridle makers, stave makers, and various other associated occupations declined with the changes. Additionally, cottage industries in the towns served by the railroad also suffered. No longer would people want to purchase hats, shoes, furniture, and other household items from local vendors when a factory produced product could be purchased at the same price from Nashville or one of a multitude of large cities connected by the N&C.

---

6 Dain L. Schult, *Nashville, Chattanooga & St. Louis: A History of "The Dixie Line."* 2001, page 45.
 J.D.B. DeBow, *Nashville, Chattanooga & St. Louis Ry. Legal History of the Entire System.* 1899, page 199.

There were also those who disliked the noise, grime, and perceived bad elements the trains would bring. They saw the railroad as an unwanted intrusion into their lives. There are several documented reports where communities discouraged the N&C from coming through their towns. The city of Macon, Georgia was one of those places that at first refused to allow the railroad through their community. Landowners in Bedford County, Tennessee were another, though eventually a branch line was constructed from Shelbyville to Wartrace in that county. This of course was the exception to the rule and for the most part the Nashville & Chattanooga and those rail lines that would some day become part of the NC&St.L system brought nothing but prosperity and growth.

The coming of the railroad opened commerce, developed the region's infrastructure, and generally made life much easier for the people in the areas it served. Railroads strengthened America and bound all parts of the country together with bands of iron.

NC&St.L yard switching crew. *-Terry L. Coats Collection*

History of the Nashville, Chattanooga & St. Louis Railway

Railways and the Church have their critics, but both are the best ways of getting a man to his ultimate destination.
... Rev. W. Autry

The history of the Nashville, Chattanooga & St. Louis Railway spanned 112 years. Its infancy sprang from an era when railroading replaced foot, horseback, the wagon, and the flatboat as the primary means of transporting goods. Its demise ushered in the era of Sputnik and the first space explorations.

At the height of its business enterprise, the Nashville, Chattanooga & St. Louis Railway routed just over 1,240 miles of track[7] and called at over 135 terminals, stations, depots, and flagstops across Kentucky, Tennessee, Alabama, and Georgia.

The Nashville, Chattanooga & St. Louis Railway system was divided into five divisions. Connecting to these divisions were eleven branches. The largest of the divisions by mileage, was the Western & Atlantic Division that ran from Atlanta, Georgia to Chattanooga, Tennessee, a distance of 289 miles. This was followed closely by the Paducah, Kentucky to Memphis P&M Division at 254 miles; the Fayetteville, Tennessee to Gadsden, Alabama Huntsville Division at 203 miles; the Nashville to Hickman, Kentucky Nashville Division, known as the *Windy*, at 168 miles; and the Chattanooga to Nashville, Chattanooga Division at 151 miles. The latter was the original Nashville & Chattanooga Railroad that was chartered in 1845 by the State of Tennessee. Added to these main lines were the branches that served coal and lumber reserves, stretched to interchange with other rail lines, or carried train cars to river landings such as those at Guntersville, Alabama, Perryville, Tennessee, and Hickman and Paducah, Kentucky.

Before the Coming of the Railroads

Because of its geographic location and because of the configuration of the river flow, East Tennessee was at a distinct transportation disadvantage to the other two sections of the state. Materials shipped on the Tennessee River from Knoxville had to travel south as far as Huntsville, Alabama then back north though middle Tennessee and then west for hundreds of miles before they reached an outlet at the Ohio River near Paducah, Kentucky. Because of this drawback, a great deal of the early commercial traffic that could have gone to Knoxville passed instead to Nashville. Not being blessed with the waterways of its neighbors in central

---

7   *The Nashville, Chattanooga & St. Louis Railway 1866-1942*, The Nashville, Chattanooga & St. Louis Railway Employees Education Service, Lesson Number 4. Nashville, Tennessee. December 1942, page 17.

and west Tennessee, citizens in the eastern part of the state saw the railroads as a way to place themselves on a more level field with their counterparts. As early as the late 1820s businessmen in east Tennessee entertained the idea of building the first rail system within the state's borders. These men envisioned building a line from the Knoxville area east to Charleston and other eastern ports. Additionally, should a projected rail line be built from Virginia to the ports at Mobile, Alabama, the line would have to be built through east Tennessee giving them a seacoast outlet both to the east and to the south.

Tracy City, Tennessee. Branch Engine #64 before 1915. -*William Turner Collection*

About this same time, men in the Memphis area advocated the building of a rail line from the Bluff City to Charleston, South Carolina and another line to Baltimore. Unfortunately, President Andrew Jackson had curtailed the flow of federal funds to the state of Tennessee shortly after his election in 1828. The refusal of Jackson to accept federal aid was his stand against centralized government. Jackson's stand may have maintained states rights, but at the same time it severely curtailed federal funds flowing to Tennessee for internal improvement projects such as railroads.

Despite the lack of outside help from the Federal government, the state legislature granted six charters for railroad construction in 1831. The first railroad to be chartered was the Franklin Railroad to run between Franklin, Tennessee and the state capitol. Other charters would follow for other companies, but not one mile of railroad track was built as a result of this early chartering. Those who proposed the building of railroads in the state were unable to garner appreciable amounts of capital on their own and the state refused to supply additional financial help.

City of Memphis, ca. 1948. -*H. C. Hill photographer, Nashville Chattanooga & St. Louis Railway*

In the early 1830s, there was considerable argument for and against state aid for internal improvements. Those in favor believed that railroads would stimulate business, increase the value of farm products, and encourage growth in manufacturing. Those in opposition to the aid argued that taxes would have to be increased to raise the monies needed to give to the railroads. They went on to say that the railroads would only benefit a certain portion of the citizenry, but it would be all taxpayers that would have to endure the costs. They saw this as unfair.[8]

---

8 Joseph H. Parker, PhD, *The Story of Tennessee*. 1973, page 192.

After some consideration on the matter, the state legislature sided with those in support of giving aid for internal improvement. In 1836, as a way to promote commerce, the State legislature enacted the Bank and Improvement Act to promote railroads and turnpikes across the state. This act allowed the State of Tennessee to purchase one-third of the common stock of any company engaged in the construction of any railroad or turnpike. Any company that raised money for two-thirds of its stock received the other one-third from the state. No railroad companies came forward to accept the offer at the one-third support level. In 1838, the state enhanced the offer and offered to purchase one-half of a company's stock if a company would raise money for the other one-half. Even after the bounty was raised, the act spurred only three railroad developers hoping to take advantage of these new investment dollars. All in all, the entire Act was a dismal failure. The only tangible benefit of the Act was the building of several turnpikes in the middle Tennessee area. Businessmen split into two factions, those who wanted to use the state subsidies to build roads or to improve waterways and those who wanted to invest in railroading. The factions battled one another and the battling was counterproductive toward both camps. Bonds issued to the railroads and turnpike companies were sold by the companies at disastrous discounts, sometimes as little as fifty cents on a dollar.

The first of the three roads, the Louisville, Cincinnati & Charleston Railroad, never got past the proposal stage. The second, the Hiwassee Railroad, began building from Knoxville to the Georgia line. This line was to pass through Athens and Cleveland, Tennessee. This was the first railroad to actually start construction in the state. The company built about 65 miles of track before construction stopped and the Hiwassee declared bankruptcy in 1842. In Memphis, the LaGrange & Memphis Railroad was the first railroad to qualify for a state subscription and to actually operate a train … well almost. They started construction in 1837 and by 1841 had laid a few miles of track. The year 1842 saw the arrival of the first steam engine for the company, as well as the first in Tennessee. A grand parade was held celebrating the arrival of the *Iron Horse* to the city, but the fan fair was short lived. After being placed on the tracks, the engineer could not get the locomotive to power up. Within weeks after the operators finally got the engine running, the local sheriff unceremoniously confiscated the engine because the company had entered into receivership.[9]

Four years later in 1846, the Memphis & Charleston Railroad chartered and took over the abandoned LaG&M project; they built across north Alabama and eventually connected with the N&C at Stevenson, Alabama in 1857.[10]

After a fledgling start to railroading in the mid 1830s, construction came to a complete stop in 1839. Most of the blame for the collapse in an interest in railroad construction can be attributed to an economic depression known as the *Panic of 1837*. This national depression

---

9   Ibid, page 193.
10   Ibid, page 196.

virtually brought all railroad construction to a halt across the country. Additionally, in 1840, the Bank and Improvement Act was repealed curtailing any other companies from taking advantage of this state money and further depressing the building of any railroads in the state.

The first half of the 1830s was a time of prosperity and expansion fueled greatly by the construction of railroads. The government sold millions of acres of public land to speculators. It was hoped that the expansion of canals and railroads into these areas would greatly advance the values of these parcels as settlement and traffic developed.

Windfalls from the land sales as well as duties collected from the Tariff of 1833 allowed the government in 1835 to pay off the national debt and to accrue a surplus. Federal legislation in effect at the time dictated that any federal surpluses were to be returned to the individual states in the form of loans.

The godsend to the states was used for internal improvements … railroads and canals. Many of these improvements were paid for using paper bank notes in lieu of gold- and silver-specie. In some cases, states issued as much as ten dollars in paper for every dollar in specie they had to back them. In order to ebb the flow of devalued paper as payment to the government, the Jackson administration issued the Specie Circular. The Specie Circular was an order requiring payments to the government to be made only in coinage. The domino effect of this order was that banks called in old loans and restricted new credit. A run on the banks by depositors in the latter half of the 1830s created a panic and virtually shut down the economy.[11]

RAILROADING IN ITS INFANCY

After a few years, the state of Tennessee was able to shake off the effects of the Panic. In 1837, the same year Andrew Jackson returned from Washington, Shelby County's William Armour introduced a bill in the Tennessee state legislature to unite the Mississippi with the Atlantic by a railroad from Memphis through Nashville and Knoxville. A short time later, railroading was able to gain a small footing in east and west Tennessee. East Tennessee farmers who were hemmed in by the Allegheny Mountains to the east and Cumberland Mountain to the west saw the railroads as a way to effectively ship their goods to market. West Tennessee farmers saw the railroads as a marked improvement over the quagmire of muddy roads they had to navigate to take their cotton and tobacco to market.

It took middle Tennessee a little longer to share the enthusiasm for the railroad held by the other two grand divisions. Middle Tennesseans, in fact, saw the railroads as a threat to the dominance they held over the other two geographic sections of the state. If the railroads were

11   Panic of 1837. www.UShistory.com website.

built in east and west Tennessee, it would put them in direct competition to middle Tennessee. Middle Tennessee was blessed with good roads as well as the Cumberland, Tennessee, and other rivers. So at least at the outset, there was no rush to embrace the railroads.

Instead of building railroads, middle Tennessee chose to use the state offered aid to build macadamized turnpikes. It would not be until 1845 that interest in railroading would re-emerge and it would be a few more years before construction actually started.

The picture was not quite as dismal in Georgia, but that state also shared from the fledgling start syndrome. In 1836, the state incorporated the Western & Atlantic Railroad. The railroad was to be constructed at the state's expense from a point at the future site of Atlanta, Georgia to the Tennessee River in southeast Tennessee near Ross' Landing (Chattanooga), and was to serve as an extension of other railroad lines to be constructed or in prospect in Georgia.[12]

Construction on the Western & Atlantic began on July 4, 1837, but was severely curtailed a short time later. Because of the Panic of 1837, construction on railroads in Georgia ground to an almost complete halt later that year. Construction did not resume until 1840. Only a small amount of grading and some survey work was accomplished by the W&A during that period.

Back in Tennessee, the citizens of Ross' Landing, eager to have the railroad come, held a meeting on March 25, 1837 and adopted a resolution advocating the selection of Ross' Landing as a terminal of the Georgia road. The people of Ross' anticipated that one day there would also be an extension of this line to Louisville via Nashville.[13]

The predicted coming of the railroad to Chattanooga renewed hopes in Memphis and Knoxville. Even Nashville took note that something new and exciting was just over the horizon. The latter part of the 1840s and early 1850s would finally see a resurgence of interest in railroading.

A region wide gathering, the Southern and Western Convention, was held in Memphis in July and November of 1845. More than 600 delegates from sixteen states and territories attended the November session presided over by the honorable John C. Calhoun of South Carolina. The Convention reawakened interests that had lain dormant since the Panic of 1837 had quashed many of their plans. Spurred by this renewed interest, old projects were revived and new ones started. Delegates from the Southern states of Georgia, North Carolina, South Carolina, Mississippi, Alabama, and Tennessee formulated plans to develop a web of interlinking railroads within the participating states that would create trans-state commerce.

---

12   U. B. Phillips, *History of Transportation in the Eastern Cotton Belt*. 1909.
13   Knoxville Register. April 12, 1837.

There was also much talk about the creation of a Southern based transcontinental railroad. These Southern politicians and businessmen had become increasingly concerned by the amount of railroads under construction in the North and that these Northern rail companies would build a transcontinental railroad of their own. The delegates were afraid that the conventional north-south trade in lumber, farm goods, and manufacturing goods would shift to an east-west route instead. There were concerns that if a transcontinental railroad was created that neglected the Southern states, trade between the eastern United States and the Orient would exclude them. These men formulated a plan to build a railroad from the Southern states to El Paso, Texas and then from El Paso to extend the line to the west coast.

Birth of the Nashville & Chattanooga Railroad

The seeds of the railroad that would be known as the Nashville, Chattanooga & St. Louis Railway would be planted in 1843 when A. O. P. Nicholson and Dr. James Overton, both of Nashville, advocated to the Tennessee Legislature that a railway should be built from Nashville to Chattanooga.

At the time of the proposal, Chattanooga was nothing more than a shipping hamlet on the Tennessee River. Boxed in by high mountains on three sides, the precarious location of the city made many skeptical that the town could be reached by rail without great difficulty. Many persons ridiculed Overton's proposal as nothing more than a delusional dream of a fanatic. Undaunted, Dr. Overton saw the trade potential of a link over the forthcoming Western & Atlantic Railroad from Nashville to the cotton growing states of Georgia and South Carolina. He pressed on in an attempt to persuade the people of the mid-state to support his idea.

Around 1845, an upturn in the economy of middle Tennessee allowed the area to shake off the effects of a crippling recession. The improved economy brought with it an increased amount of trade in and out of the region. Steamboats on the Cumberland River soon became taxed near or beyond capacity. It became apparent that Nashville could use a secondary transportation outlet. That outlet would manifest itself in the form of a railroad. With just a small nudge, Dr. Overton's dream of a ribbon of iron to Chattanooga was about to come to fruition.

The subject of a railroad to connect Nashville and Chattanooga was brought before the Legislature and on December 11, 1845, an act was passed to incorporate a railroad from Nashville on the Cumberland River to Chattanooga on the Tennessee River. The seventeenth section of that act authorized, "Any state or citizen, corporation or company, to subscribe for

and hold stock in said company, with all rights and subject to all the liabilities of any of the stockholders."[14]

The next step was for the city of Nashville to raise $500,000 in subscriptions. A Nashville merchant, (later Nashville & Chattanooga president) Vernon K. Stevenson latched upon the opportunity to promote railroading in Tennessee. Stevenson took it upon himself to visit every household in the city and through his efforts was able to secure the signatures of fully two-thirds of the public in favor of the subscription. Mr. Stevenson worked diligently for almost two years before succeeding in his quest. Through his efforts, 1,347 shares of Nashville & Chattanooga stock were sold to individuals.[15] On December 9, 1847, the legislative act of 1845 was amended allowing the city of Nashville through its mayor and aldermen to subscribe the $500,000 through the sale of bonds. The money was raised in this manner.

Vernon K. Stevenson, G. P. A. Healy, artist.
-Tennessee State Library and Archives; -Neal Savage Mahoney Papers Collection

After securing approximately $602,000[16] of subscriptions in Nashville, Stevenson traveled to Charleston, South Carolina in an attempt to procure financial aid from that city as well. A decade earlier, foreign trade had declined sharply for the city of Charleston. Much of the trade had shifted to the city of Augusta, and through the port of Savannah, Georgia. In order to find a viable alternative to the lost trade, Charleston as well as Savannah, bid to build rail lines westward. While Charleston was laying rail toward business in the cotton states, railroads in Georgia were being built east toward South Carolina. Charleston certainly had a stake in investing in the Nashville & Chattanooga. The N&C would build to Chattanooga and there connect to the line already under construction to the sea. Investing in the N&C would help open a trade route of 550 miles all the way back to middle Tennessee. A supply route to the materials of the middle Tennessee area would make Charleston competitive to other seaports in Georgia and all the way north to New York City and beyond.

So intent was Charleston to develop business when Vernon Stevenson offered stock subscriptions in the Nashville & Chattanooga Railroad, Charleston invested $500,000 in the startup company. Charleston's subscription made it one of the principal investors in the new

---

14 W. Woodford Clayton, *History of Davidson County.* 1880, page 213.
15 *The Nashville, Chattanooga & St. Louis Railway 1866-1942*, The Nashville, Chattanooga & St. Louis Railway Employees Education Service, Lesson Number 7. Nashville, Tennessee. March 1, 1943, page 8.
16 *Glimpses into Nashville's 176 Years – Stevenson Built Railroad Empire with First Train Leaving In '51.* The Nashville Banner. Undated 1956.

company. Citing the potential for future business between the two companies, Stevenson approached the Georgia Railroad & Banking Company. The GR&B subscribed $250,000 toward the Nashville & Chattanooga, making it the second largest of the initial stockholders. Other investors were the cities of Atlanta and Augusta, Georgia, and Murfreesboro, Shelbyville, and Winchester, Tennessee. The Central Railroad of Georgia proposed investing an additional $250,000, but the stockholders later failed to ratify the plan and those monies never materialized.

With new financial incentives granted by the state of Tennessee in hand, the Nashville & Chattanooga stockholders held their first meeting on January 24, 1848 and elected Vernon K. Stevenson as the company's first president. In March, the N&C began pushing its way from Nashville toward Chattanooga. By April 13th, there were 9.7 miles of track laid and, on that date, the first train ran to the end of the line at Antioch. By December, the N&C had extended the line 61 miles from Nashville, and was running two trains a day.

At about the same time as the start up of the N&C, other railroads across Kentucky, Alabama, and Georgia sprang to life and began to stretch their tentacles as well. In east Tennessee, the East Tennessee & Georgia and the East Tennessee & Virginia Railroads were completed in 1856 and 1858 respectfully. Later, these two roads would merge to form the East Tennessee, Virginia & Georgia Railroad. From north of Nashville, Louisville subscriptions as well as aid from the state of Tennessee had allowed the Louisville & Nashville Railroad to incorporate in Kentucky. The L&N connected to Nashville in 1859. To the west of Nashville, the Hickman & Obion and the Nashville & Northwestern Railroads were building toward one another. To the east of the capitol city, the McMinnville & Manchester Railroad and the Winchester & Alabama Railroad were in their infancy. The latter two were building to join the newly constructed N&C mainline at McMinnville and Winchester, Tennessee respectfully. By 1848, the Western & Atlantic Railroad was pushing its way toward the Tennessee border and to the river ports of the Tennessee River in the city of Chattanooga.

The W&A reached Chattanooga in 1850 after forcing its way across the mountainous region of north Georgia. With this advancement, dormant interests in railroading were revived in Knoxville and Memphis as well as sparking additional interests from other businessmen in Nashville. With a railhead developed in Chattanooga connecting Atlanta and another from Atlanta to the seaports of Savannah and Charleston, there was a rail connection from the Atlantic Ocean ports to east Tennessee. In early 1854, the Nashville & Chattanooga Railroad reached Chattanooga, connected with the W&A, and in doing so extended rail service from middle Tennessee to the markets on the Atlantic Ocean.

In 1852, the state of Tennessee passed the General Internal Improvement Law to promote economic growth. This law allowed the state to issue loans to the railroad companies at the rate of $8,000 per mile. This action on the part of the state spurred an outpouring of applicants from start-up railroad companies. Years later, all but one of these railroads defaulted on the loans made to them by the state of Tennessee; the Nashville & Chattanooga Railroad was the only company not to default on their loan. The Nashville, Chattanooga & St. Louis Railway would lease or purchase nineteen of these defaulted roads and encompass them as part of the system.

In the latter years of the 1850s, the railroads of Tennessee were linked over several lines to the seaports of the east coast. The next step would be to turn attention toward linking the state to the Pacific Ocean. Tennesseans formulated dreams of projecting lines in a westward direction; they wanted to connect the major cities of Knoxville, Nashville and Memphis to Little Rock, El Paso, and onward. However, the war to come would dash those dreams.

Prelude to War

Between 1850 and 1860, 1,253 miles of railroad were built in the state of Tennessee. Established were lines from Memphis to Louisville over the Memphis & Ohio Railroad as far as Paris, Tennessee to Guthrie, Kentucky over the Memphis, Clarksville & Louisville Railroad; and on to Louisville over the L&N Railroad. The Mobile & Ohio Railroad stretched between Columbus, Kentucky and Mobile, Alabama. Connecting with the M&O at Jackson, Tennessee and extending to Grenada, Mississippi was the Mississippi Central Railroad. The Mississippi & Tennessee Railroad connected Memphis to New Orleans via a link at Grenada to the Mississippi Central.

In 1850, there were only about 7,500 miles of railroads in the entire United States and by 1860 the number of miles had increased to 30,500.

Nashville & Chattanooga Railroad: The War Years

*"The Southern railways ... meant more than the mountain ranges
and scarcely less than the great rivers in determining the
lines of advance and defense."*

So wrote noted Civil War historian Dr. Douglas Southall Freeman as he related the importance of railroads to the outcome of the fighting during the War for Southern Independence.[17]

The War years of 1861 to 1865 would be a combination of windfall and disaster for the Nashville & Chattanooga. The upside was that the first years of the War were very lucrative for the company. The Confederate government used the line to transport men, munitions,

---

17 *The Nashville, Chattanooga & St. Louis Railway 1866-1942*, The Nashville, Chattanooga & St. Louis Railway Employees Education Service, Lesson Number 3. Nashville, Tennessee. November 16, 1942, page 1.

and materiel for their armies. So productive was the early War business, that it allowed the N&C to pay off the bonds that had been issued by the state of Tennessee for its initial construction. Paying off the bonds gave the N&C the honor of being the only railroad the state aided that caused it no financial loss. The downside was that as the War progressed and the states of Tennessee and Georgia were falling to advancing Federal forces, the railroad became a strategic focal point for disruption by the retreating Confederates. After the railroads fell to Federal hands, they became the target of attacking Confederates in an attempt to cut Yankee supply lines.

Nashville, Tennessee USMRR Engine Facilities. The complex of buildings in the center of this photograph are engine repair, machine shops, and a roundhouse used by the USMRR. To the left is the N&C freighthouse. The building seen above the roof to the right is the 1854 N&C passenger station. -*Tennessee State Library and Archives*

With the escalation of the War, Nashville soon became the largest Federal supply depot of the Western theater. Needing a mass quantity of storage space for these supplies, the Federals set to leveling many of the smaller railroad building surrounding the depot and replaced them with large warehouses. Stored in the warehouses were shoes, coffee, tents, blankets, and gunpowder. At any given time over fifteen million rations were being stored in the *gulch*. With the end of hostilities, these storehouses would become the property of the N&C. The *gulch* area was a very busy locale for the invading Federals. In addition to the storehouses, they built stables and barns for horses, barracks, mess houses, medical facilities, and car repair and maintenance shops near the old 1854 N&C depot. There was even a printing office attached to the north side of the depot.

USMRR printing office in Nashville, Tennessee. This building was used for the printing of materials related to the operations of the United States Military Railroads during the War. The building was attached to the side of the N&C Nashville Depot. -*Tennessee State Library and Archives*

Nashville fell to Federal hands in February 1862 and with it went the N&C Railroad in middle Tennessee. Over the next two years, the two armies would seesaw control of the line between the cities of Nashville and Chattanooga. After Confederate General Braxton Bragg marched his army into middle Tennessee in the fall of 1862, the N&C tracks to the south of Nashville returned to Confederate hands. They stayed in Confederate control until just after the battle of Murfreesboro fought in the waning days of December. General Bragg withdrew from Murfreesboro down the railroad to Tullahoma, Tennessee where he stayed through the spring of 1863. With Bragg's retreat, the N&C from Tullahoma to Nashville returned to Federal hands. As General Bragg abandoned Tullahoma, he continued to follow

Lookout Mountain and the N&C Railroad, ca.1864 From a print by artist A.E. Mathews. -*Tennessee State Library and Archives*

the N&C tracks toward Chattanooga. Proceeding south, his army used the N&C Bridge at Bridgeport, Alabama to cross the Tennessee River and in doing so he was able to place the river between himself and the following army of U. S. General William S. Rosecrans.

As the War continued to rage in southeast Tennessee and on into north Georgia, the N&C and the W&A played vital roles in the outcome of the battles. At the battle of Chickamauga just south of Chattanooga, Confederate General James Longstreet used the railroads, including the W&A, to move troops from Virginia through the Carolinas to Atlanta and then north to Ringgold. The September 20, 1863 battle of Chickamauga was a victory for the South because Longstreet was able to move enough forces quickly by rail and was able to out maneuver and out number the Federals. General Rosecrans was forced to fall back to Chattanooga after the battle.

On October 3rd, Federal reinforcements for Chattanooga, the advanced elements of what would be twenty-two thousand men, their horses, mules, artillery, and supplies started arriving at Bridgeport. These two corps of troops under the direction of General Joseph Hooker arrived outside Chattanooga after a trip that carried them over several northern railroads and finally arriving in Nashville. From Nashville, the reinforcements were transported over the N&C to Bridgeport. In just eight days, Hooker's army was able to move an astounding 1,159 miles to arrive just in time for battle. After making the thirty mile march from Bridgeport to Chattanooga, these troops took part in the decisive turning of the tide at Missionary Ridge.

General Bragg was forced to abandon Chattanooga. The movement of troops turned the tide of battle for the Confederates at Chickamauga and less than two weeks later the movement of troops by rail saved the Federals at Chattanooga.

After Chattanooga, General Joseph Johnston replaced General Bragg as the commander of the Army of Tennessee. In the winter of 1863 to 1864 the area around Tunnel Hill on the W&A became the boundary between the two resting armies. When fighting resumed in the spring of 1864, Johnson used the W&A Railroad as his base of attack in several delaying hit and fall back battles. The armies skirmished at Dalton, Resaca, Adairsville, Cartersville, Allatoona Pass, Dallas, Acworth, and Kennesaw Mountain before the Confederates finally withdrew to Atlanta.

After the fall of Chattanooga, the Federal emphasis was to keep pressure in the face of the Confederate Army of Tennessee as they made their way toward Atlanta. To accomplish this, the Federals needed to transport a vast amount of men and supplies to northern Georgia.

In the spring of 1864, the United States Military Railroad (USMRR) completed the unfinished section of the Nashville & Northwestern Railroad between Kingston Springs, Tennessee and the supply depot at Johnsonville. To construct the railroad, the government hired, at $20.00 per month, freed Blacks and many runaway slaves that had made their way into Nashville. The construction was completed and the line was opened on May 10, 1864.

The Federals needed to open this vital supply line from the Tennessee River to Nashville and then to forward this materiel to General Sherman on his Atlanta campaign. The Nashville & Chattanooga and the Western & Atlantic played an inertial part in the movement of these supplies.

N&C and USMRR Nashville Depot. Seen in the center and lower part of this photograph are a line of USMRR engines. The Tennessee State Capitol building can be seen in the upper right corner. *-Library of Congress*

Back in Nashville in early 1864, the Federal Army turned the operation and reconstruction of the war damaged Nashville & Chattanooga over to the United States Military Railroad. Between 1864 and the end of the War, the USMRR was kept busy restoring the damage done by raiding Confederates as well as the effects natural disasters had taken on the lines. Additionally, improvements were made to the N&C rights-of-way, new sidings were installed, and new water and telegraph facilities were built. Next to the Union Station at Nashville, new warehouse facilities were built to accommodate the mounds of supplies brought into that city for the army.

The N&C saw its last action of the War in the winter of 1864. As General John Bell Hood moved his Army of Tennessee from Atlanta toward Middle Tennessee for an attack on Nashville, the Federals moved troops from Chattanooga to Nashville for a defense of that city.

The War ended in April 1865. With the conclusion of hostilities, the Federals returned the N&C to company control on September 15, 1865.[18] [19]

---

18   Richard E. Prince, *Nashville, Chattanooga & St. Louis Railway: History and Steam Locomotives*. 1967, page 12.
19   *The Nashville, Chattanooga & St. Louis Railway 1866-1942*, The Nashville, Chattanooga & St. Louis Railway Employees Education Service, Lesson Number 4, Nashville, Tennessee. December 1942, page 1.

1870s to 1890s: The NC&St.L Comes of Age

Destruction of Nashville & Chattanooga Locomotives and Cars during the War Years. This illustration depicts the type of destruction done by raiding parties of both armies as they fought for supremacy of the railroads.
-*Terry L. Coats Collection*

The War had been devastating, not only in its loss of life, but also in its destruction of personal and public property across the South. The tracks and structures of the N&C were mostly in shambles, the condition of the railroad as a whole was appalling. Bridges were either gone or in such pitiful shape as to rendered them unsafe for use. Station houses and machine shops had been destroyed or left in unusable condition; locomotives and rolling stock were almost nonexistent. Of the 380 passenger and freight cars owned by the N&C at the start of the War, the Federals returned only 118 cars. Of these, only a meager 82 were made serviceable, and then only after an extensive overhauling.[20] The company estimated their losses at $1,891,022.[21] The story of the locomotives was worse. Of the thirty-five locomotives owned by the company in 1861, only nine could be placed back into working condition and eighteen were scrapped completely.

The railroad would need more locomotives with which to operate. During the War, the U. S. Government purchased all available new locomotives. Even if there had been locomotives for sale, the N&C was strapped for cash and their credit was exhausted. The only option was to purchase used USMRR equipment from the War Department. The N&C was able to purchase thirty-four of the war engines and immediately put them to use.

In 1866, the N&C was near the point of financial and physical ruin. After the War, the Federals relinquished control of the railroad, but they did not simply hand the railroad back to the N&C and just walk away. The U. S. Government would return the property to the N&C only on the condition that the N&C pay an estimated $1,600,000 within two years. The $1,600,000 dollars was restitution for repairs and improvements made by the occupying Federal troops to the N&C and to its subsidiary the Nashville & Northwestern Railroad. The N&C acquired the debt for the N&NW as part of its operating expenses for that company.[22]

---

20   Ibid, page 22.
21   *Carpetbaggers at the Throttle!* The Nashville Tennessean Magazine. August 25, 1957
22   A portion of the $1,600,000 included the purchase of 34 USMRR locomotives. During the War, the motive power of the N&C had been moved as far away as South Carolina and, additionally, most of it was in pretty poor shape. Michael Burns chose to purchase these USMRR locomotives as replacements for the worn out N&C units.

In addition, the government mandated that the N&C give bond as a guarantee that it would pay a fair market rate for all equipment, supplies, and buildings acquired from the USMRR upon the return of control of the railroad by the N&C.

As stated in the order that returned the railroad to company hands, the government was to make restitution to the N&C for the use of the railroad between 1862 and 1865. In reality, no compensation came. The government allowed no repayment for the use of the road or for any of the N&C equipment by the military authorities. They also declined any reimbursement for any property or equipment destroyed as a result of the fighting. It was a black and white issue with the Federals mandating the terms.

In time N&C president Michael Burns negotiated the $1,600,000 down to the sum of $1,000,000. Nevertheless, in the days of Reconstruction this was still a very handsome sum for the money to raise for the strapped Nashville & Chattanooga. During the War the company had invested over $922,000 in Confederate bonds. They had Confederate money, but what they did not have was United States currency. Over time, the entire amount of encumbrance, including additional interest payments of 7.3 percent, was paid to the U. S. Government. At the same time the N&C was paying monies to the Federals, they were also forced to replace tracks, structures, and equipment destroyed during the War. Making these payments and paying for the needed repairs greatly burdened the railroad financially. The N&C (NC&St.L) would eventually pay off its indebtedness, but the toll it would take on the company would come at a high cost.

Michael Burns, N&C RR President, 1864-8.
-*Nashville, Chattanooga & St. Louis Railway*

The USMRR returned the N&C and the Nashville & Northwestern Railroad to their respective owners. By 1867, the N&NW was able to bridge the Tennessee River at Johnsonville, Tennessee and from there push tracks westward to McKenzie, Tennessee, the point at which they had culminated the proposed Hickman to Nashville line in 1860. President Burns was able to accomplish this task by using the extensive labor pool of former soldiers looking for work after the War.

The N&NW was able to fulfill its chartering obligations by linking the Mississippi River to Nashville, but soon found itself in default on its state loans. Shortly afterward, the company declared bankruptcy. The N&C leased the N&NW from the state in 1869 and ran it as leased property until it bought the railroad outright on August 1, 1872. After its takeover, the NC&St.L would refer to the newly acquired N&NW trackage as the St. Louis

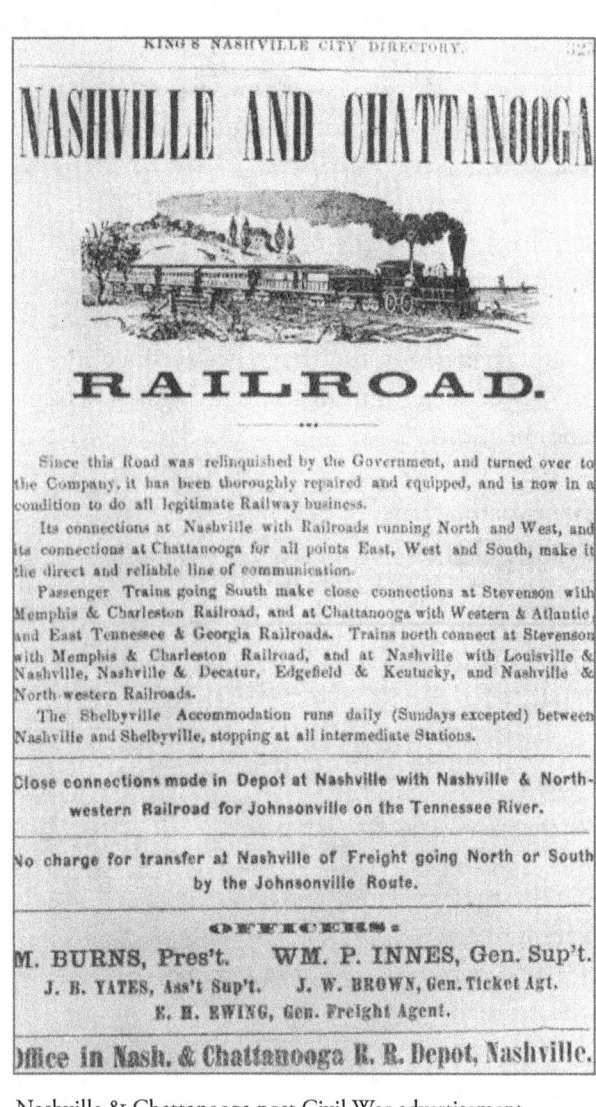

Nashville & Chattanooga post Civil War advertisement.
-Tennessee State Library and Archives

Division, then the Northwestern Division, and finally the Nashville Division.[23]

Just after the N&NW acquisition, the N&C Railroad petitioned a Tennessee chancery court to change their name from the Nashville & Chattanooga Railroad to the Nashville, Chattanooga & St. Louis Railway. In 1873, the petition was granted. The court granted permission for the railway to add the words *St. Louis* to its name because it deemed that the railway was making progress toward gaining access to the Missouri city.[24] With the name change, the railroad also adopted a new company slogan. Soon the company was placing on its timetables the slogan … *From St. Louis to the Sea*.

The acquisition of the N&NW would be the first of more than twenty railroads the NC&St.L would garner in the next twenty years. During the following decade, the NC&St.L would acquire the McMinnville & Manchester (Sparta Branch), the Sequatchie Valley Railroad (Sequatchie Branch), the Winchester & Alabama (Fayetteville Branch), and the small Nashville to Lebanon, Tennessee & Pacific Railroad (Lebanon Branch). In the last three months of 1887, the company acquired the Huntsville and Elora Railroad that had been chartered to run between those named cities, but on which no construction was ever completed. The NC&St.L completed the line after the acquisition. Likewise, the Duck River Valley line from Columbia to Fayetteville was purchased and an extension of the line from Sparta to the coal mines at Bon Air, Tennessee was built.

The NC was fortunate in that it had in close proximity its own bountiful supply of low cost coal reserves on the Tracy City and Sequatchie Valley Branches. Taking advantage of this abundance, in 1870, the railroad installed heavier grates in all their locomotives and all were converted from wood to coal burners.

---

23   Dain L. Schult, *Nashville, Chattanooga & St. Louis: A History of "The Dixie Line."* 2001, page 33.
24   Ibid, page 33.

Under the direction of NC&St.L president, Edmund W. "King" Cole, the railroad made great strides to expand its empire over the two decades between the 1870s and the 1890s. Under the leadership of the flamboyant Cole, the NC&St.L had not been satisfied to simply add the words *St. Louis* to its name. There was a legitimate attempt by the company to gain a physical presence into that city. Cole set his sights on building the NC&St.L into a trunk railroad starting in Savannah, Georgia and culminating in St. Louis.

1875 NC&St.L Pass. *-Terry L. Coats Collection*

Cole's ambitions did not go unnoticed by the L&N and would set in motion one of the most dramatic chapters in NC&St.L history.

In 1875, the NC&St.L and the L&N had entered into a contractual obligation where each would agree to allow the other to operate within a mutual area of interest. The NC had rights to transport freight destined for Atlanta and other Southeastern cities while the L&N had exclusive rights into St. Louis and Northern cities.[25] However, within a few years, the L&N broke the contract when in November 1879 they issued a tersely worded statement saying, "All freights destined to Georgia and South Carolina points received by the Louisville and Nashville Railroad will be shipped by Montgomery after this date."

Taken as an affront to its sovereignty in Georgia the Board of Directors and the stockholders of the NC held *called meetings* of their respective groups to discuss what actions they would take in retaliation to the L&N's breach of contract. Both bodies gave Cole carte blanche to do whatever it would take to expand the NC from its small nucleus into a vast railroad empire.

Sixteen days after the L&N's proclamation of change of intent, the NC&St.L issued its own statement. In it, the NC Board stated, "That it regretted that the L&N had taken a course of such aggressive policy by invading… territory in the South hereto awarded to the (NC)… by contract between the two Companies; and that such action is considered a menace to the rights of this company…" The statement went on to say that, "The management of this Company will be sustained in adopting such measures as it may see fit to hold that territory which legitimately belongs to this Company…"

Edmund Cole, President of NC&St.L, 1868-1880. *-Nashville, Chattanooga & St. Louis Railway*

---

25   Dain L. Schult, *Nashville, Chattanooga & St. Louis: A History of "The Dixie Line."* 2001, page 48.

The gloves were off; the L&N had started a war. If these were the rules by which the L&N wanted to abide, the NC would do the same.

In actuality, the first sparing between these two behemoths had begun earlier that spring. Between April and July, 1879 the L&N had acquired the Kentucky and Tennessee division of the St. Louis & South Eastern Railroad. This line between Henderson, Kentucky and Nashville had been a thorn in the side of the L&N for years. This division of the St.L&SE ran parallel to the L&N's Louisville to Nashville trunk line and had using rate-cutting freight tariffs undercut the L&N's freight rates at every turn. The purchase of this portion of the St.L&SE effectively quashed the competition for Nashville traffic.[26]

In a counteracting move, president Cole and the NC attempted to gain a controlling interest, first by lease and then by purchase of the Illinois & Indiana Division of the same St. Louis & South Eastern Railroad. This Division ran from Evansville, Indiana to St. Louis, Missouri[27] and Cole was one step closer to achieving a foothold in St. Louis. In the spring of 1879 when the NC bought an interest in the Owensboro & Nashville Railroad and laid 40 miles of track southward from Owensboro to Central City, Kentucky. Their plans were to continue laying track all the way to Nashville.

Had all these acquisitions come to fruition, all that would be left to do for the NC to reach St. Louis would be to bridge the gap between Owensboro and Evansville. With the permission of both the Board of Directors and the stockholders in hand, Cole suddenly found himself on a fast track to gain egress into St. Louis.

At the same time, Cole was also actively trying to acquire a lease of the Central Railroad & Banking Company of Georgia (later the Central of Georgia) and the Western & Atlantic Railroads. The W&A went to Atlanta and the Central Railroad all the way to Savannah. If Cole could connect the lines from Nashville to Central City and from Owensboro to Evansville, the NC would have had a direct line from St. Louis through Nashville and Atlanta to Savannah, Georgia. If the NC could cobble together a system of rail from St. Louis to Savannah, it would become the largest railroad in the entire South.

Cole's attempt at control of the vast W&A and Central railroading system was more than the L&N could stand. If Cole made good on his attempt, the L&N would be completely shut out of Georgia and the NC&St.L would have access to the heart of the Midwest.

Although Cole understood he was about to truly gain the upper hand, suddenly he stopped his brilliant surge and offered an olive branch to the L&N. In December 1879, he proposed that the two companies merge into one company with each receiving an equal share

---

26   Maury Klein, *History of the Louisville & Nashville Railroad*. 1972, page 154..
27   Ibid, page 153.

of the new venture. The L&N was not interested in any such proposition. They wanted no part of a merged railroad; they wanted it all. The L&N began a campaign to purchase large blocks of NC&St.L stock and to purchase the NC&St.L outright.

Acting L&N president Horatio V. Newcomb took it upon himself to personally travel to New York City to persuade former N&C president and majority stockowner Vernon Stevenson to sell his 134,000 shares of NC&St.L stock. When Stevenson was not convinced to sell through friendly persuasion, Newcomb threatened the old man by telling him if he and the other major stockholders did not sell, the L&N would build a railroad line to parallel the NC's entire system. In reality, the L&N could never have accomplished such a feat, but the bluff worked. Vernon Stevenson garnered about $4,000,000 from the sale of his stock.

President Cole tried with all his might to head off the purchase. He knew that even though Stevenson, his son, and their associates owned the majority of stock, it would actually take two-thirds of the stock to control the railroad. New York speculators in a syndicate held the stock that would make the difference. These speculators had purchased a large block of NC stock upon the word of a proposed merger between the NC&St.L and the L&N. Stocks rose to $121 per share. When the merger fell through the price of NC stock started to fall. The speculators panicked as prices fell. Cole made a direct appeal to the syndicate to hold on to their shares until he could make a counter offer to one made by the L&N. In the end, Newcomb had more of what the speculators wanted … money. Newcomb and the L&N bought the syndicate's stock at a price of $95 per share, which was well above the current market price. The L&N took controlling interest in the NC&St.L.[28]

On January 17, 1880, Stevenson delivered the majority of the NC stock to Newcomb and the L&N[29] so the L&N would now own $7,177,600 of the $10,000,000 outstanding NC&St.L capital stock. It is ironic that the same approach in 1902 would happen to the L&N, as it was the subject of a hostile takeover by the Atlantic Coast Line Railroad.

An immediate merger between the two companies might have taken place in 1880 had it not been for the outcry from the citizens in Nashville. The L&N management took seriously threats that were made in Nashville and other parts of Tennessee, that if the L&N attempted to merge the railroads, the citizens would destroy L&N rolling stock and property.[30] The L&N had seen the destructive power southerners like John Hunt Morgan and Nathan Bedford Forrest had perpetrated during the War and one would guess they wanted no part of having a re-occurrence of those actions.

When the facts of the takeover were learned, there was much disappoint expressed in the editorial of newspapers in Nashville and even in Louisville:

---

28 *L&N's Opposition' Stirs Memories of Old Feud*. The Nashville Tennessean. November 6, 1977.
29 Dain L. Schult, *Nashville, Chattanooga & St. Louis: A History of "The Dixie Line."* 2001, page 50.
30 *Nashville, Tennessee's Railroad Heritage*. NC&St.L Preservation Society website, www.ncstl.com.

"No event has occurred since the fall of Fort Donelson in the late war that has more profoundly agitated this community," Nashville Daily American.

"Cole's best friend stabbed him in the heart," and then when president Cole resigned over the incident, "Colonel Cole has the sympathy and good will of all who know anything about the duplicity that undermined him," Louisville Courier-Journal.

The route into St. Louis via Evansville that president Cole had all but tasted was suddenly snatched away from him by the L&N. The NC&St.L had gotten so close to its goal only to be denied the prize.

1882 NC&St.L Pass. *-Terry L. Coats Collection*

With the absorption of the NC, the Nashville & Owensboro reverted to L&N control and the L&N suspended Cole's ongoing negotiations with the Central Railroad of Georgia. Cole was livid, but powerless to act on his frustration; he resigned his position on February 1, 1880. He stayed at the helm of the NC for four more months and was then replaced on June 30th by the L&N with James D. Porter, a former Confederate general and Governor of Tennessee from 1875 to 1877. Porter served until September 1884.

The acquisition of the NC&St.L by the L&N did not stop the railroad from fulfilling its Georgia aspirations. In 1890, the NC&St.L completed the mission embarked upon by its president Cole by acquiring from the state of Georgia a lease for all Western & Atlantic properties. The NC had now gained entrance to Atlanta and had extended its system by 289 miles.

In what had to have been one of the most miraculous coincidences in railroading business history, when the lease for operation of the W&A was offered, the NC outbid the Richmond & Danville Railroad by one dollar per month to obtain the lease over their opponent. More than likely the NC had been tipped off with insider information from the Southern Railroad. Some years before the N&C had helped the Southern Railroad gain access to Chattanooga and in all likelihood, the Southern returned the favor.[31]

1896 NC&St.L Pass. *-Terry L. Coats Collection*

---

31   Dain L. Schult, *Nashville, Chattanooga & St. Louis: A History of "The Dixie Line."* 2001, page 63.

In 1896, the NC&St.L leased two more lines, the Paducah, Tennessee & Alabama in Kentucky and the Tennessee Midland in Tennessee. The Paducah, Tennessee & Alabama Railroad had acquired the Tennessee Midland Railway under a thirty year lease agreement in 1892. This arrangement was short lived. The PT&A was only able to hold on to its new acquisition until the following year when both railroads went into receivership. The receivership lasted until December 1895 when both were sold in foreclosure to the Louisville & Nashville Railroad. Immediately the L&N turned around and put in place a 99-year lease of its new acquisition to the NC&St.L.

With the acquisition of this new line the NC&St.L now could travel over their own tracks from Nashville to Bruceton then through Jackson to Memphis. They were no longer dependant on the L&N for egress into the Bluff City. Before the lease, the NC had to exchange Memphis bound passengers at their interchange with the L&N in McKenzie, Tennessee and they had no freight service to Memphis at all. Not only did acquiring these two lines give the NC its own access to Memphis, it added 230 miles of track to the system and added a second river connection at Paducah, Kentucky. This line would become the Paducah & Memphis Division of the NC&St.L.

At the other end of the system, the NC&St.L acquired the Rome Railroad, an 18 mile long Rome to Kingston, Georgia track. This acquisition took place in 1896 as well.

Tennessee 1897 Centennial Exposition

Visionary, Major Eugene C. Lewis saw the Centennial as a great cultural and business opportunity. Versed in the classics, Lewis had always envisioned Nashville as the Athens, Greece of the new world. When approached by some of the most prominent leaders of the Nashville business world and asked if he would co-chair the exposition with Major John W. Thomas, president of the NC&St.L, Lewis welcomed the opportunity to serve.

People placed a great deal of faith in a developing society heightened by commerce as well as a growth in science and technology. Major Lewis saw the Centennial as an opportunity to bring to the public the latest advances in those fields, to showcase Nashville, and because the Nashville, Chattanooga & St. Louis would handle most to the passenger traffic to and from the Centennial, he saw this as a great business boon for the railway as well. Fashioned after the 1893 Chicago Columbia Exposition, the Centennial opened to the public on May 1st. Six months and 1.8 million visitors later, the Exposition closed on October 31, 1897.

The Centennial was one of the largest and more spectacular of a series of industrial expositions that became predominant in the latter part of the nineteenth century. It featured exhibitions on the industry, agriculture, commerce, machinery, and transportation of the state as well as displays on educational and cultural advancements.

Map of 1897 Tennessee Centennial. *-Terry L. Coats Collection*

The Centennial Exposition gave much attention to, among other things, the social progress of woman, Blacks, and children. Entire buildings were dedicated to these three aspects of Tennessee society. The Woman's Building featured displays of domestic arts and home economics and sponsored lectures by leaders of the emerging feminist movement. The Negro Building was filled with displays of African American products and educational achievements. Advocates of racial progress and cooperation were invited to address the exposition, and several Negro Days were set aside to honor the free, educated, aspiring *new Negro*. A Children's Building offered displays of children's artwork and hosted lectures on school reform. Throughout the exposition there was an ever-present emphasis on improvement through science, technology, and education.

Though the organizers of the Exposition sought to present the New South image of a rural antebellum culture giving way to a progressive industrial society, they did not forget their Southern roots. At no point did they forget the sacrifice made by its native sons on the Civil War battlefields a short thirty years earlier. The NC&St.L Railway transported free of charge, sixteen thousand former Confederate soldiers for a military encampment held on the grounds of the fair. To honor these old men, the Exposition held a Confederate Veteran's

Day. Members of the Grand Army of the Republic Veterans group were honored with a day specially held in their honor as well.

The grounds consisted of twenty-seven major buildings created on the site that once was the home to a city horse racetrack. Erected at the center of the grounds was an exact scale model of the Parthenon of ancient Greece. This structure overlooked two man-made lakes and housed the Fine Arts Building. Surrounding the lake and the Parthenon were the Memphis Pyramid of Cheops, the Negro Building, the Cuban Building, a Agricultural Building, Knights of Pythias Building, Commerce Building, Transportation Building, combination NC&St.L Terminal and Exhibit Building, a huge Auditorium Building, and more than a dozen more exhibit halls. After visiting the exhibits in the buildings, visitors to the Exposition could make their way to a *fair-like* midway containing rides and exotic shows from around the world.

Today, all the exhibits, rides, and buildings are gone, save a 1930s reconstructed model of the Parthenon. The old Exposition grounds are now the home of Nashville's premier city park … aptly named Centennial Park.

The 1890s

The waning years of the 1890s brought about several major changes on the NC&St.L system. In 1893, the NC&St.L and the L&N operated a joint terminal and yard in the *gulch* in Nashville. In August 1898, they broke ground for the new Union Station in that Nashville yard. Officials for the city, and the NC had wanted to build the new depot as early as 1872, but the location for the new depot would not be chosen until 1884.[32] Much of the delay can be attributed to the fact that the L&N had postponed lending financial support to the project. A stock securities fraud scandal involving the L&N lingered from 1881 until near the end of the decade and almost took the company into bankruptcy. The L&N Board of Directors was able to finally bring the company back to solvency only to have to fight another major battle. The U. S. Congress passed the Interstate Commerce Act in 1877 that Act was instrumental in establishing the Interstate Commerce Commission. The ICC was a regulatory agency formed to address the issues of railroad abuse and discrimination. As one of the country's larger railroads, the L&N was at the forefront of the ICC's investigations into abuses and bore the brunt of much of the agency's rulings. The L&N was tied up for a number of years fighting off federal regulation that attempted to restrict its use of power and its growth.[33] The station project was further delayed when the L&N lent money toward the building of the Tennessee Centennial Exposition. After the Exposition closed, the L&N was finally able to turn its attention to the financing of a new depot.

---

32 *When You Took a Train to Town*. The Nashville Tennessean Magazine. September 1, 1957.
33 Joe Sherman, *A Thousand Voices, The story of Nashville's Union Station*. 1987, page 14.

Delays in the start of construction brought on another set of problems for the NC&St.L. Major Lewis truly would have loved to have had a sparkling new depot in Nashville as a show place for the visitors the NC&St.L brought to the Centennial. This did not occur. The NC was forced to make substantial renovations to the only structure available, the 1850s era Church Street Depot. In 1896, the station was remodeled, refitted, and enlarged to serve as a welcome center for the guests to come. A short time after the new station was finished the old one was razed.

Trackage rights were obtained in 1899 over the Illinois Central between Martin, Tennessee and the terminal at Fulton, Kentucky. It was over this section that the NC could route the Dixie Flyer to and from Chicago.[34] The NC&St.L had been deprived of gaining access to St. Louis when the L&N threw up the roadblock in 1880. By becoming a bridge over which the Dixie Flyer could pass on its way to Florida, the NC&St.L could at least get its Pullman equipment into St. Louis. From Martin, the Dixie Flyer made its way to Nashville over the Nashville Division then on to Atlanta via the Chattanooga and Atlanta Divisions.[35]

In 1902, the Needmore Coal Company along with the NC&St.L began construction on a 10 mile railroad branch line north from Bridgeport, Alabama to its coal mines in Orme, Tennessee. The project was completed in 1904 and the operations were then sold to the Campbell Coal & Coke Company. On May 9, 1904, the NC&St.L acquired the railroad from the Campbell Coal & Coke Company and made it the last purchase the NC would ever make of a rail line. With this acquisition, and the expansion of existing trackage to mines at Ravenscroft and Clifty on the Sparta branch, and to Coalmont on the Tracy City branch a few years later, the railroad grew to its apex as a system. At that time, the NC&St.L had taken over twenty-two other companies and was operating just over 1,200 miles of trackage in four states.

Back in Nashville, 1902 saw a shift in the railroad dominance held by the NC&St.L and L&N. Jere Baxter, at the helm of the newly formed Tennessee Central Railway, was able to make a crack in the monopoly the two roads held on the city. It was in that year that the Nashville & Knoxville Railroad, the line from Lebanon to Monterey, Tennessee was acquired by the Tennessee Central. After gaining control of the N&K, the TC built a parallel track to that of the NC's from Lebanon into Nashville. By 1904, the TC had built on east of Nashville to Hopkinsville, Kentucky, and west from Monterey to Harriman, Tennessee.

Since the mid 1890s the NC&St.L had maintained a working relationship with the Nashville & Knoxville, including the sharing of a joint passenger station in Lebanon. With the acquisition of the Nashville & Knoxville by the Tennessee Central, the NC&St.L no

---

34 Richard E. Prince, *Nashville, Chattanooga & St. Louis Railway: History and Steam Locomotives.* 1967, page 151.
35 Dain L Schult, *The Dixie Trains*. Presentation at the Kudzu Railroad Convention, Kennesaw, Georgia. May 2004..

longer had a through connection toward Knoxville. The NC maintained its Lebanon Branch until 1934 when it asked permission of the ICC for abandonment of the 27 miles of the branch. Permission was granted and the last train on the NC&St.L departed Lebanon on July 13, 1935.

Between 1900 and 1925, railroading in America hit an apex in the amounts of trackage, revenue, freight hauled, as well as the number of transported passengers.

In 1860, there was 30,500 miles of track in the United States. By 1900, that number had expanded to 192,000, and in 1916 there were 254,057 miles of track, and more than 85,000 depots.[36] Unfortunately, after 1916, short lived would be the period through which the railroads would rein as king.

The NC&St.L struck its prime for freight revenue as well as net income in the 1920s.[37] Almost immediately, the emergence of the mass-produced automobile and a national road-building program took an enormous bite of the business held by all railroads including that of the NC.

In 1926, after declining patronage on the Tracy City branch, the NC&St.L purchased three buses and a cargo truck to run on this line in lieu of running passenger cars on the trains. The NC was forced to abandon this experiment in alternate trafficking in 1930. Unable to generate passenger interest on the buses, they were retired and afterward combination passenger-freight caboose service was used.[38] This decline continued until the years of WWII when the transportation of troops and war materiel gave the railroads a much-needed revitalization.

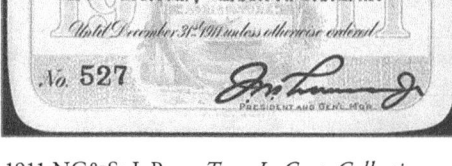

1911 NC&St.L Pass. -*Terry L. Coats Collection*

Between 1900 and 1912, the NC&St.L built or upgraded three of its four terminal depots. Construction began on a new Union Station in Nashville in 1898 and the station was opened to the public in 1900.

Additionally, in 1900 the NC&St.L performed an extensive remodeling and refurbishment of the 1882 Union Station in Chattanooga. During the renovations, extensive interior details were and new floors of Georgia marble were added. The transformations were said to have been a beautiful freshening of the old depot.

---

36 Michael Ray O'Neal, *Historic Railroad Depot Architecture in Middle Tennessee*. A thesis presented to the Graduate Faculty of Middle Tennessee State University in partial fulfillment of the requirements for Masters of Fine Arts Degree. August 1983.
37 Dain L. Schult, *Nashville, Chattanooga & St. Louis: A History of "The Dixie Line."* 2001, page 119.
38 Terry L. Coats, *Tracy City Bus Service 1926-1930*. The Dixie Flyer, Nashville, Chattanooga Preservation Society Newsletter. November 2007.

In 1909, the Memphis Railroad Terminal Company chartered to build a new passenger station in Memphis. Five railroads including the NC&St.L bought equal amounts of stock for the erection of a new union station. The new terminal was completed and opened in September 1912.

During the latter part of the nineteenth and the early part of the twentieth century, the NC&St.L outgrew two of their facilities and moved them to larger quarters. In 1890, the old shops located in the *gulch* near the old 1854 Church Street Nashville depot was abandoned and an entire new repair-erection center was built on Charlotte Avenue about two miles away from the old location. The new facilities would be called the *New Shops* and would serve the NC&St.L through the L&N merger in 1957.

NC&St.L Shops Mile Marker 2.0. *-Tennessee State Library and Archives*

At the apex of operations in 1945-6, the New Shops would employ over two thousand people and was the center of operations for all repairs and building of NC&St.L equipment. Located in the 45-acre complex were an erection shop, car repair facilities, storehouse, paint shop, a massive roundhouse, foundry, locomotive repair shop, and smith shop. There were a total of fifteen major buildings. If the NC needed something, it was more than likely done in-house at the Charlotte Avenue Shops.

The buildings of the shops were razed in July 1960 after the facilities closed and the last employees were transferred to Nashville's Radnor Yards in February 1959.

Chattanooga, Tennessee Cravens Yard. *-Nashville, Chattanooga & St. Louis Railway*

By 1907, the yard adjacent to the Chattanooga depot known as the *City Yards* had grown too small to handle the increasing load the NC&St.L was demanding. In February of that year, the railroad completed the building of a new yard at the foot of Lookout Mountain and hugging the Tennessee River at Moccasin Bend. Cravens Yard, as it would be named, had the capacity to hold 1,000 freight cars and had 25 tracks open on both ends. The NC retained its freight transfer and passenger station at the old City Yards facilities. In 1916, the repairs shops from the downtown yard were moved to Cravens as well. Cravens Yard was surpassed in 1961 when the L&N railroad opened Wauhatchie Yards approximately six miles west of the city. Because of its proximity to the downtown area, Cravens is still in use today as a small switching yard.

United States Rail Administration

When America was suddenly thrust into WWI against Germany and the Axis powers in 1917, it was found that American railroads proved inadequate to the task of handling the increased burden of transporting the men and materiel. Years of federal regulation of the rail companies had so weakened them that they had been unable to keep up with inflating costs. By 1915, between fifteen and twenty percent of all United States rail companies were in bankruptcy. After a failed attempt by the railroad companies to band together in a coordinated War effort, the Interstate Commerce Commission (ICC) recommended federal control of all American railroads to be organized for a common goal.

On December 28, 1917, President Wilson placed in effect the Federal Possession and Control Act to nationalize a majority of America's railroads. The result of Wilson's actions was the formation of the United States Railroad Administration, or the USRA; the USRA remains today as America's greatest experiment in nationalization.

Changes to the United States rail system under the USRA were swift and merciless. Terminals, shops, and other facilities were consolidated, passenger train runs duplicated on more than one railroad were eliminated, and costly Pullman services on many trains were curtailed or eliminated all together. The USRA changed the names of railways to railroads and most of the passenger trains that up until that time had been identified by name were suddenly simply shown on USRA timetables as numbered trains. On the NC&St.L, only the Dixie Flyer retained its name.[39]

Though some of the changes made by the USRA would prove an object failure, some would set the standards that the railroads would retain even after the demise of the USRA. The Rail Authority standardized the design of locomotives and cars. Using the new standardized design, the USRA ordered 2,000 locomotives and 100,000 freight cars for use on the nationalized railroads.

In 1917, the USRA also nationalized the rail express businesses of the Adams Express Company, the American Express Company, Southern Express Company, and Wells Fargo and Company Express into the American Railway Express. American Railway Express would change its name in 1929 to the Railway Express Agency and would remain in business until 1975.

---

39   Personal interview with Dain L Schult. May 23, 2003.

The USRA changes had a profound effect on the NC&St.L … eliminated was the Dixie Flyer route between Fulton, Kentucky and Martin, Tennessee that the NC had obtained ten years earlier. On the other end of the NC&St.L system, the Dixie trains that up until that time had called at the old 1871 Atlanta Union Depot were now arriving at Atlanta's Terminal depot a few blocks away. Terminal Station suddenly became an ultra busy facility. Not only were the southern bound Dixie's arriving there, but also the trains of the Southern, the Central of Georgia, and those of the West Point Railroad as well.

Dutchman's Curve: Worst Passenger Train Wreck in American History

Dutchman's Curve 1918 Accident. Shown are two cars from the Nashville bound train. In the center of the photo can be seen the wheels and frame of locomotive No. 281. The boiler of that locomotive was stripped away in the accident and is in the corn field to the right in this photograph. *-H. C. Hill photographer, Henry Hill, III Collection*

A history of the first twenty years of the twentieth century on the NC&St.L Railway could not be written without a mention of the events of July 9, 1918. On this date, at approximately 7:30 AM, two NC&St.L trains, one northbound (though predominately southwest in direction of travel, the timetable called this north) from Nashville to Memphis and southbound Memphis to Nashville collided head-on approximately five miles west of Nashville. In brief, the crew of the Memphis bound train mistook a local switcher and a cut of cars working in the yards for the superior Nashville bound train to which their train was supposed to yield. Thinking that the superior train had passed, the engineer entered his train onto the single main to the west of the NC&St.L shops at Charlotte Pike. A short distance hence, the two trains collided. It was estimated that the combined speeds of the trains was in excess of 100 mph. Both engineers, both firemen, and an additional 26 on- and off-duty railroad employees were killed. The official passenger death toll was listed as 79. The combined death toll for this wreck was 109 with an additional 84 injuries. To date, the wreck remains the most deadly passenger train wreck on American soil.

Boom or Bust

During the decade 1917 to 1927, the NC&St.L increased through-freight business by increasing its interaction with other railroads in the states of Tennessee and Kentucky. Prior to the earlier date, the NC and the Chicago, Burlington & Quincy Railroad had operated a joint car-ferry between Metropolis, Illinois and Paducah, Kentucky. In 1917, they built a double track bridge across the Ohio River eliminating the ferry. This 5,442 foot bridge became the longest truss bridge in the world. The two railroads operated this link across the river as the Paducah & Illinois Railroad. After the completion of the bridge, traffic at this point increased exponentially. Seeing the magnitude of traffic generated by the new span, the Illinois Central Railroad would, in 1924, purchase a one-third share in the crossing and would eventually make it a major part of their north-south main line between Chicago and New Orleans.

In August 1926, the Gulf, Mobile & Northern (later the Gulf, Mobile & Ohio) entered into an agreement with the NC&St.L for track rights between Jackson, Tennessee and Paducah. The GM&N used the 145 miles between the two cities as a bridge between Mobile to the Burlington at Metropolis. In 1933, the GM&N changed the routing to the Illinois Central and the traffic over the Dixie Line ceased.[40]

By 1928, the 78 year-old Tunnel Hill tunnel, made famous during the "Great Locomotive Chase" was too small to handle the traffic on the NC&St.L; so a new larger bore was made directly beside the original. Today the old original tunnel serves as part of a walking trail in the city of Tunnel Hill, Georgia.

In Atlanta, the NC&St.L began construction on a new Union Station to replace the beautiful but aged depot that had served since 1871. The new structure was begun in 1928 and opened two years later in 1930.

As was the case in all of America, the NC&St.L took a devastating financial blow starting in 1929 as the years of the depression swept the country. Suddenly the railroads that had been riding a wave of prosperity in the early to mid 1920s were almost overnight

---

40   Richard E. Prince, *Nashville, Chattanooga & St. Louis Railway: History and Steam Locomotives*. 1967, page 69.

The Dixie Flyer departs Chattanooga, Tennessee in this 1936 photo.
-*Photographer unknown; -Dain L. Schult Collection*

cut down in their prime. As the years of reversal dragged on, the NC was forced to eliminate jobs for many workers and to reduce hours and pay for almost all remaining employees. The railroad was forced to abandon and remove over 40 miles of track as a cost saving measure. It was during the depression years that the NC abandoned the Lebanon to Nashville branch. During this same period, portions of the McMinnville branch were, in part, shut down. The number of passenger trains operated by the NC was cut in half, but the combination of all these cost-cutting measures was still not enough.

Adding to an already cumbersome load of heavy taxation, the federal government had in effect a mandatory rate structure to which the railroads were required to adhere. This repressive structuring was not mandated equally to the truck and barge companies and, in essence, gave both industries a leg up in competition against the trains.

Fighting against the federal government's unfair burden and the poor economy, the NC was somehow able to steer clear of the receivership that beckoned at its door throughout the 1930s. By 1937, the picture looked a bit brighter. However, even after conditions stabilized and the economy began to float back to a more normal state, irreversible financial damage had been done to all railroads in this country. The railroads would never overcome the foothold gained by the trucking and barge industries during the decade between 1931 and 1941.

1941–1950: Decade of Re-growth

Slowly, America shook off the effects of the depression and, as a modicum of prosperity returned, an upturn in business spread optimism for better days ahead spread throughout the NC&St.L. Additionally, the World War II years that followed brought an increase in business to the NC. The transportation of troop and war materiel increased the workload and the profits for the NC.

Parlor Car, 1930s. -*Nashville, Chattanooga & St. Louis Railway; -H. C. Hill photographer*

In 1941, the company set about on a reconstruction and modernization program. President Fitzgerald Hall, sensing the magnitude the effects the war would have on the company purchased 1,000 new boxcars, 1,250 hoppers and gondolas, as well as additional used passenger cars from other railroads.[41] Business on the NC&St.L expanded expediently.

During the War, the army established training Camp Forrest just outside of Tullahoma and Camp Campbell outside of Clarksville. Thousands of men as well as the supplies and equipment needed for training poured into these camps over the NC. Over the next few years the railroads of middle Tennessee would see more than their fair share of business.

Locomotive #534, Nashville to Atlanta, March 1941. -*Marietta Museum of History*

As the War geared up in Europe the need for petroleum products skyrocketed. Fearing the repercussions of trying to transport oil and gasoline by ship from the refineries in the Gulf of Mexico to demarcation points on the east coast, the army chose to carry the petroleum products overland by train. Tank car after tank car of aviation fuel, oil, and gasoline were handed off to the NC&St.L at Memphis to travel across Tennessee to Chattanooga and from there carried to Atlanta or handed off to the Southern for transport through Knoxville to Virginia. During 1942 and 1943 the NC was handling on average six to eight tankcar trains daily over its system.[42] In 1943, it would not have been an unusual sight to see a fifty car NC unit train of tankcars rolling through the Tennessee and Georgia countryside. Over the course of the War, the NC&St.L delivered over 34,000 cars of fuel to the Atlantic coast.

World War II Train. Civilians depart Union Station in Nashville on NC&St.L passenger cars to report for induction into military service. -*Tennessee State Library and Archives*

The increase in business enhanced the NC's revenues, but for the operations department, it proved to be a very taxing situation just to keep pace. The NC&St.L needed more motive power to help with the increased load and it could not come any too soon.

In the 1930s to 1940s, diesel electric locomotives were beginning to develop as the motive power of the coming generations. The NC attempted to purchase new diesels for use

---

41   Stewart Covington, *NC&St.L: Dixie Success Story*. Trains Magazine. January 1948.
Dain L. Schult, *Nashville, Chattanooga & St. Louis: A History of "The Dixie Line."* 2001, page 147.
42   David P. Morgan, *Gliders, Yellow Jackets, and Stripes*. Trains Magazine, December 1963.

Magazine advertisement depicting a string of tank cars of WWII petroleum produces being transported by trains over America's rail system. -*Terry L. Coats Collection*

Cowan, Tennessee, March 1946, locomotive #532. -*Marietta Museum of History*

in their yards as well as for road power. They were able to purchase some early production switchers from Alco, Baldwin, and EMD for the yards but by the time they tried to acquire diesels as passenger road locomotives, the Federal Office of Defense Transportation curtailed all purchases of diesel power. The NC&St.L would have to operate throughout the war years with steam engines as their road engines.

The NC&St.L had not purchased any new motive power since the procurement of the 4-8-4, J2s, from ALCO in 1930. To keep up with the increased workload created by the War it was imperative for the railroad to supplement its aging fleet. After having rousing success with the J2s, the NC again contacted the American Locomotive Company (ALCO) of Schenectady, New York to build its latest fleet of locomotives. Using the J2s as a base on which to develop a new engine, ALCO and the NC&St.L's superintendent of machinery Clarence M. Darden retained the best of the J2s and incorporated the latest improvements in the creation of the new power. Designated as J3s, the new engines were ultra sleek in design. With their red-capped smokestacks and wide yellow striped sideboards these locomotives were quite a site to behold. The engines sported a conical nose and a Commonwealth pilot. They were equipped with Timken roller bearings on both the locomotive and tenders. This was a major improvement over the J2s. The old timers would tell you that the roller bearing and the precision of machinery on these engines made you think you were *driving a Cadillac*.

The emphasis for the NC&St.L during the 1940s was modernization and speed. The new J3s were much faster than their sisters' engines the Mountains and Mikados. High speed traffic could only be accomplished by upgrading the rails. Between 1945 and 1947, major improvements were made to reduce curvature and grade on the entire line from Memphis to Atlanta. At the same time these improvements were being made to the track, the NC&St.L finished installing Central Traffic Control (CTC) between Bruceton and Memphis.

Begun in 1943, the CTC system, with the exception of 38 miles of double-track between Chattanooga and Bridgeport that needed no signals, had been extended to Nashville by the fall of 1944. By June 1947, CTC was extended into Memphis. At that point there was 384 miles of NC track under block signal control. Control towers were erected at Bruceton and Cowan, Tennessee and Tilton Yard in Atlanta. The Tilton tower would eventually be closed and those operations moved to Dalton, Georgia. Freight trains from Bruceton to Atlanta shaved four hours off the scheduled running time after the installation of CTC.[43]

---

43 S. Kip Farrington, Jr., *Railroads of Today*. 1949, page 158.

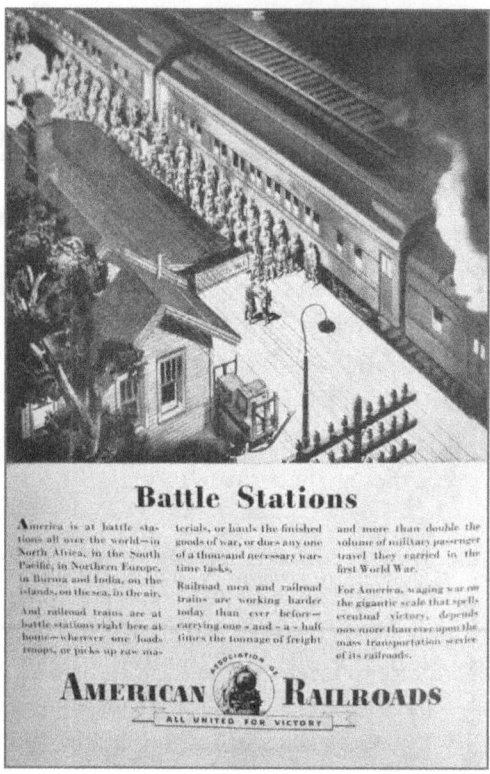 

Battle Stations and Darkest Hour. Seen here are two magazine advertisements from WWII expounding the virtues of American Railroad's war efforts. *-Terry L. Coats Collection*

A short time after the merger of the NC into the L&N, most of the traffic over the P&M division was re-routed through McKenzie to Nashville. The CTC from Memphis to Bruceton over the old P&M was removed a short time later.

Other improvements along the lines included the installation of a new bridge and route straightening at the Etowah River as well as improvement of the bridge at the Chattahoochee River, both on the Atlanta Division. The bridge at Bridgeport, Alabama saw improvements and major changes took place at Johnsonville on the Tennessee River west of Nashville. Ten miles of the Nashville Division between mileposts 74.4 and 84.5 had to be diverted when the Tennessee Valley Authority constructed a dam downstream at Gilbertsville, Kentucky. The blocking of the river created a lake from the dam site all the way to the Mississippi state line.[44] The completion of the new dam allowed the Illinois Central to reroute their tracks atop the structure freeing the old bridge to be used for a new assignment. The bridge was taken down from its pylons and placed on a barge for movement. The bridge was floated upriver and re-erected at the NC&St.L's new crossing approximately three-fourths mile south of the previous Johnsonville to the Eva crossing site. The establishment of the newly formed Kentucky Lake placed the towns of Eva and Johnsonville under several feet of water. A new community of New Johnsonville was established on the east approach to the bridge and a modern depot was

---

44   Ibid, page 159.

erected. This would be the last station built by the NC&St.L. The New Johnsonville depot is still in use today by the CSX railroad. Because of the relocation of the tracks away from Eva, that station closed as a stop on the NC's timetables.

Chattanooga Attempts to Evict the Railroads

In the 1850s, Chattanooga had welcomed the railroads with open arms. Ninety years later, the story changed dramatically. The Western & Atlantic Railroad entered the city in 1850 followed by the Nashville & Chattanooga in 1854. In those days, Chattanooga was not much more than a small hamlet. As the city expanded east and south from the river it enveloped its tracks of the railroads. By the 1940s, the NC&St.L, Southern, Central of Georgia, and Tennessee, Alabama & Georgia Railroads served Chattanooga, calling at two passenger stations … Union and Terminal. Additionally, these railroads were delivering and receiving freight cars from hundreds of industries and warehouses within the city limits. Almost without exception, all of the track crossings of the railroads were at grade level with city streets.

A survey completed in the mid 1940s showed that these four railroads were on average shuttling thirty passenger trains and over 7,500 freight cars across city streets each day. The survey went on to say that in a 14-hour daily period, these trains delayed an average of 4,538 trucks and automobiles and that there had been several fatal accidents involving train-car collisions. The situation got completely out of hand. In a letter presented to the four railroads on January 14, 1946, the city proposed the moving of the NC&St.L mainline from the north end of Cravens Yard to the east end and that the two present downtown terminals be abandoned and replaced by a new larger terminal to serve all lines; this proposal was immediately rebuffed by all lines. The refusal by the lines to cooperate was just the latest in a string of several similar proposals by the city.

Chattanooga had had enough. The city went to the Tennessee State Legislature for help. In March 1947, the Legislature passed a bill creating the Chattanooga Terminal Authority (CTA). Using the newly formed Authority, the city now had the power to evict the railroads at their own expense. Sensing that the CTA would actually have the muscle to force the rail companies into submission, the railroads decide to come to the negotiation table with the city.

Proposals wavered back and forth for years. In the end, Cravens Yards between Lookout Mountain and the downtown area was reduced in importance and Wauhatchie Yards, a much larger facility, was built on the opposite side of the mountain. On the other hand, passenger service to Union Station continued through the merger of the NC&St.L into the L&N and up until the L&N discontinued service in Chattanooga at the birth of Amtrak in 1971. This discontinuance brought to a close 121 years of passenger service to Chattanooga. Southern Railroad retained its own passenger service for a number of years after the creation of Amtrak. In the end, both the city and the rail companies won a portion of the negotiations. The yards were moved but the lines into the two terminals were retained until the railroads withdrew service.[45]

Passenger Train Travel after World War II

During the War years, the public was severely neglected in favor of the transportation of materiel and soldiers. After Pearl Harbor, servicemen traveling on trains were given priority for Pullman space on sleeper trains. This left only the day coaches for the general public. After the war, in an attempt to re-establish support of the traveling public, railroads across the nation, including the NC&St.L, rushed to refurbish and revamp their passenger services. A two pronged attack would be needed to draw the public back to using the trains. New equipment and an expansion of services would be needed.

The passenger cars on most railroads, some dating to the 1920s, had served dutifully during the War, but were now far beyond their time of useful service. Budd and Pullman-Standard, the two largest car builders in America, were inundated with orders for new passenger cars. There was no way these car builders could make production to match the kind of demand that had besieged them. Both companies were quoting delivery times up to four years from the time orders were placed.[46] If the NC&St.L wanted new passenger equipment, they would have to find another company to build them or they would have to build the cars themselves.

Dixie train at foot of Lookout Mountain. -*Nashville Chattanooga & St. Louis Railway*

For some time, the NC&St.L had looked to add a new train on its Memphis to Nashville run. Adding a new train to this route could be the answer to adding that second prong to their revamping plans. Many high profile trains such as the *Lookout, the Quickstep,* and the *"Dixie"* trains journeyed the tracks of the NC&St.L only to be handed off to another rail line. The NC&St.L wanted a train it could call its very own ... enter the *City of Memphis*. The NC saw in the *City* a way to add a new element to its roster.

Superintendent of Machinery, Clarence M. Darden, who had designed the cylinder-integrated steel framed beds for the NC's J's was called upon to *home build* a fleet of streamlined cars

---

45   Warren Stephens, *Relocation of Mainline Railroads out of Downtown Chattanooga: 1945 to 1975.* Presentation to the L&N Historical Society, Chattanooga, Tennessee. September 2009.
46   Dain L. Schult, *Nashville, Chattanooga & St. Louis: A History of "The Dixie Line."* 2001, page 158

for the new train. Darden and the men at the West Nashville Shops set to kitbashing a set of six 1920s style heavyweight Pullmans. These cars were stripped of roofs, and interiors, and then completely retrofitted with, new larger windows, air conditioning, a new streamlined roof, and roller bearing trucks.

NC&St.L Locomotive #535. Rebuilt and streamlined in 1947 for service as the City of Memphis train. The locomotive served from 1913 until 1949 when it threw a side rod and was retired from service. -*Robert J. Foster photographer; -Terry L. Coats Collection*

Dieselization of road engines was just over the horizon. But for now, the City of Memphis would have to settle for steam power for the new streamliner. Thirty-three year old Pacific class, engine No. 535 was chosen for the haul. No. 535 was the engine known on the NC&St.L as engine *Marie*. In 1913, at the time of the delivery of a group of new engines to the NC, president John Thomas requested a former engineer turned minister to christen and name one of the new engines. No. 535 was chosen for the naming and the annotating. Rev. Thomas Harrison christened the engine and named it for his five-year-old daughter, Marie.

City of Memphis. -*Nashville, Chattanooga & St. Louis Railway*

In 1946, just as the cars had been, the engine was reworked for the new duty. She received the same cylinder integrated type frame and Timken roller bearing wheel sets Darden had used on the J3s. The boiler and firebox were completely rebuilt, and a sleek new shovel nosed shrouding was installed to give her an ultra-modern appearance. The entire train set was given a new paint scheme. The Confederate gray and blue that would become the standard for the next generation F3s and passenger GP7s diesels was introduced with the train. Engine No. 535 entered service and made its inaugural run of the City on May 17, 1947. The new train was introduced to the public with great excitement and fanfare. The public immediately fell in love with the train.

The City left Memphis each morning at 8:05 AM and arrived in Nashville at 1:05 PM and made the return trip to Memphis each evening. The engine would be serviced in the Bluff City overnight, only to be called for duty the next morning to make the run again.

The upkeep of this hectic schedule finally proved to be too much for *Marie*. One morning in the fall of 1948, the NC&St.L literally ran the wheels or at least the running gear, off the engine. Marie had been turning as much as 14,000 miles per month making

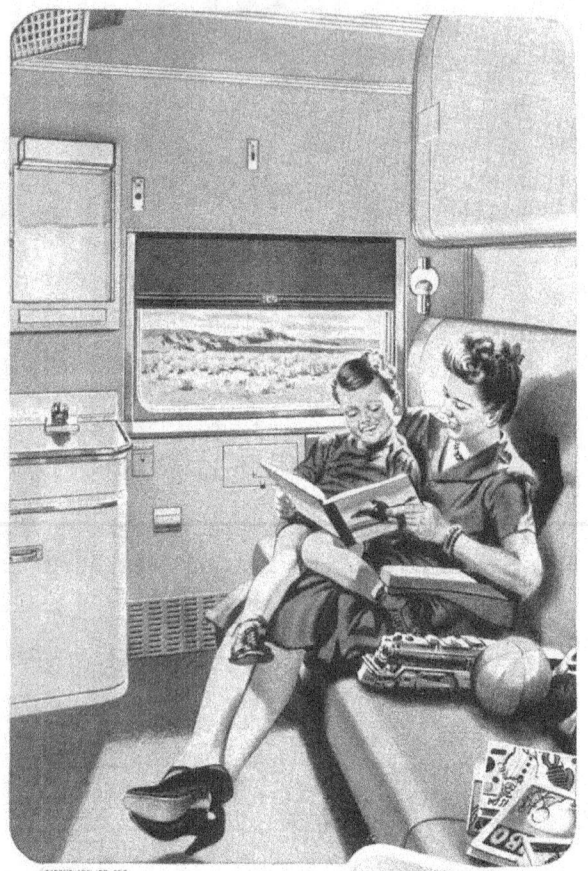

Pullman Advertisement. -*Terry L. Coats Collection*

Dixie Flagler Advertisement. *-NCS&L Railway*

1950s Air Travel Advertisement. With a return to a peacetime economy after WWII, the airlines tried to attract passengers as seen in this 1946 advertisement. -*New Yorker Magazine;* -*Terry L. Coats Collection.*

the Memphis to Nashville run on a daily basis. All that mileage caught up with her on a run toward Nashville. As the train passed though Vaughn's Gap about ten miles from her destination, the engineer suddenly felt underfoot a great wobbling and realized that there was something terribly wrong with the locomotive. He had just enough time to react to the danger and to leap from his pilot's seat when the drive rod on his side of the locomotive came loose and wiped the right side of the cab completely off the engine. Remarkably, neither the engine nor any of the cars left the tracks, but the long career of the old engine was over. Knowing that the new road diesels were ordered and that they would soon be able to make the run, it was simply not worth the effort to rebuild her. *Marie* was scrapped in 1949 and the NC used the J3s as its primary source of power until the delivery of five GP7 steam generator equipped diesel blue and gray beauties, Nos. 750 to 754, were placed in service.

As profitable as passenger business had been to the NC&St.L and other railroads during the War years, the latter half of the 1940s and the 1950s would witness a continuous slide in the opposite direction. No amount of new trains, new cars, and superlined equipment could seduce post-War riders away from the influence of the automobile and the airplane. Automobiles would supply the freedom and the planes the speed that passenger trains could never deliver. Passenger trains became a dying class. The railroads continued to lose passengers to the airlines and, in 1957, the number of people traveling by airlines finally surpassed those traveling by rail.

How did the railroads fall so far behind? Blame it on our love affair with the automobile and a historic indifference of legislators for subsidizing the nation's railroads. Our government's disdain for trains began with President Franklin D. Roosevelt when, in the 1930s, he turned his back on the railroad barons asking for federal handouts. Two decades later, President Eisenhower certified our commitment to the automobile when he authorized the building of the Interstate highway system. These were two substantial factors in the demise of passenger train service in this country.

The final chapter for the NC&St.L took place between 1948 and 1957. The NC entered the diesel age in 1941 with the delivery of four 660-horsepower, SW-1s from ALCO. By the end of the War, there were twelve diesels working the yards at Nashville, Chattanooga, and

GP7 #752 shown ahead of the City of Memphis in Lexington, Tennessee on September 6, 1954. -*Jim Ozment photographer;* -*Western Rail Images Collection*

Diesel Instruction Car, ca. 1952. The company converted this old NC&St.L passenger car and pulled it from location to location as a mobile classroom. The car was used for the instructing engineers on the operation of the EMD and Alco diesels the NC purchased. -*Nashville, Chattanooga & St. Louis Railway*

Atlanta. In 1948, the first of 52 EMD, F3s and F7s, and in 1950, the first of 37 EMD, GP7s began to fill the NC&St.L rosters. The new diesels would take over the domains that once ran with Pacifics, Consolidations, and the Dixies.

January 4, 1953 marked a day of finality for the company. On this day ran the last passenger train on the Bruceton to Union City section of the Nashville Division. This part of the line had seen passenger service since the 1860s as first the Nashville & Northwestern Railroad and then as the NC. In the waning years before secession of service, passenger trains were only averaging three riders per run, way to little patronage to warrant continuation of service. This last passenger run on the Nashville Division also marked the last steam engine run on the entire NC&St.L system. Steam locomotion on the NC&St.L had lasted 103 years, The honor given to an engine to make the last steam run was not to one of the J3s, the newest and biggest on the NC roster, (these giants had been scrapped in September the year before), but was given to one of the oldest and smallest locomotives … the railroad chose 2-8-0, Consolidation No. 406. Ironically, this same engine had just a few months before been at the head of the last passenger run on the Paducah to Memphis Division.

Train No. 6 departed Bruceton on Sunday afternoon, but this last run was different from previous runs at its regular stops in Huntington, McKenzie, Gleason, Dresden, and Martin; at each stop dignitaries, newspapermen, and politicians from the respective towns boarded the train. All were the guest of the NC&St.L Railway and all were carried to the end of the line at Union City for a farewell dinner that evening.

Crew of the Last Steam Run on the NC&St.L System. This locomotive was also on the last passenger run on the Paducah & Memphis Division three months earlier. -*Nashville, Chattanooga & St. Louis Railway*

Last Passenger Run on the P&M Division, Paris, Tennessee, 1953. -*Nashville, Chattanooga & St. Louis Railway*

All along the 59 miles of rail to Union City, people turned out by the hundreds to witness the end of an era in Tennessee history. *Old Smoky,* as someone dubbed her that day pulled a mail-baggage car and one coach on her final run. Engineer C. S. Morrow used up much of the old engine's steam pressure on the last mile into Union City. Morrow reportedly played a swan song in steam on No. 406's whistle.[47] [48]

"Lament of the Last Steamer"

I'm heading for the last Round-house,
You're using 'Old Smoky' for the last time to ride;
So long old pals, my boiler's almost dry,
I'm heading for the last Round-house.
Roll along, old drivers, roll along, roll along,
Roll along, old drivers, roll along,
Roll along, old drivers, roll along, roll along,
Roll along, old drivers, roll along,
I'm heading for the last Round-house,
To the far-away Shop of the Super in the sky;
Where all old 'steamers' are torch-ered', there go I,
I'm heading for the last Round-house.

... Author unknown

The steamers were given up as too costly to maintain and diesels would rule on both passenger and freight trains after this date. All the steamers went to the torch except one. In September 1953, the NC&St.L donated one of its pride and joys, J3, No. 576 to the people of Nashville. On September 30, 1953, the mighty engine rolled down a temporarily constructed track into Centennial Park in Nashville. Her resting place was within sight of the Charlotte Avenue Shops where she had been carried countless times for maintenance or for turning on the 110 foot turntable alongside the roundhouse.

The railroad also saved the tenders from the J's and used them in maintenance of way service. As late as the 1990s, one of the old tenders was seen in a MOW consist serving as a water reservoir for the work train.

By 1952, the NC had on its roster all the diesels that it would purchase. The reddish-maroon and yellow, GP7s were relegated to freight service while the F3s and F7s pulled both freight and passenger service. Only the F-unit "B's" were equipped with steam generators,

---

47   Union City Daily Messenger. January 5, 1953. McKenzie Banner. January 9, 1953.
48   NC&St.L Railway Bulletin. February 1953, page 4.

meaning that any passenger train headed by the F's had to include one of the "B" units to supply power for the cars. Five of the GP7s were also ordered from EMD with steam generators. These five units, Nos. 750 to 754, were painted in the blue and gray scheme and were used on the City of Memphis.

1954 would see the opening of an expanded Radnor Yards. Radnor was an immense classification yard located five miles south of downtown Nashville. This joint venture between the NC&St.L and the L&N Railroads was a foreshadowing of the venture that awaited the two rail lines in 1957. Compressed into a 2.5 mile stretch of land, Radnor had over 100 miles of tracks capable at peak capacity of handling 3,000 cars a day. The L&N had maintained a yard at Radnor for over 40 years; the expansion would make it one of the most important on the L&N System. The increase in business for the two railroads made the Kayne Avenue Yards behind Nashville's Union Station antiquated. There was not enough room to expand the Kayne Avenue Yards, so the only alternative was to expand the Radnor site.

END OF A DYNASTY

Speaking in 1951 before a meeting of Security Analysts of New York, L&N president John E. Tilford told his audience that as soon as the L&N and the NC&St.L completed the building of their merged yard facilities at Radnor Yards in Nashville, he had all intent in merging the railroads into one company.[49]

With the opening of the new merged yards at Radnor, Tilford set in motion his plans to make good on his promise of merging the two companies once and for good. By December 1954, the headlines in The Nashville Tennessean newspaper were all ablaze over the announced merger of the NC&St.L and the L&N. A vote taken by the board of directors of the L&N meeting in New York sealed the fate of the NC&St.L.

The people of Nashville were distraught at the loss of the hometown NC&St.L to the Louisville based L&N. They did not understand how the vote taken by a small group of men

---

49   *Merger in a Regulated Industry, Case Study of the Proposed Merger of the L&N and the NC&St.L Railway.* Committee on the Judiciary, House of Representatives. March 30, 1956. Dain L. Schult, *Nashville, Chattanooga & St. Louis: A History of "The Dixie Line."* 2001, page 191.

in New York could make such an impact affecting an institutional icon in Nashville. Fuzzy in their minds were the events of 1880 when Vernon Stevenson had sold his majority block of 134,000 shares of N&C stock to the L&N. In one fell swoop, Stevenson's actions gave the L&N controlling interest in the N&C and stopped in its tracks the aggressive strides made by philanthropist, N&C president Edmund W. Cole. The events of 1954 played the final card from a hand that had been dealt the NC&St.L 75 years before.

The actual date of the merger would not occur for almost three more years but the die had already been cast. The NC would be forced to live in a lame-duck purgatory until August 1957.

The Nashville, Chattanooga & St. Louis Railway for its 112 years of existence was quite a progressive railroad. It had the enviable position of being a trunk system connecting America's Midwest with the Atlantic Ocean to the east and the Gulf Coast to the south. The railroad had connections to four rivers, the Ohio in Paducah, the Mississippi in Memphis, the Cumberland in Nashville, and the Tennessee in Chattanooga and Perryville. It traversed the heart of the richest sections of the state of Tennessee traveling through the Great Nashville Basin, extending branches at Wartrace, Cowan, Tullahoma, Decherd, and Jasper. From these departure points the NC reached out to rich coal and mineral reserves, cotton fields, and iron furnaces.

- In Nashville, the NC intersected with the L&N and the Tennessee Central giving it an outlet to Louisville, Evansville, St. Louis, and Chicago to the north, Alabama, Mobile, and New Orleans to the south, and Knoxville and the upper mid-Atlantic to the east.
- From Memphis and Atlanta, connections were made to both coasts.
- At Stevenson, connections were made with the Memphis & Charleston Railroad.
- Connections with the Illinois Central and the GM&O in west Tennessee provided gateways to the Midwest.
- In 1942, the NC&St.L in conjunction with Vanderbilt University developed an educational course for all its employees. The course covered every aspect of the railroad from it history to how the company was organized, to how each department within the company was structured and operated.
- Not only was it the first successful railroad in the state of Tennessee, during its tenure it went on to be one of the most progressive railroads in America. Many innovative firsts in railroading occurred on the NC&St.L.
- The NC was the first railroad in the world to

Railway Express Agency advertisement from a local 1944 newspaper. *-Terry L. Coats Collection*

experiment with dispatching freight trains using radiotelegraph. Up through 1920, the NC&St.L had to pay an excessive amount in long distance phone charges each month to keep the Huntsville Division headquarters in Tullahoma in touch with the line at Guntersville. A radio transmitter was purchased and E. W. Crabtree, a former WWI wireless operator, was placed in charge of the experiment. Though the experiment ran into several problems and was eventually abandoned, the railroad pioneered the radio system used on all railroads today.[50]

- The NC was the first railroad to offer its employees a retirement pension plan. Long before the adoption of the Railway Retirement Act on the federal level, the NC&St.L had a fully company-funded pension in place.
- The NC developed a means of billing for freight movement that was adopted by railroads across the nation.
- The NC was the first railroad in the nation to offer its customers an "en-route" processing service. A farmer's grain would be taken off the train, milled and processed, making it ready for market. The processed grain would then be held free of storage until market prices were favorable. The transportation and storage would be charged as one trip. The NC&St.L enacted this practice in 1872. Years later this would be a standard practice on hundreds of other lines.
- The NC was the first railroad in the south to add 4-8-4 class locomotives to its roster. In 1930 the NC purchased the first of what would become a total order of thirty J2 and J3 locomotives. It was these thirty locomotives that were the backbone for transportation of materiel on the NC&St.L during WWII.
- The NC was the first southern railroad to use Camelback and Duplex engines over its mountainous regions.
- First southeastern railroad to go intermodal in two areas. The NC operated a steamboat ferry line between Hobbs Island and Guntersville, Alabama, a distance of 22 miles, the longest rail-ferry crossing in the world. On the Tracy City branch, the NC also operated between 1926 and 1930 a passenger bus between the main line in Cowan up and down the mountain from Tracy City.
- First railroad in the region to exclusively dieselize (1952).
- The NC was the first southern railroad to build and operate a Dynamometer Car.
- In the 1920s, the NC&St.L operated a special Agriculture Train, something akin to having a demonstration farm on wheels. The train operated across the entire NC&St.L system exhibiting cars on poultry, cattle, crops, and the domestic arts.

These were but a sampling of some of the innovative firsts and exclusive attributes that were unique to the NC&St.L.

---

50   NC&St.L Employees Bulletin. November 1950, page 11.

Down at the Depot

*"Went down to the depot, never got there on time.
Well, my train done left, she's a'rollin' down the line."*
Big Railroad Blues ... Grateful Dead

From the 1850s to the first decades of the twentieth century, the telegraph wire and the steam locomotive traversed the land as the forbearers of today's Internet, cell phones, and airplanes. If it was important to the community, it traveled by train. People, produce, consumer goods, and information were all commodities that either came or left by the railroad. If it traveled by train, it arrived or departed from the depot. The train station was such a mainstay in American society that in 1916 it is estimated there were some 80,000 depots in this country[51].

From the trains onto the station platform, stepped the backbone of American culture; the teacher and the students, the minister and the sinner, the farmers and the construction worker, the accountant and the drummer with their wares. Each person had his or her own story, each one using the train as transport to their next great adventure, or maybe just the next phase of their lives.

If you were a farmer, it would be through the freight depot the product of your labors would go to market. If you operated the local gin, mill, or small manufacturing plant, it would be the portal through which your manufactured goods would ship. At journeys end, your product would make its way via some other depot to the consumer.

Parents sent their children to college on the train, mothers and wives sent their sons and husbands to war, men left for business trips, and cousins came to visit ... all by train. When grandma came to visit she would step from the train followed by a porter loaded down with her luggage and parcels. If you were to die in a distant place your remains came home in a coffin carried in the baggage car. America moved by the railroad.

The local station served a multitude of functions. In addition to supplying an area for passengers to wait for their trains, it served as an office for conducting company business. The agent-operator was an intermediary between the

Denver, Tennessee Depot. *-Bob Bell, Jr. photographer; -Terry L. Coats Collection*

---

51   John A. Droege, *Passenger Terminals and Trains*. 1916, page 259.

train and the dispatcher. It served as a telegraph office, a REA agent's office, a freight house, and in most towns would have been the local gathering place as well.

Given its diverse functionality, the depots were in many cases the most important building in town. They touched more lives than did the city hall, the schoolhouse, and even the local church buildings. They were the building through which the lifeblood of the community flowed. The depots were the hubs of activities. The approaching locomotive; ground shaking, steam hissing, whistle blowing, and bell clanging, was sure to gather those within earshot of the depot to see what new discovery would alight from the cars. At any given time, the platform outside the station would be piled high with dry goods, groceries, trunks, barrels, boxes of clothing, sides of meat, and milk cans.

Not all freight activities could be carried on at the depot. Adjacent to the depot was usually a *team track* used for the offloading of the larger items such as lumber, farm machinery, and the raw materials for the local manufacturing plant not served by its own track. It was common for there to be an area directly next to the depot for such activities, close enough to be managed by the agent, yet far enough away as to not interfere with the business at the depot. In many cases, the coal yard, stock pens, and icehouse would be located on this track as well.

In their day, people would frequent the depots as commonly as people today commute to work in their cars, board a plane, or use their computers. Replete with a roaring hot potbelly stove, a spittoon, and maybe even a cracker barrel, the depot was the place to gather, to chew the fat, to catch up on the latest news, debate politics, and to pass along the latest gossip.

There was an allure to the depots of the *Nashville, Chattanooga & St. Louis Railway*. Whether it was the hustle and bustle of one of the four major terminals, one of the divisional points where several trains met at one time, passengers scurrying to make a connection to the next part of their destination, or a small rural station with a single agent-operator, there was an attraction to the depot that can not quite be explained.

Railway Express Agency freight truck. *-Terry L. Coats photographer*

A station on the NC&St.L was a busy, noisy, and fascinating place. People and trains would come and go as baggage, mail, and freight moved back-and-forth between platforms and trains. Travelers hurried to make their way to their departing trains or to make connections between trains on which they had just arrived and those going on to farther destinations. Passengers in the waiting room warmed themselves around a potbelly stove while the station agent went about his or her duties of dispensing tickets, completing paperwork, and keeping the trains progressing safely along his branch of the railroad. The sounds of the activities at the depot were ones of movement and change accented sharply by the staccato sound of the *tap, tap, taping* of the telegraph key on the agent's desk. No other place on earth could generate such a vivid atmosphere!

Stations along the branches of the NC&St.L, though they may stretch over many miles, constituted a community. On these branches, an accommodation train would make a run from a starting point in the morning and would return in the evening to its home base. Boys in knee-high britches would peddle their bikes to the road crossing to get an opportunity to wave at the engineer and crew of the train. Fresh eggs would be transported from the hen house of a farm along the right-of-way and would gently be handed to the general store proprietor at the end of the route.

People depended upon the daily run of the train for a multitude of reasons. The people supported the train by their patronage; the railroad returned the favor by running specials for the people. Once a year, usually in the fall, the NC&St.L would offer half-fare excursion rates so its patrons could travel to the cities in order to experience the latest fashions, shopping and entertainment. Merchants in large cities would hold special sale days to accommodate the patrons the trains brought to them. It was a win for the merchants, railroad, and the customer alike.

Stories abound of trains stopping in mid-route, for the crew to de-board, and help one of the locals pull a mud stuck tractor out of the muck, or for the crew to stop to participate in a pick-up baseball game. By the 1920s, the railroad was tightly entwined into the weave of all the communities it served. Almost every aspect of daily life was touched in some way by the train. After 1920, automobiles, buses, and trucks began to unravel the plait that had been the railroad's hold on these communities. As the years passed, the traffic on the tracks decreased, and branches withered. Over the years as the branches were abandoned and the trains withdrawn, a major piece of the communities died.

Lexington, Tennessee Depot. Aerial photos of the Lexington depot and surrounding area.
-*William Arnold Studios, Lexington, Tennessee*

GONE BUT NOT FORGOTTEN

*"The City Council met last night, the vote was four to three
To tear the home town depot down and build a factory
To take that stretch of history and tear it off the map
And to take old engine number nine and turn it into scrap."*
Blue Water Line ... Anonymous

Of the nearly 175 plus stations and depots that once served the large cities and small towns along the NC, only a handful of these wonderful old buildings still exist to serve us. As will be covered in the chapter titled "Adaptive Uses" there are a few of the stations that have been converted for use in some continuing service, but for the most part, when the NC&St.L abandoned their stations, no one else wanted or needed them and they were abandoned and eventually razed.

#252 arrives at Waverly, Tennessee. -*Tennessee State Library and Archives*

Factors contributing to whether a town depot was retained for some other purpose or whether it became the prey of the wrecking ball depended on several circumstances. In most cases, when the railroad abandoned the depot, the town was not large enough to need the depot for any other purpose. Many of the stations were not located in the town center and so they were not in a position to be used for some municipal activity. In other cases, a depot on the outskirts of town was usually clustered with other mercantile stores that also were abandoned as the population dwindled over the years. Few, if any, of these abandoned buildings were adapted for other use. As the years passed and the depots fell into disrepair, they were simply demolished to remove them as a tax liability to the NC&St.L, the L&N, or the CSX railroads.

The stations that survived did so because someone made the effort to save them. Some of the factors that may have saved a depot from demolition were the structure's state of repair or disrepair, its location, and its construction materials. Masonry, stone, or brick buildings stood a better chance of being salvaged.

Across the old NC&St.L system there were exceptional examples of railroad architecture that survived for an extremely long time or are still with us. On the Western & Atlantic Division, the stations at Ringgold, Tunnel Hill, Calhoun, Cartersville, Cass, and Kingston, Georgia, all were built before the Civil War and all were of stone construction. On the Sequatchie Branch there is the Victoria station. On the original Nashville & Chattanooga a portion of the Smyrna, Tennessee depot built in 1873 is incorporated in the current station. A survivor well into the late twentieth century was the antebellum freight house at Fayetteville, Tennessee. All of these depots were constructed of brick or stone that accounted for much of their longevity. Unfortunately we no longer have the Fayetteville freight house or the depots at Cass and Kingston, Georgia, but all the others remain today.

The feature that weighed heaviest on a depot's survival was whether a need could be found to revitalize the building for some other use. An overwhelming number of the smaller depots were saved because some farmer or a landowner purchased them for use in a storage capacity. Today, one can still find several of these depots in use for the storage of hay and feed, used as an auxiliary attic, or as a workshop.

The decades of the 1950s through the 1970s were extremely harsh for all architecture in America. At the end of World War II, as our war veterans returned home, a wave of revitalization swept this country. As a result, many of America's aging buildings were demolished and replaced with newer structures. The recycle and reuse trend of the modern era had not yet occurred. Unfortunately, so many of the houses and other structures that we now would love to refurbish simply no longer exist. During this period, a countless number of local small depots and stations along the right of ways succumbed to the wrecking crews.

It was not just the small rural stations of the railroad that fell to the wrecking ball. Of the four Nashville, Chattanooga & St. Louis Railway terminal buildings ... Memphis, Chattanooga, Atlanta, and Nashville ... only the latter still stands. Gone now are three of the monuments that stood to give testimony to the days of grandeur when great named trains such as the City of Memphis, the Dixie Flyer, and the Georgian prowled the rails of the NC&St.L Railway.

The Union Station in Memphis gave way in 1969 for a central post office. The Atlanta Union Station site is now a plaza under which is now Underground Atlanta. The Chattanooga Depot was razed and in its place now stands an office building. The Nashville Union Station stood abandoned for a number of years and came very close to being destroyed before a last minute reprieve saved it. It has since been refurbished and today is a 125-room luxury hotel.

In doing research for this book, this author tried to seek out and document as many of these buildings as possible. Still standing are depots, freight houses, CTC towers, tool sheds, Nashville's Union Station, and the old roundhouse in Bruceton. What may have been missed in my research, and are not counted in my estimate of the number of structures still standing, are many of the section houses that are now private residences and have been revised in appearance over the years.

As sad as it is that so many of the NC&St.L structures are gone, we are fortunate that between fifty and sixty railroad structures of diverse types are still with us. The wonderment that so many of these depots have survived to today is a testament of how well they were constructed, the materials used in their construction, and the devotion of people who found a use for these old buildings and saved them.

Adairsville Section House. -*National Archives*

Train Management and the Agent-Operator

"A Freight Agent must possess many attributes. Loyalty to duty, in all aspects, should take first place with competence and a proper amount of self-reliance necessary qualifications. The successful agent is one who knows how to deal with the public and is sensitive to the needs off all types of patrons. Public relations are entrusted to his care because to most people, he is the railroad."

Virgil Wright, station agent at Wartrace, Tennessee.
-*Ernest Robertson Collection*

So wrote J. F. Scarbrough, Agent in Lewisburg, Tennessee, in an article that appeared in the July 1944 issue of the NC&St.L Employees Bulletin.

Only a handful of people in a town held as much prestige and status as did the railway station agent. He would be considered along with the mayor, the town council, and the ministers as one of the most important and well known town's personalities.

The station agent would have to be of superior intelligence, the complexity of his or her job would demand it. The agent would have to combine the talents of town ambassador, safety director, travel agent, and parcels coordinator, in addition to his or her regular duties assigned by the railroad.

Where the agent was in charge of the business at the station house, the operator was in charge of the movement of trains. The regular duties of an NC&St.L agent would sometimes be complicated by the inclusion of *operator* status. If required, he would be known as an *agent-operator*. As well, he fulfilled a role as baggage agent, station maintenance man, and bookkeeper; and most importantly, he was a vital link in the safe and smooth passage of trains along the lines. The agent had all these responsibilities in addition to taking care of ticket sales. The hours were long and in most cases he or she was subject to call out when there was trouble on their section or branch of the NC&St.L Division.

It was common for them to act as the local travel agent as they would have to be familiar with distant places with exotic names. They might be called upon to perform the duty as policemen against the rowdy traveler or as traveler's aid to a traveler out of money and down on his luck. Long before the days of UPS and FedEx, the local agent was the person to whom people turned for delivery of the latest horticulture item from a distant seed company or the latest mail order parcel from Montgomery Ward or Sears & Roebuck.

NC&St.L Advertisement.
-*Nashville, Chattanooga & St. Louis Railway*

Through the freight portals of the depot, came everything to carry on daily life in rural America. By train came the latest in ready-made clothing, sewing machines, and patterns and bolts of cloth for homemade clothing. The farmer counted on the train for delivery of harnesses, wagons, plows, and the tools for everyday work. From the cradle to the grave the articles to sustain us came by train. Everything from the clothes for the newborn, to the suit coat or dress worn for burial, everything came by train; and in many cases delivered the casket itself.

Communities relied on the railroading system to relay the latest news. Whether it was from the next town up the tracks or from around the world, the last link in the communication chain was the local depot agent. The agent was the equivalent of today's radio or television newscaster. His reporting source was his telegraph sounder, or the crew of the last train that had passed his station. He would gather the news from his sources and shortly afterward the latest information would be passed along to the entire town.

The agent-operator was a part of a much larger system that spread far beyond the local station. Each depot or tower on a division was an inertial part of a vast order of other components. To understand the importance of the agent, one needs to have a sense of the agent's role in the movement of trains. The depot was a single spoke on a vast wheel. The telegraph allowed the agent to be in communication with the other stations so he or she could report the position and movement of trains in their locale and at the same time keep them moving safely along.

As can be seen in the organizational chart below, the Station Agents, Operators and Dispatchers are answerable to the Chief Dispatcher. The Chief Dispatcher answered to the Train Master. On a daily basis, the actual movement of trains would more than likely have gone no further up the chain than the Chief Dispatcher and unless there was some anomaly the local agent would probably not have had any contact any further up the chain than the dispatcher.

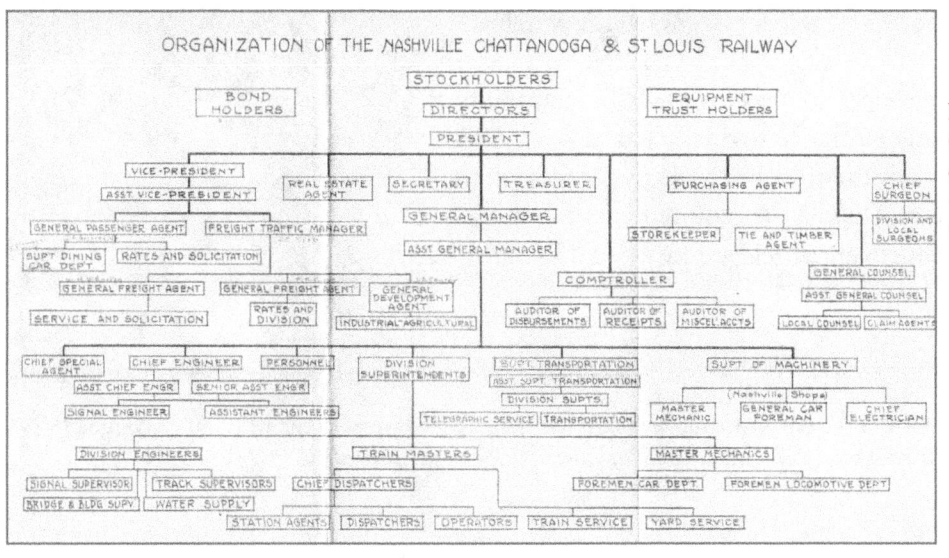

NC&St.L Railway Company general organization chart.
-*Terry L. Coats Collection*

The Telegraph

Initially the railroads used telegraphy only to verify the arrival at their destination of commodities that had been shipped by train. Within a short time, it was realized that the use of the telegraph could be expanded and could be utilized to control the meeting and overtaking of trains along the rights-of-way.

From its creation, almost all the way through its demise in 1957, the NC&St.L relied on the experienced telegraph operator as well as the telephone and radio as a form of communication. In the mid 1940s, it was still a requirement for many of those hired to work for the NC to be versed in telegraphy.

To distinguish one telegraph office from another, each control tower and depot was assigned a one or two-letter designation much the same as the modern airports are assigned a three-letter designation today. Each message to that station would start with that two-letter designation.[52]

In the days before long distance phone service, people relied on the Western Union office for the dissemination of personal messages. Families would communicate news of births, deaths, and other happenings at the local depot. The depots of the NC&St.L were the local representatives for the Western Union, Postal Telegraph, and other firms. It would be through the nimble fingers and skillfully trained ear of the agent-operator that these messages would be sent.

The agent-operator was versed in telegraphy. Most of the agents on the Nashville, Chattanooga & St. Louis Railway had hired on in the first decades of the twentieth century. One of the requirements for the job was for them to be fluent at telegraphy.

Morse code used by the dispatchers, operators and agents on the railroad. *-Terry L. Coats Collection*

Telegraph Sounder. *-Terry L. Coats photographer*

---

52   Some examples of the one or two-letter telegraph designations were; Glencliff (GN), LaVergne (VN), Antioch (AN), Murfreesboro (DI), Tullahoma (B), Cowan (CN), and Smyrna (MY).

Timetables and Train Orders

The conductors and engineers of trains did not simply pull away from a terminal or out of a railroad yard without guidance. Train movement was controlled by a strict set of orders and/or signals. Train movement on the NC&St.L Railway was handled prior to World War II by train order and after 1943 either by CTC (Centralized Traffic Control), or a combination of timetables and train orders.

A railroad timetable is a list of times for arrivals and departures of trains on a particular railroad system. There were two types of timetables. One was for the general public. A public timetable listed arrivals, departures, and other pertinent information, such as the times for connecting trains on the same railroad or trains of another line at a union depot.

The second type of timetable was one intended for the specific use of an employee of the railroad. This timetable was much more in-depth. Included in an employee's timetable was a listing of all the stations on a territory of the railroad as well as a listing of the regular trains that ran on that territory, the days and times the trains would normally run and the locations at which scheduled trains would meet another scheduled train. This *meeting point* would always occur at a station, a place designated by name on the employee's timetable. In this case, a station is not to be necessarily confused with a geographic location that had a physical depot. A station could be any point at which there was a siding long enough to accommodate moving a train off the main track and allowing a train of superior class to pass.

When traffic on a division was heavy, it became imperative that some trains be given precedence over others operating on the same tracks. This precedence gave a train authority by train order or timetable to hold the main track over, ahead of, or against another train. A train could be granted precedence in three different ways; 1) by *right*, which would be granted by train order, 2) by *class*, which would be granted by timetable, or 3) by *direction*, again granted by timetable between trains of same class. This rule applied to trains running in the same direction as well as those moving in opposing directions. The rule mandated that the train of a lesser class would have to clear the main line allowing the other to pass without impedance. In most classes, classification of trains was usually done by type. Passenger trains were classified as a first class train. Though most railroads in America would designate a through freight as second class and a slow moving local freight as a third class train, the NC&St.L never designated any of their trains as second class. Trains on the NC&St.L were designated either first class or third class.[53]

Operating the railroad solely by means of a timetable worked well when all the regular trains were running on time and they all met at their assigned meeting points. But there were many cases where trains were not running on their assigned schedule. What would

---

53 A personal interview with Mark Womack, former NC&St.L employee. November 11, 2006.

happen if one was not running on time? Under the governing rules of the railroad, if a train was delayed too long from its normal schedule, the dispatcher could issue train orders related to the diversion from its schedule, it would lose its superiority and would be designated a train of secondary status. There were also cases when the traffic became so heavy a second train had to be added to handle the increased load. This added train would be labeled as a *section* and could then be allowed to follow directly behind the scheduled train using the same schedule as the first unit. In the case when a train was not given an authorization by timetable, it would be designated as an *extra*. The train crew of other trains on the system would have no way of knowing about the extraordinary situations. If that crew arrived at a given meeting point and then proceeded by the right of time allotment alone, this could certainly cause an accident. Another tier of protection was needed. The railroads needed some way to notify the train crews of the change of conditions. The answer was the train order.

Train orders are written dictates issued by railroad personnel, in this case a dispatcher. Dispatchers were responsible for all train movement on their division and worked at the mandate a chief dispatcher. The chief dispatcher's job was to control and supervise the safe and efficient movement of the trains under his control.

For the movement of a train, the dispatcher would issue a clear and concise set of written instructions directed to everyone to whom they would effect. The primary recipients of these train orders would be the train's conductor and engineer. A copy of the same orders would be issued to the stations where the two trains would pass.

Train orders followed a protocol. First, orders were always written. If at some point there arose a question as to what had been conveyed in the orders, there was a paper document to verify exactly how actions had been transacted. Second, one person issued these orders, this way there was no possibility two or more people would give conflicting instructions concerning the matter at hand. Third, the same order was issued to everyone at the same time. In this way everyone knew what everyone else knew and no one could act on a matter before others were aware of what was going on. These orders were passed by telegraph, telephone or in later years by radio. Orders were received and then repeated back so there was little chance the order was not understood. If the trains on a division were running according to schedule the operators job was made much easier, if not, and many times they were not, the operator-agent had to stay atop the situation to make sure he knew the location of all the trains in his area. It was also his responsibility to report the passing of each train to the dispatcher miles away. This way the dispatcher could be certain of the status of the trains on the entire division. A second unit or *extra train* might follow many times the regularly scheduled train. An extra train as defined by the NC&St.L Rules book was, "A train not authorized by a timetable schedule."

The NC&St.L railroad was controlled by two types of train orders, the *Form 19* and the *Form 31*. The order forms were made of tissue paper called *flimsies*. This thin tissue paper allowed carbon paper to be inserted between the sheets so duplicate copies of the orders could be made for tower operators, train crews and station agents alike.

Form 19 could be delivered to a passing train without stopping it. The order contained on the Form 19 would not jeopardize the safety of the train or its crew if the order was not read immediately. Form 31, on the other hand dictated the movement of superior trains, a serious factor on the railroad. Considering the seriousness of such an order, it was imperative a signature be obtained from the conductor before the order could be considered *complete*.

If it was in any way possible and the safety of the train was not placed in jeopardy, it was much preferred for a train not to have to stop for orders. It could take an extremely long time to stop the train, pick up the orders, walk the train, pump up the brakes, and start it rolling again. This is why a Form 19 order was much preferred over a Form 31.

If the order to the train crew were written on a Form 19, there needed to be a way the operator could pass the order to the engineer and the conductor of the train without stopping it. This was accomplished by the use of an order hoop. The early hoops were just that, a bamboo hoop approximately four-feet in height and formed into the shape of a figure nine. Connected to the hoop was a metal clips capable of holding a folded train order. As the train passed the station, it was usually the fireman who would reach out the window of the engine and would extend a bent elbow toward the ground. He would run his arm through the open part of the hoop and would snatch the loop from the agent as he extended it up toward the passing train. As the caboose passed the agent the conductor in the *crummie* would do as the fireman had done and would snatch a second set of orders from a second hoop. At this point, the fireman and the conductor would both quickly remove the folded set of orders and would immediately throw the hoop to the ground for the agent to retrieve. In later years, the figure nine hoops gave way to a *Y-shaped hoop* with clips located at the top of the handle and at the tips of the arms of the Y. Instead of having the orders folded and clipped at one location, the orders would be tied to a string and the string was attached to the hoop at the three clips. This hoop was a marked improvement over the older version in that the open top of the Y allowed the recipient to catch only the string and the paper attached instead of the entire hoop. There was no longer a need for the crew to have to return the hoop since they never received it.

Hoopin' Up the Orders. William Ernest Arnold, telegraph operator for the NC&St.L, is seen hoopin' up train orders to the fireman of fast moving NC Mikado 2-8-2 locomotive #665. The second hoop on his shoulder holds orders for the conductor of the same train. Photograph from the 1940s was captured in Lexington, Tennessee. -*Beth Arnold Lee Collection*; -*William Arnold Photography Studio, Lexington, Tennessee.*

Semaphore Signal

Train order signals (usually a semaphore) were used to signal trains at telegraph stations concerning the delivery of orders from the dispatcher. These semaphores, visible both day and night to an approaching train were located at NC&St.L station offices and could convey one of two messages depending on the position of its blades. The indications were either stop or clear.

Stop: The blade was raised to a horizontal position. This would indicate that there was an emergency or that the agent needed the train to stop for orders. If the dispatcher had sent an order to a station for delivery to a train, the operator positioned the signal to notify that there are orders. If a train for which no order had been issued precedes the one for which orders are held, the operator would hoop them a, "Clearance Form A, stating that the signal is posted for _____." Filling in the name of the train for which the orders are held.

Clear: The blade pointing straight up or straight down. This would mean the agent has no orders for the crew.

CTC on the NC&St.L

The NC&St.L installed automatic block signals on the Western & Atlantic (Atlanta Division) in the 1920s. This was single trackage and the signals were used to keep the trains on that division running safely and as smoothly as possible. All other divisions were known as being in *dark territory*, a section of the railroad having no mechanical or electrical signaling system for the control of the trains. The one exception to this dark territory was the section of track between Sherwood and Cowan over Cumberland Mountain that was controlled by manual block signals.[54]

Starting in the 1940s, the railroad phased in a system of Centralized Traffic Control (CTC). Starting with the section between Atlanta and Cartersville, Georgia installed in 1943, the progression of installation was ... 1944 from Stevenson, Alabama to Nashville, Tennessee, 1946 from Cartersville, Georgia to Chattanooga, Tennessee, and before the War was over CTC was installed on the main line from Nashville through Bruceton down to Memphis. With the amount of traffic generated during World War II this improvement was a necessity. The NC&St.L had neither the time nor the materials to upgrade to double tracks so the CTC was the simplest solution.[55]

---

54 A personal interview with Mark Womack, who worked for the NC&St.L from 1942 until the merger in 1957 and then worked for the L&N and CSX until his retirement in 1983. November 11, 2006.
55 Dain L. Schult, *Nashville, Chattanooga & St. Louis: A History of "The Dixie Line."* 2001, page 152.

Even with the upgrading of sections of the railroad to CTC control, it was still a monumental task to keep trains operating safely. Light years before the use of a computer to monitor train movement, the dispatcher, the station agent, and the tower operator were the primary lifeblood that kept the trains moving along.

CTC Signal at Florence, Tennessee. -*Bob Bell, Jr. Collection*

Hand, Flag & Lamp Signal Illustrations

Fig. 5, APPLY AIR BRAKES—Swung horizontally in a circle.

Apply Brakes

Fig. 1, STOP—Swung across the track.

Stop

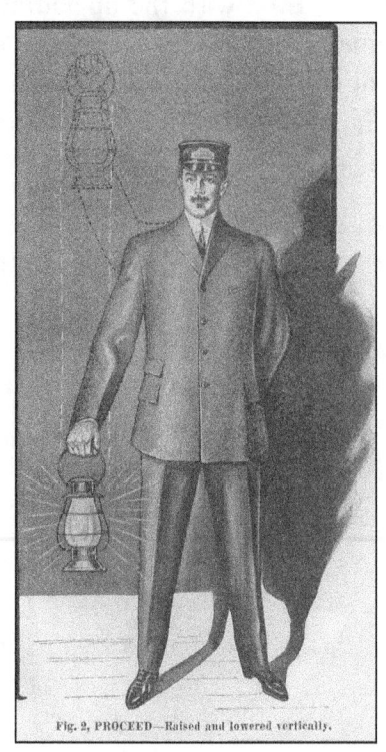

Fig. 2, PROCEED—Raised and lowered vertically.

Proceed

Fig. 6, RELEASE AIR BRAKES—Held at arm's length above the head.

Release Brakes

Fig. 3, BACK—Swung vertically in a circle across the track.

Back

Fig. 4, TRAIN HAS PARTED—Swung vertically in a circle at arm's length across the track.

Train Has Parted

Segregation on the Railroad

Born in a time of Black servitude, the NC&St.L Railway closed just before America saw its greatest advancement in the Civil Rights movement. Railroads played an inertial part in some of this country's darkest days of discrimination and ultimately were the platform that launched some of its greatest advancements in Civil Rights.

In the case of the Nashville & Chattanooga Railroad, it would be slaves owned by the company that would do much of the building of the initial railroad. When manpower ran short, the N&C placed an advertisement in newspapers in Tennessee as well as surrounding states asking for slave owners to lease those in servitude to the railroad. The N&C needed a massive number of laborers for the backbreaking work of pick and shoveling through Cumberland Mountain and carving out the passage that would come to be known as the Cowan Tunnel.

Black Gandy Dancers repair the right-of-way near Murfreesboro after the battle of Stone's River. This photo was taken around 1863. Up until that date, N&C ran its trains on 5-foot gauge 55# and 65# pound "U" rail. This rail had been laid on runners akin to the way strap rail had been laid. As can be seen in this photo, the men are installing the newer "T" rail. When laying the "T" rails, track was tacked to rough hewn crossties without benefit of tie plates. -*Library of Congress*

The following want ad appeared in several 1848 Tennessee newspapers.

Negroes To Hire Advertisement. -*Tennessee State Library and Archives*

100 Negroes Wanted to Hire

To labor on the Nashville and Chattanooga Rail Road at the Tunnel now being excavated through Cumberland Mountain. For likely Negroes, between 20 and 35 years old a liberal price will be paid. To correct an erroneous impression in regard to danger from laboring in rockwork, it is proper to say the hands have nothing whatever to do with blasting. This altogether done by blasters of supervisors immediately under the direction of the Superintendent.

Applications to the undersigned at Winchester Post Office will be promptly attended to.

HUGH STUART & CO.
Contractors
Refer to, V. K. Stevenson, Esq., Nashville

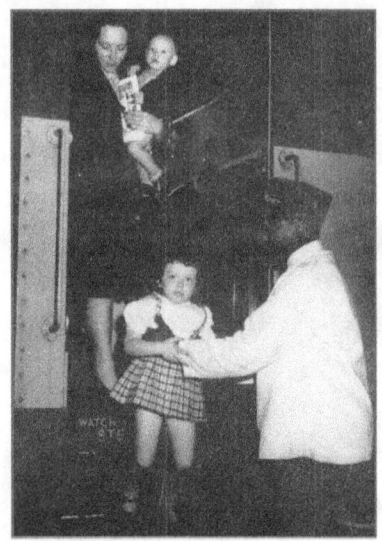

NC&St.L Porter. -*Nashville Chattanooga & St. Louis Railway*

Runaway Slaves and Black Freedmen Civil War Era Photo. Blacks known as contraband assemble outside primitive shelter. Thousands of Blacks flocked to Nashville for refuse during Federal occupation. -*Library of Congress*

Freight Car Shops Employees. A group of NC&St.L Car Shops employees at the Nashville New Shops, ca.1928. -*Nashville, Chattanooga & St. Louis Railway*

With the coming of the War Between the States, it would be runaway slaves and the Black freedmen who built and maintained railroads between the years 1861-1865. In 1864 when the USMRR needed to complete the unfinished Nashville & Northwestern Railroad line between Kingston Springs and Johnsonville, hundreds of men of color were recruited in Nashville to complete the job. After the line was completed, some of these same runaway slaves and freedmen joined the Federal Army and were assigned to guard the trestles and bridges along the road.

From the 1870s to the 1880s, former slaves began to work for the railroads as firemen, machine shop laborers, porters, and baggage handlers. From their positions as porters on early passenger trains, Black employees would develop one of America's first labor groups, the Brotherhood of Sleeping Car Porters. The Brotherhood of Sleeping Car Porters would be instrumental in taking some of the first steps in the struggle for black equality.

Progress by this early labor union could never erase the fact that until the coming of such landmark Supreme Court cases as Brown versus Board of Education and the Civil Rights Acts of the mid 1960s, this country was segregated.

After the end of slavery, laws across the United States continued to segregate Blacks from other segments of America. Many of the harshest, most discriminatory rules of this segregation were associated with the railroads. In fact many landmark court decisions upholding segregation involved the railroads.

In 1890, a New Orleans shoemaker named Homer Plessy was told to vacate the train seat in which he was riding and to give that seat to a white person. Upon his refusal, he was forcibly evicted from the train. His defiance led to a trial in Louisiana State Court. In 1896, the case made its way to the United States Supreme Court. In the case of *Plessy vs. Ferguson*, the high court ruled that the states were allowed to provide "separate-but-equal" transportation, education, and other services. These "separate-but-equal" clauses opened all manner of doors for states to continue practices that had come to be known as Jim Crow Laws. Jim Crow Laws, named after a character in a popular 1800s minstrel show song, regulated the separation by race of public facilities and accommodations.

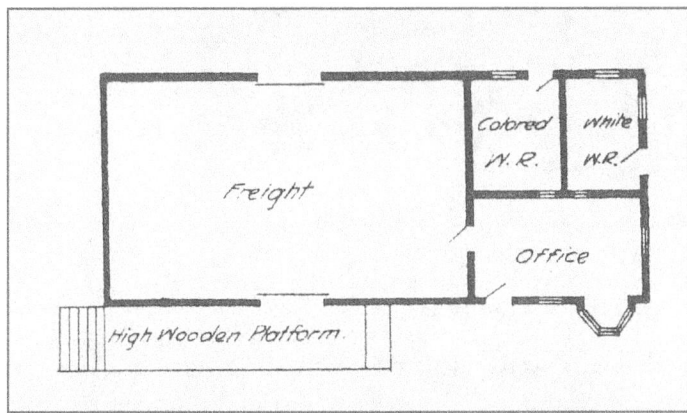

Typical NC&St.L Rural Station. Almost without exception all NC&St.L rural stations had separate waiting rooms for Blacks and Whites. Note the dual ticket windows in the agent's office for serving each room. -*L&N Collection, University of Louisville*

As it related to the depots and stations of the NC&St.L, these separate-but-equal standards demanded that the waiting areas in all stations be separated for whites and those of color. From the smallest rural depot to the terminals in the major cities, all NC&St.L passenger depots maintained a waiting room for the separation of the races.

The segregation laws dictated that there could not be a mixing of blacks and whites, even while the patrons stood in line to purchase train tickets. In order to conform to this regulation, the configuration of the rural station either placed the waiting rooms for whites and blacks at opposite ends of the building with the agent's ticketing office separating the two, or if the building was designed to where the waiting rooms were side by side, the agent's office would contain two ticket windows each serving one of the rooms. At the terminals, there were usually three waiting rooms. There was the large main waiting room that was always designated for white patrons, there would be a smaller room that would be reserved only for white women, and there would be a room always smaller than the main waiting room that was reserved for blacks, both male and female. Black females were never allowed their own parlor, as were their white counterparts.

The segregation did not stop at the station door. Once upon the train, the train consist was usually assigned a "Jim Crow" car. Since the start of business, the Nashville & Chattanooga had segregated blacks from whites. The first cars on which blacks were allowed to travel were the baggage cars. During the next generation of development Southern railroads created the combination car. This car was used on roads that could not generate enough business to warrant separate baggage and passenger cars for each race. The combination car was typically divided into three parts. One end was assigned to the blacks, in the middle was located a small baggage handling compartment, and on the other end was a section usually set aside as a smoking area for the whites on the train. The placement of the baggage compartment between the sections created a buffer between the two other portions of the car. The segregated cars and, thus, those riding within were the subject of further discrimination in that these cars were usually the more dilapidated units on the train. When new steel

Jim Crow Car. This Louisville & Nashville car #668 was identical to those used on the NC&St.L Railway during the years of segregation. Note the baggage handling compartment separating the smoking lounge "whites only" from the "colored" passenger end. -*Steve Johnson Collection*

cars were placed in service, the older wooden cars were relegated to stay in service as the Crow cars. They were the last to gain air conditioning and blacks were usually forced to give up seating so that train crewmembers could use those seats for their needs. Worst of all, these cars were always placed directly behind the steam locomotives forcing those inside to get the brunt of all the smoke and cinders from the engines. The placement of the Jim Crow car directly behind the engine involved in the 1918 Dutchman's Curve accident on the NC&St.L accounted for the disproportional number of blacks being killed in that wreck.

With the coming of diesels and the increase of black ridership on the NC&St.L, the Negro traveler was no longer forced to ride in the baggage car. Trains like the City of Memphis were all steel and air-conditioned; the car the blacks rode in was the same quality as the cars for the whites, but to the end of the NC in 1957, it remained segregated.

Colored passenger lounge on the City of Memphis. The introduction of the NC&St.L train, City of Memphis, in 1947 finally allowed blacks separate, but equal facilities. -*Nashville Chattanooga & St. Louis Railway*

STANDARDIZATION

As the Nashville & Chattanooga pushed forward across the vast countryside, the need for depots to service freight and passengers expanded. In the fledgling years of the nineteenth century the railroad hastily built structures or used existing houses, stagecoach way stations, or even, at least on a temporary basis, a boxcar was used as their depots. It was common for the ticket offices to be located in a hotel or some public building. Early depots were simple one-story buildings with their long sides running parallel to the tracks. In the 1870s the addition of bay windows or rounded corners allowed station agents to more easily observe the movement of trains near the station.

Boxcar Station. Until a more substantial depot could be built or in places where a permanent depot was not warranted, a makeshift depot made from an old boxcar was used as the station. *-Drawing by Terry L. Coats*

The N&C Railroad started construction on the Nashville to Chattanooga trackage in 1848. In the annual president's report to the stockholders of 1849, N&C President Vernon Stevenson reported that the N&C had an expenditure of $14,998.50 for depots at Chattanooga and at Nashville.[56] In 1850 and 1851 the Nashville & Chattanooga was constructing depots, woodsheds, and water stations across the route between the terminus cities. The 1851 annual report to the stockholders reported that by the end of that year there was an engine house under construction in Nashville. There was also a third class combination passenger and freight station under construction at Smyrna and Wartrace, Tennessee. Completed that year was a second class freight house at Murfreesboro, Fosterville, Christiana, and LaVergne, in Rutherford County, Tennessee[57] as well as in Shelbyville on the new branch line to that city. Woodsheds and water stations were also completed at Antioch, Smyrna, and Christiana.[58]

In a 1851 letter to President Stevenson and the stockholders, Nashville & Chattanooga Chief Mechanical Engineer James H. Grant (a third cousin to United States president Ulysses S. Grant) wrote, "It will be necessary to construct passenger houses at Nashville and Chattanooga, a freight house at Chattanooga and third class depot buildings, wood sheds, and water stations at division houses at all the way stations between Nashville and the Tennessee River not already provided for."[59]

---

56   Annual Report to the Stockholders of the Nashville & Chattanooga Railway. 1849.
57   Judy Lee Green, *A History of Rutherford County Railroad Depots.* Rutherford County Historical Society, #18. Winter 1982.
58   Annual Report to the Stockholders of the Nashville & Chattanooga Railway. 1851.
59   Ibid.

It can be seen from the statements made in the stockholders report that the N&C was committed to a building program of facilities to maintain their locomotives and cars as well as providing for the comfort and needs of persons using the passenger services.

Shortly after track construction began the N&C built its first depots. The first two depots built were in the terminus cities of Nashville and Chattanooga at a cost of $2,497.25 and $2,501.25 respectfully.[60]

James H. Grant. -*Tennessee State Library and Archives*

Nashville had developed as a leader in politics, commerce, and culture. The Nashville & Chattanooga wanted to make its presence known within this thriving political and cultural hub.

Unfortunately, some of the NC depots built in the first years of the company's existence were destroyed during the War. These depots represented vital communication centers and were the targets of repeated raids by Confederate Generals' Forrest, Morgan, and Wheeler. Many were severely damaged or destroyed. For example, the depot at Tullahoma (following page) was intentionally torched in 1863 by retreating Confederates rather than let its ammo repository, as it was being used, fall into Federal hands.

This Tullahoma depot was one of the original stone stations built by the N&C in the years of the company's startup. The Nashville & Chattanooga built many of its first stations to a standardized pattern.

Illustrated on the next page are pre-War drawings of stations at Anderson and Tullahoma, Tennessee and a Civil War photograph taken in Stevenson, Alabama. Note that each of the three stations illustrated are the same size and contained the same window and door arrangement. All three depots had a center freight door on both sides of the building; all were built of brick, and all apparently had the same floor plan. Although only three of the stations of the original N&C line are illustrated here, it can be assumed that many more of the more substantial stations on the line were identical to these three.

A few years after the War, the N&C depots that survived were approaching a quarter of a century in age. Some had been of crude construction and had never been intended to last for any real length of time. For instance, the depot built in 1855 on the mountain at Tantallon was of log construction. It was time to replace these aging depots, replace the damaged ones, or to build depots at the new locations blossoming along the lines. In addition to having to

---

60   Annual Report to the Stockholders of the Nashville & Chattanooga Railway. 1849.

Anderson, Alabama. -*Terry L. Coats Collection*

Tullahoma, Tennessee. -*Terry L. Coats Collection*

Stevenson, Alabama. -*Terry L. Coats Collection*

replace the aged depots of its own railway, the N&C inherited a multitude of stations of the companies they bought in the decades just after the War. Many of these stations would need attention as well.

By the last quarter of the nineteenth century, a majority of Tennessee railroads chartered in the 1850s had fallen into bankruptcy. The War Between the States had been devastating, both financially and physically, on all the railroads in Tennessee. Several of the rail lines had been shut down completely during the War; all had been affected in some way. On several occasions, in order to keep their supply lines operating, the Yankees uprooted rails from many of these smaller railroads and transferred them to the main lines of the N&C Railroad toward Chattanooga, the L&N Railroad toward Louisville, and the Nashville & Northwestern Railroad toward Johnsonville, Tennessee. Because the state of Tennessee had fallen into Federal control so early in the War, all three of these lines had been in the hands of the Federal armies and, toward the end of the War, the United States Military Railroad used them as supply lines for its armies in the field. After the War, almost all of the smaller railroads were unable to recuperate

By 1871, only Tennessee's two largest railroads, the Louisville & Nashville and the Nashville & Chattanooga were financially healthy enough to weather the economic trauma that had been caused by the War. All others, unable to recover from the loss of business, the wanton destruction by both armies, and the financial devastation of the Federal Reconstruction era were forced to default on the loans granted to them in the early 1850s.

Reluctant to call the loans on these struggling rail lines, in 1869 the Tennessee state legislature made an attempt to bolster these sagging railroad companies by offering them a bailout. The state of Tennessee appropriated nearly $14 million to be used to rebuild the railroads. Unfortunately, little of the monies would be legitimately used to replace missing track, or to replace damaged or destroyed rolling stock. Within a short time the state was inundated with Carpetbaggers ... ruthless men from the North ... who saw Tennessee railroad property as prime "plums for the pickin'." With the state of Tennessee reeling under the despot heel of Yankee Reconstruction, these men swarmed into the state to buy up property and to establish themselves in governmental positions. Many of these racketeers were appointed to *receiver* positions to oversee financially weak or bankrupt railroads during these troubled times.

Under the crooked Reconstruction administration of Governor "Parson" William G. Brownlow, most of the $14 million in appropriations made its way into the pockets of corrupt railroad officials, the receivers, and the Radical Carpetbagger legislators who were working hand-in-glove to illegally divert this money. One example of the corruption perpetrated on the state during this time was that of a railroad, that existed only on paper. The owners received $100,000 in state financing but never had any intention of building any track. This Knoxville promoter admitted that his Mineral Homes Railroad ... "Begins nowhere and ends nowhere." The corruption was widespread and left dozens of railroads that had been in business before the War penniless and primed for more affluent companies to purchase them at bargain prices.

Such a bad taste was placed in the legislators' mouths over the corruption that they rewrote the state constitution in 1870 to preclude the state from giving future financial aid to any railroad company. The corruption was so pervasive that it took the state nearly ten years of investigations and hearings to uncover the depths of dishonesty.[61]

After the 1869 debacle, the state of Tennessee had no choice but to foreclose on the bad loans granted twenty years before. In 1870 and carried on into 1871, foreclosures were begun on all railroads' loans in the rears. Most of these loans had originally been granted under the General Improvement Law of 1851-2.

Colonel Edmund W. Cole ascended to the presidency of the Nashville & Chattanooga Railroad in 1868. During his twelve-year tenure, the dramatic Cole would expand the N&C at a maddening pace. The Nashville & Chattanooga Railroad changed its name to the Nashville, Chattanooga & St. Louis Railway in 1873. That year, the NC&St.L was celebrating its silver anniversary as a railroad. Between 1872 and 1877, the NC&St.L Railway would embark on an aggressive campaign to purchase at forced sale several of the companies taken over by the state. Purchased by the Nashville & Chattanooga were the Nashville & Northwestern and the Hickman & Obion in 1872, the Jasper to Pikeville portion of the Sequatchie Valley Railroad, the Tennessee & Pacific, the Winchester & Alabama, the McMinnville & Manchester, and the Southwestern Railroads in 1877.[62]

---

61   Robert E. Corlew, *Tennessee: A Short History, 2nd edition*. University of Tennessee Press. 1981, page 342.
62   J. D. B. Debow, *Legal History of the Entire System of the Nashville, Chattanooga & St. Louis Railway and Possessions*. 1899, Foreword.

With the addition of these seven new railroads, the NC&St.L inherited the rolling stock, tracks, structures and depots of the defaulting lines. In some instances, these depots were probably nothing more than a converted barn or some other lowly structure, in others, substantial depots had been built in the larger towns along the lines. Each of these railroads had built their more prominent stations to a standard style. When added to the original N&C depots, this new collection of depots was certainly a varied one. By the 1890s the look of the stations along the N&C was as diverse and colorful as a 1972 Amtrak passenger train consist. Just as Amtrak at its startup had obtained cars from a multitude of railroads, so too had the NC&St.L obtained a multitude of depots from the railroads now in their control. In the years to follow, the Nashville, Chattanooga & St. Louis Railway would add trackage in the states of Kentucky, Alabama and Georgia. With the acquisition of each new railroad, the diversity in the style of depots owned by the company would multiply many times over. In many cases, a town started out with a small shelter or a small station, only to have that structure replaced with a more substantial depot as the population increased and the use of the depot expanded. Transversely, the use of a depot sometimes decreased and the railroad could no longer justify the cost of paying to maintain a fully staffed office. In this case, the station was closed and a small flagstop shelter was substituted.

In the late 1870s, the NC&St.L started replacing outdated depots or began building new structures. They developed two standardized styles of architecture for their rural stations. The first of these two styles was the Carpenter Gothic. A few years later, as American architectural tastes changed, the NC&St.L developed a Queen Anne style for its stations. Today, several examples of both these styles of stations still remain. The new industrial age brought interchangeable parts for manufactured goods. It only made sense that the railroad would follow suit by repeating design elements in their new structures giving them interchangeability as well. A standardized station plan would allow the railroad to utilize mass-produced and interchangeable parts.

Along with the industrial developments imported from Europe, came a movement of enlightenment in the fields of literature and architecture. Though Gothic architecture in England never completely went out of vogue, around 1800 a revitalization of the Gothic known as Gothic Revival or Victorian Gothic became a popular style. This revival began to gather momentum around 1840, spurred surprisingly not by the architects, but by the social critics and philosophers. A moral reformation in Victorian England had harkened them back to architectural styles of times past. Shortly afterward, designers in America began turning to the Romantic Gothic as their choice to replace the more classical styles of Greek and Federal. The latter two forms of architecture had exemplified for the founding fathers a sense of the republican style government after which they had patterned the new American government. It was now time to explore new frontiers.

In the early nineteenth century, Gothic was considered more suitable for church and university buildings, whereas classical style was thought more appropriate for public and commercial buildings. By the latter part of the century, Gothic was gaining favor for use in public and commercial buildings.

Gothic architecture is exemplified by strong vertical lines, battlements, steeples, sharply pointed gables, pinnacles, and tall narrow windows with tracery and topped with lancets (sharply pointed) arches. Other characteristics were the hexagon or square towers. Gothic Revival retained many of the elements of the medieval English architecture that it was imitating. The aforementioned 1854 brick NC&St.L depot in Nashville was a fine example. This building had tall narrow windows and hexagon towers on eight corners. The roof exhibited a row of battlement, and it had the distinctive sharp arches over the track doors on the attached train shed.

The use of Victorian Gothic would not be limited to the masonry building. Designers began to incorporate many medieval elements into wooden structures as well. Wood buildings such as churches, houses and railroad depots began to exhibit these elements. The ingenuity of the American craftsman to take the elements of a stone building and to incorporate these elements in wood structure became so synonymous with the rural carpenter; these wooden structures began to be referred to as *Carpenter Gothic*.

It was the development of the steam powered lathe and the jigsaw that allowed the carpenter to emulate the tracery designs found in the windows of Gothic architecture. With the steam-driven jigsaw, the cuts and turns of the intricate designs used on gingerbread and bargeboard trim became much easier to produce. The use of these tools allowed the ingenuity and craftsmanship of the local carpenter to shine.

Obviously the railroad could not justify using masonry on all the depots across the system, but a standardized wood depot with Carpenter Gothic detailing was very much within the NC&St.L budget. Opting for a more utilitarian design for their depots, the NC&St.L did not incorporate all the lavish scrollwork of the Gingerbread trim. Instead, they chose to include some of the stronger elements of the design. The standard depot of the NC&St.L was a rectangular wood frame building, one story in height. The exterior walls were covered with board and batten, usually placed over a three-foot tall lower band of vertical tongue and groove siding. Windows were single hung sash type; narrow and tall usually with a 4/4-window light arrangement. Adornment over the windows varied; sometimes a simple flat lintel was used, at other times eared molding or a triangular louvered pediment was used. Transoms were standard additions over both pedestrian and freight doors. The building exhibited a low pitch Gable roof with large overhangs and verges supported by a decorative bracket.[63]

---

63 Michael Ray O'Neal, Historic Railroad Depot Architecture in Middle Tennessee. A thesis presented to the Graduate Faculty of Middle Tennessee State University in partial fulfillment of the requirements for his Master of Arts Degree. August 1983.

Gothic Revival or Carpenter Gothic Architecture

When we think of the depots of the NC&St.L, it would probably be the charming wood station that would first and foremost come to mind. Shortly after 1870, a large number of picturesque simplified Gothic Revival railroad stations known as Carpenter Gothic began to appear as the standard station on the NC&St.L.

Carpenter Gothic included many of the architectural features seen in stone Gothic buildings, but the designs were simplified and refined when applied to wooden commercial buildings, such as train stations. Gone were the battlements, but the vertical theme was repeated in the board and batten siding covering the exterior walls. The octagon towers were represented in the angled windows of the agent's bays and all windows and doors were adorned with pointed arches at the tops of the frames. Seen also were the heavy timbers used as roof supports and the use of wood vergeboards used where walls met rooflines, a carryover from a similar adornments used in stone structures. The most distinguishing feature of the NC&St.L Carpenter Gothic station would be its low, widespread roof line. The standard roof carried no more than a four/twelve pitch with large overhangs that protected both passengers boarding the trains as well as giving much protection for the loading of freight.

The company developed stock sets of blueprints for the construction of these depots. Included in these sets were several styles of drawings that could be used as the need dictated. A standard depot design was needed for the small rural depot, a combination passenger-freight depot and a plan for a union depot at which the NC&St.L would share its facilities with another railroad company. The company could then expand these standard designs by developing several sizes of each style. For example the stations at Dickson, Huntington, and Gleason, Tennessee were all the same architectural design, but they were not the same size. The Dickson depot measured 30 feet, 4 inches by 140 feet, 0 inches, while the Gleason station measured 30 feet, 4 inches by 80 feet, 9 inches. The Dickson station built in 1882 and the Huntington station built in 1896 were within inches of being identical in size, but in the fourteen years between the dates when these stations were built, the railroad chose to adorn the Huntington station with three dormers and a more elaborate set of roof brackets. (See the photos of these two stations in the chapter titled *Nashville Division*). If a town wanted a larger or a slightly more ornate depot than was called for in a standard drawing, any of the standard plans could easily be altered to fit the requirements. It was such an alteration that accounts for the changes to the Huntington station. The addition of a dormer, the change of roof brackets, or an acroteria added to the end of a roofline was a small, but significant, deviation from the norm.

By the 1890s the NC&St.L had prospered and began to incorporate a few more elaborate details into their structures. Tongue and grove siding began to replace the board and batten. Clapboard was added in some cases and the company began to use tin, clay, or asphalt shingles in place of the wood shingles of earlier construction.

Many railroads in America developed a two-story station, a standard combination structure with living quarters on the second floor. This was not a pattern of design used on the NC&St.L. If the NC built a two-story station as they did at Cowan and at Bridgeport, the second story was used for office space.

Because of the symmetry of these depot designs, the same building crews who were assigned to the bridge and building departments of the railroad could do most of the construction. As many of the design elements of these depots were repetitive, each of the depots, no matter their size or style, the parts could be mass produced in railroad car shops and then shipped by rail to the building site. It is thought that much of the standardized parts for these depots were built in Nashville at the shops and shipped to a depot building site in kit form.

Standardization of these depots was a great cost savings. Additionally, by giving a *family* resemblance to the buildings, the NC&St.L could give these structures a unique look … something akin to establishing a corporate image. Long before there was a McDonald's arch, a Xerox "X", or even an Atlantic and Pacific Tea Company "A&P", there was the standardized train depot. In the twentieth century the NC would be known for its red and white "bowtie" logo, its boxcars with the distinctive yellow stripes, and the black and gold "Stripes and Glider" J3 steam engines, but in the nineteenth century, it would be the dark forest green and ochre yellow low pitch roofed depot that would serve as the distinctive corporate image.

When the NC&St.L built their standard Carpenter Gothic depots and then painted them in distinctive Goldenrod and Green paint, they were setting their depots apart from the depots of other railroad companies. This amounted to the building of a corporate icon in wood, glass, and iron.

Inherited Depots from Other Lines

Between the years of 1875 and the early 1920s, many of the depots inherited through mergers would eventually be replaced. Most of these depots stood the test of time and remained as viable structures through the company's history. Just as the N&C had standardized their depots from the 1850s on, there was often a sense of family in the style depot these other companies used in the construction of their depots. Almost without exception, every branch line inherited by the N&C had built on its own standard set of depots.

We know that the stations of other companies were standardized. A reference was made to such standardization in the 1861 will of Alexander Roulston of Weakley County, Tennessee. Alexander Roulston donated two acres of land to the Nashville & Northwestern Railroad and agreed to build a station at his own expense using a standard building plan of the Nashville & Northwestern Railroad.

A. Roulston

To
Proposition Depot House
N. N. Rail Road

In consideration Nashville North Western Rail Road Company locating and Establishing a Station and Depot House on my Land for Transacting their passengers and Freight Business at that point such depot to be known as Roulston Station. For and in consideration of the above consideration I have agreed and do agree to donate to the said Rail Road Company and their successors forever two acres of Land for depot purposes to be laid off by the Engineer of the Said Company in such a position and location that may be required by the company for such purposes and I further agree to build and complete a depot House on the said Land in accordance with the declarations and plans of said Company at a cost of 500 Dollars which said Depot House when completed to the satisfaction of said Company myself my heirs and assigns relinquishing all right claims and peaceable possession of same to the said Company their successors forever. I further agree to bind myself my heirs and assigns to build the Said Depot House within seven months from date of the acceptance of this proposition by the said Company.

Dresden Tennessee Janry. 17th 1861

Attest
Allexander Roulston   Seal

E. Culverhouse
H. T. Gardner

In consideration of the within proposition being fully carried out by the said Alexander Roulston the said Nashville & North Western Railroad Company accept the within proposition.

Dresden Tennessee, January 17th 1861
E. Culverhouse agent N & NW RR Co.

Inherited Depot — Cartersville, Georgia

In 1895, the NC leased from the L&N the trackage that would become the Memphis and Paducah Division. As part of that agreement, the NC&St.L inherited the tracks and structures of the Tennessee Midland Railway and the Paducah, Tennessee & Alabama Railroads. The Tennessee Midland ran from the Aulon interlocking tower near Memphis through Lexington, and then an additional 24.5 miles to the Tennessee River at Perryville, Tennessee. The PT&A ran from Paducah, Kentucky and intersected the Tennessee Midland at Lexington. The depots inherited from these two lines had been built by those two companies to a standard gothic design. But, if one were to compare the gothic designed depots of the TM and the PT&A to those of the NC&St.L, he or she would see a difference in interpretation. The designs of the Tennessee Midland and the PT&A included a board and batten vertical siding, as did the NC&ST.L, but included a steeper pitched roof and a simpler overall design. Whereas the NC stations were painted in a two-tone ochre yellow and dark green color scheme, the PT&A and TM depots were monochromatic in either a brown or maybe maroon color.

Likewise, early photographs of other inherited depots on other lines show a familiar resemblance. The depots of the Nashville & Northwestern Railroad, those on the Lebanon branch of the Tennessee and Pacific, as well as the depot on several other lines show that they were built from some type of patterned design.

It is apparent that all these railroads had the same idea when it came to standardization. It was much more economical to build a railroad's depots to one standard. It simplified the designing and construction, and it presented a sense of family to those seeing the stations as they passed from town to town.

Queen Anne Architecture

With the coming of the industrial revolution, Americans became caught up in the excitement of new technologies. Elaborate factory-made and pre-cut architectural decorations began to appear in the 1880s to 1890s. Architects and builders across the country rushed to include these new innovated elements into their designs. Homeowners of all classes clamored to have the latest fad sweeping the country. Those in rural areas could now emulate the houses of their city cousins and the wealthy went wild incorporating the elements of the Queen Anne style into the mansions they were building. America's railroading companies including the NC&St.L followed the wave of architectural change. Beginning in the 1890s, new Queen Anne stations began to appear along the NC.

Carpenter Gothic / Queen Anne Depot — Wartrace, Tennessee

The elements of architectural design incorporated into the standard NC&St.L Queen Anne depot include the hip roofs, large dormers supplemented with smaller eye-browed dormers (as accents), tall crowned chimneys, decorative roof ridge flashing, square instead of angle sided bay windows, and the introduction of much more detail than had been seen in the Gothic style depot. The NC&St.L built Queen Anne depots in both wood and brick veneers. In many cases, when the Queen Anne station was built, the older Gothic station was retained and from that time on would be used as a freight depot.

Non-Traditional

There were a number of depots on the NC&St.L built after the 1890s that did not adhere to the standard Carpenter Gothic or Queen Anne style of architecture. These depots were usually designed and built by the railroad with which the NC was sharing the facilities. Some examples of these stations were the ones at the NC&St.L intersection at Union City, (GM&O), Martin, and Gibbs, Tennessee (both Illinois Central), Stevenson, Alabama station that was a shared depot with the Memphis & Charleston Railroad, and the Lewisburg, Tennessee, Gadsden, Alabama, and McKenzie, Tennessee, where the NC&St.L and the L&N shared union stations. The depot in McKenzie, Tennessee followed a standard L&N design. One only has to look at the L&N depot in Humboldt, Tennessee to see a twin L&N structure.

Non-Traditioanl Depot — McKenzie, Tennessee

The last station built on the NC&St.L was in 1945 when the NC was forced to build a new depot on the Nashville Division. The construction of Kentucky Lake on the Tennessee River required the re-routing of approximately ten miles of track at Johnsonville, Tennessee. The replacement depot at New Johnsonville was built in a simple post-War style.

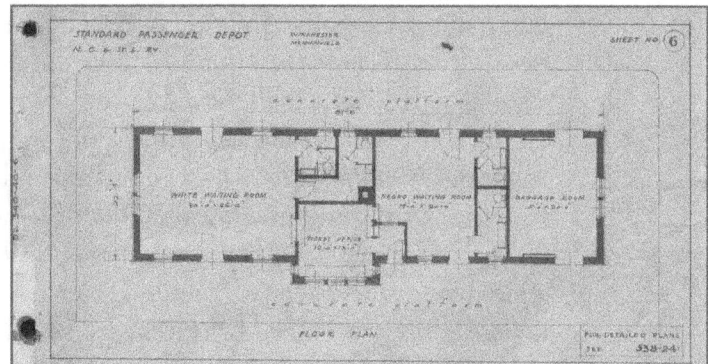

Standard Queen Anne —
Winchester McMinnville Floor Plan

Standard Queen Anne —
Winchester McMinnville Elevation

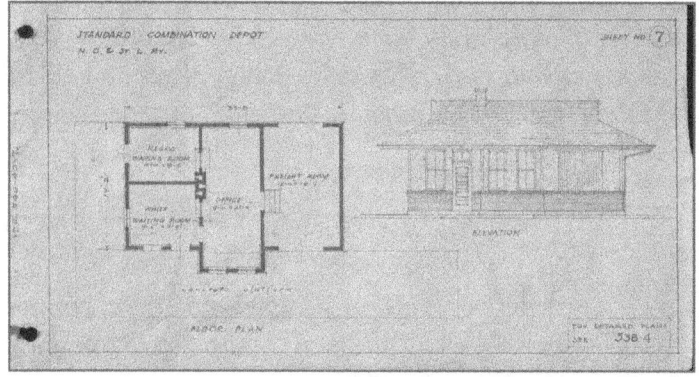

Standard Queen Anne —
Combo Depot

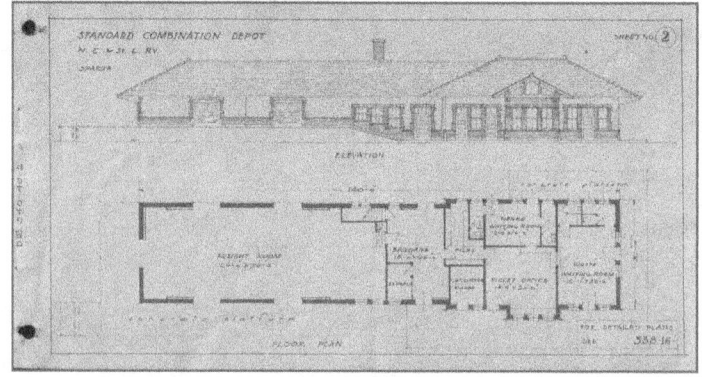

Standard Queen Anne —
Sparta Floor Plan and Elevation

Terminals

"Well, I wait around the train station, Waitin' for that train
Waitin' for the train, yeah, Take me home, yeah
From this lonesome place"
... Jimi Hendrix

To the NC&St.L, its terminal buildings … large, prominent, ornate, and towering … were symbols of technical development, commerce, and prosperity. The terminals were meant to show strength and at the same time elegance.

Shortly after the Civil War, there was a move in America to build terminal stations to rival the palatial structures in existence in Europe. Commodore Cornelius William H. Vanderbilt was the first to construct a terminal in 1872. The erection of Grand Central Terminal in New York City allowed Vanderbilt a central locale to house his three railroads … the New York City & Hudson River Railroad, the New York & Harlem Railroad, and the New York & New Haven Railroad. Following Vanderbilt's lead during the 1880s and 1890s there was an abundance of new grandiose terminals built across the country.

Walter G. Berg, in his 1893 reference manual for railroad architects and designers, set the standard for the construction of railroad structures in America. The book, *Buildings and Structures of American Railroads,* cites over forty-five major terminals built during this period.[64] In referencing the building standard for terminal depots in the twentieth century, Berg wrote, *"The structure should be built on broader and grander lines than local depots, presenting a bold and prominent front,"* he added, *"It will also prove better to follow, as rule, well-established styles as precedents, applying the same principals modified to suit each individual case, in preference to attempting to produce something absolutely new and unique."*

The NC&St.L closely followed both of these recommendations when it came to building or remodeling its stations in its four terminal cities. As related to following the well-established styles, the company trusted the styles of architect Henry Hobson Richardson for the Victorian design of its Nashville station and 1871 Atlanta depot, and Italian Renaissance design for its Memphis depot.

Though not built to the grandiose standards of a New York City Grand Central Terminal or a St. Louis Union Station, the Nashville & Chattanooga constructed very fine terminal buildings in Nashville and in Chattanooga prior to the War Between the States. In 1871, they built a magnificent terminal in Atlanta and then replaced it with a new one

---

64 Of the forty-five terminals mentioned by Berg, the stations at St Louis, Missouri (1894), Indianapolis, Indiana (1888), and Louisville, Kentucky (1882 to 1887), are still standing.

in 1930. The NC&St.L built a new grand terminal in Nashville in 1900 to replace a pre-War depot, and in 1912 built a terminal in Memphis that the NC&St.L could finally call their own. Up until that time the railroad had been co-tenants in stations around the city.

These four terminals were grand structures and the company could look upon each with pride. During their history, all four would extend a welcoming calling card to some of the most prestigious passenger trains to ever run in America. Between Memphis and Nashville ran the *Volunteer* and the *City of Memphis*, between Nashville and Chattanooga, the *Lookout*, and from Chicago and St. Louis on their way to Florida came the *Dixie Flyer, Dixie Limited, Dixie Flagler, Flamingo, Southland,* and the *Georgian*.

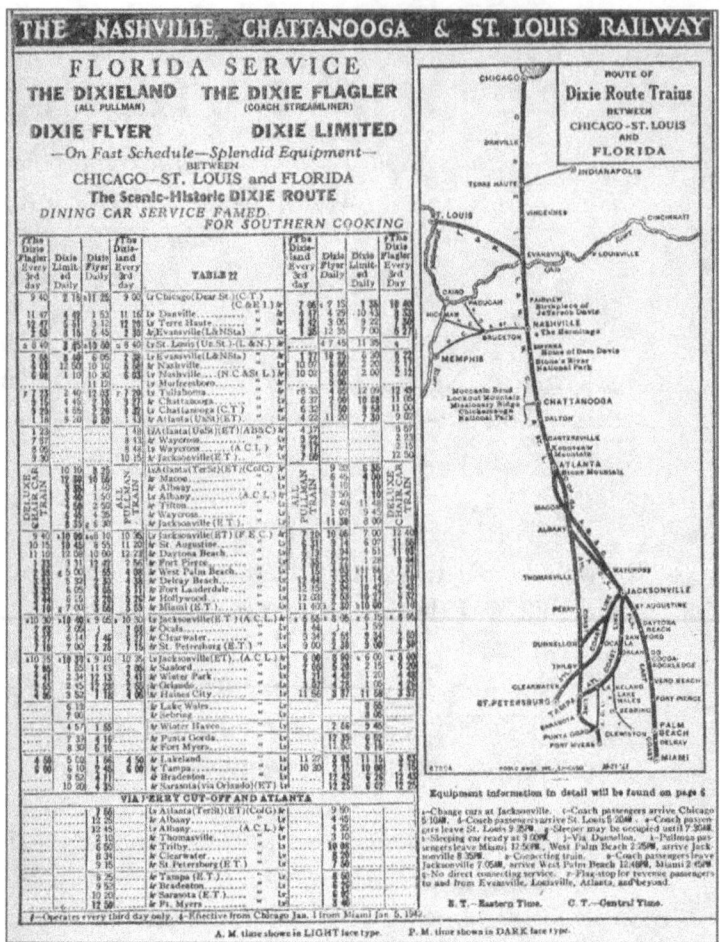

Dixie train service passenger timetable between Chicago and Florida. *-Terry L. Coats Collection*

All of the *Dixie* trains made stops at Nashville, Chattanooga, and Atlanta on their trek between the Midwest and the Sunshine State.

NASHVILLE

FIRST RAILROAD STATIONS IN NASHVILLE...

There were five railroads serving the city during the early rail history of Nashville. Of these five railroads, the Nashville & Chattanooga, the Louisville & Nashville, and the Tennessee & Alabama Railroads (later the Nashville & Decatur Railroad) built their own depots.[65]

In 1854, the Tennessee & Alabama built a large Gothic Revival masonry depot between High and Summer Streets (now 5th Avenue South and 6th Avenue South) on Broadway; when

---

65   *Speaking of Union Station.* Union Station Trust Fund, Nashville, Tennessee. 1977.

this station grew too small, it was abandoned and in 1868 the Nashville & Decatur built a new Gothic Revival depot at Cherry Street (now 4th Avenue) and Chestnut Street. This station was located only yards from the N&C right-of-way to Chattanooga. This massive structure was very similar in design to the old Broadway depot replete with lancet arches and battlements built into the brickwork. The new depot was much larger, boasted a large head house, and a completely enclosed passenger shed. Three years after the depot's construction, the L&N leased (then purchased) the N&D and used the depot as a station for trains entering and departing Nashville from the south.

The Georgian. -*Nashville, Chattanooga & St. Louis Railway*

To handle their one or two daily trains into the city, the L&N built a small depot at 159 North College Street (now 3rd Avenue North) when it entered Nashville in 1855. In 1871, the L&N leased the Nashville & Decatur Railroad. With the lease came possession of the N&D station at Cherry and Chestnut Streets. The L&N then had two stations on opposite sides of Nashville, but had no physical connection between the two.

At that time there was a track connection from the former N&D station to the station the N&C had constructed in 1854 at Church Street and Walnut Street. If the L&N could connect its College Street station to the N&C station it could use existing rails to gain access to its newly acquired property to the south of the city.

In May 1872, the L&N began construction of a set of trestles from 4th Avenue North near its College Street station. After running west for several blocks around the base of the large mound on which the Tennessee State Capitol sat, the trestles made a sharp turn to the south near 8th Avenue North. It was at that point that the tracks on the trestle connected to those of the Nashville & Northwestern Railroad arriving into the city from the west. The L&N leased track rights over the N&NW to the N&C's Church Street Station and then leased track rights from the N&C from Church Street to the Nashville & Decatur station at Cherry Street.

The trestles and the leasing of tracks gave the railroad a connection between their two Nashville depots. Bridging this short gap through Nashville gave the L&N a through connection between Louisville and Decatur, Alabama, 120 miles to the south. In September 1872, construction was completed on tracks between Decatur and Birmingham and at that point the L&N was able to run trains all the way to Montgomery, Alabama.

The small station on College Street served the L&N as well as the Edgefield & Kentucky Railroad until 1898 when it was rendered useless after catching on fire and burning.[66] The operations of this station then shifted to the already overburdened 1854 NC&St.L depot. This overcrowding was eliminated only with the construction of a new larger station, a station more befitting the growing metropolis of Nashville; the new NC-L&N Union Station in 1900.

NASHVILLE & CHATTANOOGA RAILROAD 1854 UNION DEPOT...

N&C President Vernon Stevenson, in the 1849-50-51 Annual Report to the stockholders, emphasized the need for his company to build passenger depots in its two terminals cities of Chattanooga and Nashville.

Constructed in 1854 by the Nashville & Chattanooga, the Nashville terminal at Walnut Street (now 10th Avenue) and Church Street was the northern terminus for the railroad between the two cities.

The architect of the 1854 Nashville terminal cannot be proven, but the depot's design was certainly influenced by the style of several other structures by one of Nashville's most prominent architects, Adolphus Heiman.

The Prussian born Adolphus Heiman came to Nashville in 1837 and soon made a name for himself as a designer and stonecutter. By 1845, he would be listed in the Nashville City Directory as one of only four architects in the city. After distinguishing himself at the Battle of Monterey during the Mexican War, Heiman returned to Nashville to become one of Nashville's most renowned designers. Within the next few years, he was commissioned to design over a dozen of what would come to be known as of the city's landmark buildings. Among this number was the Cathedral of Our Lady of Seven Doors (today St. Mary's Catholic Church), Belmont, the home of Adelicia Acklen Hayes, (today Belmont University), the 250-bed state Hospital for the Insane, and the Literary Department at the University of Nashville.[67] It is believed that Heiman was also commissioned to design the Nashville & Chattanooga's, Nashville depot. If the depot was not a Heiman design, the new station, a 300 foot by 55 foot structure was definitely influenced by his design. Heiman's touch can plainly be seen in the details of the structure.

---

66 After this L&N depot burned it was rebuilt in the same location, but more than likely on a smaller scale, by hotel owner W. T. Linck. This depot connected directly to the old Linck Hotel and was known as the Linck or College Street Depot. After a street-widening project in 1928, the hotel was no longer in business, but the depot was still serving three trains daily. Directly to the north of the depot and across the L&N track, stood a 500-600 foot long L&N freight house. This structure covered the entire lot between College and Market Streets. The freight house does not appear on early 1900s city maps and was more than likely made obsolete by the building of Union Station and new freight facilities.
67 James Patrick, *Architecture in Tennessee 1768-1897*. 1981, page 148.

Nashville's Original N&C Terminal as it appeared in the 1890s and before it was renovated for the 1897 Tennessee Centennial (see photo on the following page). -*Tennessee State Library and Archives*

Nashville Mental Asylum, Adolphus Heiman Architect. -*Otto Giers Photographer; -Metropolitan Nashville Archives*

The two-story N&C depot was of Gothic Revival design with a heavy reliance on roofline battlements, the use of hooded molding above the windows and the distinctive turrets on all eight corners of the building. These design features mimic almost verbatim the design the Hospital for the Insane and the University of Nashville buildings.[68] The similarities of the three buildings were striking.

The area around the Nashville depot, the 2,080 foot long property between Cedar Street (present day Charlotte Avenue) and Broadway has long been known as the *gulch*. Before the coming of the railroad in the 1850s, this area had been a residential area. The N&C purchased the houses in the immediate area, leveled them, and made way for the terminus they built there. One hundred and sixty years later, this area retrains the name the *gulch* and it still serves as the center of railroading in Nashville.

The 1854 NC&St.L depot was remodeled in 1886, receiving a second extensive overhaul again, just in time to welcome visitors to the 1897 Tennessee Centennial. This 1896 remodeling included the addition of an ornamental iron porte-cochere erected from the station entrance out to Walnut Street. The porte-cochere was built to protect station passengers from the weather while waiting for carriages. On the opposite side of the building, a 100 foot by 500 foot train shed was also added. With the addition of the new train sheds, the portion of the building previously used for the train sheds was reclaimed as offices, baggage, and passenger waiting areas. Photos made after the 1896 remodeling show that the large arches on the south ends of the building were bricked up. These arched openings had previously served as entrances to the original train sheds.

These embellishments contributed tremendously to enlarging the size of the original 1854 structure, but even with the additions, the depot was still grossly undersized to handle the growing traffic demands placed on it by the NC&St.L.

---

68 The Literary Building built in 1853 still stands at the corner of 2nd Avenue South and Lischey Street and is used today as offices by the Nashville Metropolitan Government.

1854 Nashville Depot. This 1896 photo shows the new paint job and renovations made in conjunction with the coming of the Tennessee Centennial. With the coming of Union Station in 1900 the old depot was razed and the depot was replaced with a two-story structure. The northern end of this replacement building was the Outgoing Freight Depot for the NC&St.L, the southern end was an Inbound Freight Depot. This Freight Depot was destroyed in 1940 in one of Nashville's most spectacular fires. The southern half of the building was salvaged after the fire and was rebuilt into a one-story structure.
-*Tennessee State Library and Archives*

In 1881, the NC&St.L completed construction on a three-story General Office Building at 1000 Broadway directly across the street from the future location of Union Station. This office building was the design of the esteemed architect Col. W. C. Smith, who also designed the 1882 NC&St.L Union Station in Chattanooga as well as the Huntsville, Alabama Union Station. Smith would also serve as the chief architect of structures at the Tennessee Centennial. The NC&St.L used the three-story building as its headquarters, but because of limited space in the main building, a former private residence next door was purchased and used as an auxiliary office as well. These old buildings served through the administrations of six NC presidents and were razed in 1928.

By 1923, the NC&St.L once again needed more office space and began construction of a new eight-story corporate headquarters building. NC&St.L razed the private residence used as the old auxiliary office building at 930 Broadway and used the site for construction of the new building. The former headquarters building remained until 1928 and its use between 1923 and 1928 is unknown. The new eight-story building was razed in 1965 to make way for a new hotel that currently stands on the site. The transom from the old building's front door was salvaged and today stands in Centennial Park near locomotive #576 as part of a memorial for the NC&St.L

Nashville, Tennessee NC&St.L Office Buildings, built 1881. This three-story building was built by the NC&St.L for use as its main headquarters. It stood at 1000 Broadway. The Mansard roofed building next door was a private residence before being purchased and used as an auxiliary office to the main office building. The buildings were replaced with a new 8-story main office building in 1923 and the three-story building was razed in 1928. Its use between 1923 and 1928 is unknown.
-*National Archives*

Union Station...

When NC&St.L president Major Eugene C. Lewis walked to the podium on October 9, 1900 for the opening ceremonies of the new Nashville Union Station, it was the climax of twenty-eight years of planning and the culmination of as many years of laborious work that allowed his company to boast that they had a Union Terminal. As early as 1872 the Nashville & Chattanooga Railroad had planned to build a new station in Nashville at 10th Avenue North and Church Street as a replacement for the 1850s vintage station at that location. By the end of the century, this old Union Station had certainly seen better days.

The second half of the nineteenth century was a gilded age in American railroading. At this time the railroads of the South were beginning to escape the heavy handed control of Federal Reconstruction and for the first time since the early 1860s were being returned to private ownership. This was a period for the freshly re-named Nashville, Chattanooga & St. Louis Railway to break its shackles and to put forth a new corporate image. No finer example could be found to exemplify this sought after corporate image than a new magnificently towering terminal.

As much as the NC&St.L may have wanted a new terminal, the monetarily strapped company simply did not have the finances to attempt the construction of such a massive structure on its own. The NC&St.L had no choice but to reach out to the deeper financial pockets of the L&N... but, there in lay the rub. It must have been heart-wrenching for Major Lewis to have to approach the Louisville based and New York owned, Louisville & Nashville Railroad to ask that company to become a partner in this endeavor. The NC&St.L had been a partially owned subsidiary of the L&N since a hostile stock takeover in 1880. For him to ask the L&N for the loan was something akin to a younger sibling having to ask his older brother, whom he despises, for the money.

New Office Building, built 1923. -*Nashville, Chattanooga & St. Louis Railway*

Major Lewis would have preferred for the L&N to have had no part of building a Union Station, a terminal to be located in Nashville and owned by the Nashville based Nashville, Chattanooga & St. Louis Railway. There had been open hostilities between the two companies since the former president of the Nashville & Chattanooga Railroad, Vernon K. Stevens, had vacated the state of Tennessee and moved to New York City. In 1880, Stevenson, from a lofty banking position in New York had sold the NC&St.L from under the feet of the N&C stockholders.

For the Nashville, Chattanooga & St. Louis Railway to be owned and controlled by people in Louisville and New York City obviously did not bode well with the people in

Nashville. Additionally the citizenry of Nashville despised the Louisville & Nashville as a company. The Nashville, Chattanooga & St. Louis Railway was a homegrown company. The L&N and Louisville were outsiders.

Animosity between the city of Nashville and Louisville ran very deep. The hostility became so intense that when editorials chastising the L&N began to appear in the *Nashville Banner*, a Nashville newspaper, the L&N saw to it that the ownership of the paper changed to the hands of more pro-L&N people. Soon, after the L&N started meddling in the newspaper business, Major E. B. Stahlman, an L&N board member, gained control of the *Banner* as its Editor and Publisher.[69] Shortly after the Stahlman takeover, the derogatory remarks about the L&N rescinded slowly week after week until finally there was silence.

This rivalry would simply not go away. The old adage says, "If you cannot beat them, join them." Luke Lea, an outspoken critic of the L&N turned that tenet around to say, "If you cannot join them, establish a competing newspaper to combat them." In 1907, he did just that and founded *The Nashville Tennessean* and … on behalf of the enemies of the L&N, turned the paper into a voice against the L&N.[70] In 1911, Lea was elected to the Tennessee Senate. In 1913, he attempted to launch a federal investigation of the railroads and political corruption in Tennessee; this was a direct slap at the dealings of the L&N. The coming of World War I shelved the investigation.

The board of directors of the L&N was well aware how the people of Nashville felt about them. They saw the Union Station project as a way to mend a few fences. They figured that if the L&N did lend subvention to the Union Station project, it would go a long way toward healing old wounds between Nashville and the company. In 1892, Major Lewis was able to persuade the L&N to provide financial support for the new station and in doing so diminish some of the hostilities between the NC and the L&N, at least for a short while.

The L&N might well have embraced the idea of spending money for a new Union Station in Nashville some years before they did, but for the fact that they too were strapped for funds. In the 1880s and 1890s, the L&N was forced to fight some very protracted anti-trust lawsuits that had been very costly to the company financially.

In addition to Union Station, the L&N had thrown its support behind Major Lewis' other major project, the 1897 Tennessee Centennial Celebration. The L&N wanted to wait until the end of the run of the Centennial before they embarked on the financial support of a second venture.

---

69   Dain L. Schult, *Nashville, Chattanooga & St. Louis: A History of "The Dixie Line."* 2001, page 56.
70   *Tennessean, shed have unique, controversial ties*. The Tennessean, September 28, 1994.

1897 Tennessee Centennial and International Exposition...

Tennessee celebrated its Centennial in 1896. Although planning for the Tennessee Centennial and International Exposition, a celebration of the state's 100th birthday, was in the works as early as 1893, the planners were unable to open the fair until the year following the actual centennial year. The venture was struck by several setbacks. Rivalry between the three geographic sections of the state ... east, middle and west, grew significantly. Some Nashville leaders thought a new railroad station should be built before the Exposition began. One newspaper editor declared that the, "Filthy old mule shed known as the Union Depot was not fit to receive thousands of out-of-town visitors."[71] [72] Tennessee county courts were asked for appropriations to fund the event, but the responses were slow in coming. There were concerns that 1896, being an election year, would distract from the event. It was also hoped that if the counties could shift the cost of the event to the state legislature, there would be a better opportunity for matching funds to come from the Federal government.[73]

Centennial Train. The NC&St.L toured this car across its system as advertisement for the Tennessee Centennial.
-*Tennessee State Library and Archives*

The fair finally opened to the public on May 1, 1897 for a six month run. The Centennial was the idea of Nashville architect William C. Smith who had proposed the event as a way of bolstering a sagging Nashville economy hit hard by the Panic of 1893. Smith and other leaders in Nashville called upon NC President John W. Thomas, Sr. to chair and oversee the Centennial. John Thomas brought on board Eugene C. Lewis, another prominent business leader in Nashville. The energetic Lewis took the project to heart. A scholar of Greek and Egyptian civilizations, Lewis was paramount in seeing that a full-scale replica of the Greek Parthenon was built for the Centennial. So impressive was this replica that when the temporary buildings of the Exposition were to be razed, the citizens of Nashville demanded that the Parthenon be saved ... and it was. By 1920 the old wooden replica was showing its age and was in need of rebuilding. Over the next eleven years the building was rebuilt as a masonry structure and in 1931 the Parthenon reopened to the public.[74]

---

71 Neal O'Steen, *Tennessee at 100: The Centennial Exposition in Nashville celebrated the Volunteer State's first century.* University of Tennessee website, www.tnk.edu.
72 The old Nashville Union Station would receive a facelift and expansion to accommodate the influx of almost two million visitors that would travel to Nashville, but the station was not replaced until 1900.
73 Neal O'Steen, *Tennessee at 100: The Centennial Exposition in Nashville celebrated the Volunteer State's first century.* University of Tennessee website, www.tnk.edu.
74 The Parthenon underwent another multi-million dollar renovation between 1991 and 2001 after it once again had fallen into disrepair.

Terminal Building and NC&St.L Station, 1897. *-Tennessee State Library and Archives*

The first World's Exposition dates back to 1844 when the French held an industrial exposition in Paris, though the birth of what we today would call a true World's Fair was not held until 1851 when a fair was held in London. Between that date and the end of the century these fairs would increase in popularity to the extent that by the 1890s there was an average of three expositions held in some part of the world each year. These expositions were a way to introduce to the public the latest advancements in trade and industrial technology.

The Tennessee Centennial Exposition was an exemplary way to showcase the growth and advancement the state had made in the previous one-hundred years. It was an exposition of industry, agriculture, commerce, and transportation. This was an excellent opportunity to draw attention to both the city of Nashville and the NC&St.L. Over the six-month run of the Fair the *Great White City,* as the Centennial Exposition would come to be called, welcomed 1.8 million visitors. A great number of these guests were transported to Nashville aboard NC&St.L trains. After arriving in the city, the visitors were transported from the old 1854 depot downtown, to a 100-foot square, two-story ornamental NC&St.L Terminal Station constructed on the northern edge of the Centennial grounds. The NC&St.L kept two trains running all day long for the 10-minute shuttle ride from the Church Street station to the Renaissance style Terminal. Starting at 7:30 AM each morning and running until 12:30 AM, the NC&St.L ran the shuttle at a bargain price of 5¢ each way. Every fifteen minutes a train left both the Centennial and the downtown station. They met half-way between and would exchange passengers and each train returned to its starting point. Over the six-month run of the Exposition, tens of thousands of passengers were transported in this manner. If you didn't fancy transport by steam, four electric streetcar lines also ran to the park. The NC&St.L went so far as to spruce up and create a garden setting in the West Nashville Shops Yard, through which the shuttle trains passed on their way to the Centennial.

Nashville Streetcar. The tracks for the city's streetcars went directly past the Centennial fairgrounds. Many of the visitors took advantage of the close proximity of the line to make their way to the fair. *-Tennessee State Library and Archives*

As the passengers de-trained, their first stop at the fair would be to tour the Terminal Station. The station had been appointed with two floors of exhibits that thoroughly illustrated the progress and advancements in railroading and the telegraph system in America.

Interior of Terminal Building Tennessee Centennial.
-*Tennessee State Library and Archives*

Demonstrated on the ground floor were minerals, gold, ore, agricultural products and growing plants from the state of Georgia. Located here too were the ticket office and a waiting room for the shuttle trains. Ascending to the second floor via a grand stairway, visitors viewed the exhibits of the NC&St.L Railway. The entire second floor was open as one large room. Exhibits represented every Tennessee County served by the railroad. On display were samples of every mineral, timber, and product of the soil that could be found along the railroad's right-of-way. In the center of the room was a replica of NC&St.L locomotive No. 101, constructed entirely from pumpkin, millet, and turnip seeds. A huge map of the NC&St.L system hung on one wall. The map gave the visitor a view of the vast territory served by the NC.

Two statues stood just outside the Terminal. The two persons depicted by the statues were Vernon K. Stevenson, projector, founder, and first president of the Nashville & Chattanooga Railroad, and Charles Grant, NC&St.L Railway's blacksmith and forty-seven year trusted employee.

Just to the side of the Terminal building stood a long shed under which was a large exhibit of NC&St.L rolling stock. This exhibit must have been quite a spectacle showing off the might and history of the railroad.[75]

Interior of the Transportation Building. Exhibited were the newest palatial car from the Pullman Sleeping Car and a reproduction of the first car from the same company.
-*Tennessee State Library and Archives*

The fair closed on October 31st and was a stirring success for the city as well as the railroad. The NC&St.L had delved deep into its coffers to finance the Centennial Exposition; the expenditure was well worth it. The Tennessee Centennial actually cleared less than $100 in profits, but the promotion of the railroad was a rousing success. One of the ongoing successes of the fair was an agriculture train that was developed by the company. As an extension to the farming exhibits, visitors to the Exposition had seen the trains tour the system for a number of years promoting farming and domestic arts. The train consisted of cars devoted to cattle and other livestock raising, soil testing, homemaking, crops, and farming in general. A county agricultural agent was assigned to the train to answer any of the visitor's questions. For the ladies, the train contained exhibits on the latest innovations in canning, sewing, and

---

75 Official Guide Book to the Tennessee Centennial. 1897.

child rearing. The agriculture train would pull into a town; stay for a few days and then move to a neighboring location.

CONSTRUCTION BEGINS ON THE NEW TERMINAL...

Nashville Union Station Architect's Rendering. *-Tennessee State Library and Archives*

With the closing of the Exposition, it was time to turn attention to the new Nashville terminal. Construction for the station began in August 1898. In many major cities, the coming of a train terminal or a freight yard to the center of the city would usually force out some segment of the population. This scenario held true in Nashville as well. Union Station was built in the shadow of the old 1854 terminal and the yards that it served. By the time the NC began building in the *gulch*, the more affluent Nashville residents had long since moved to areas away from the smoke, pollution and noise of the train yard. Left behind were working classes of people, some of which worked for the railroad or were laborers or teamsters in the warehouses in the area.

The Louisville & Nashville Terminal Company received a charter of incorporation from the State of Tennessee on March 21, 1893. The purpose of the chartering was for the facilitation of the construction of a union passenger station in Nashville. On April 27, 1896 the NC&St.L and the L&N Railroads leased to the L&N Terminal Company for a period of 99 years all property between Gay Street and Cedar Street. The lease provided for the construction of a new union station as well as all the tracks, terminal buildings, and other facilities needed for the L&N and the NC&St.L to operate freight and passenger services. On June 15th the Terminal Company leased back to the L&N and the NC&St.L all the property leased to it in April. On June 21st, the Terminal Company entered into an agreement with the city of Nashville in which the Terminal Company agreed to build

Two towers of Union Station. The front tower contained a clock face and the rear tower was an exhaust chimney for the fireplaces, furnace, and the locomotive smoke emanating from the tracks below the building. *-Terry L. Coats photographer*

Nashville Union Station Clock Tower. *-Terry L. Coats photographer*

the station and facilities if the city would condemn and raze all existing houses and other structures currently on the building site.[76]

At the start of construction, more than 200 homes and 57 acres of mostly residential property were condemned and leveled to make way for the new structure.[77] A deep cut into the limestone bluff was made near Broadway into what had beforehand been a rolling hill of once fashionable houses. There are conflicting accounts as to whether the people in those houses were glad to have to abandon the neighborhood. Some say the people did not want to leave, other accounts say that the noise and grime of living next to a train yard made leaving an easy proposition.

Over the next two years Major Lewis and engineer-architect Richard Monfort assembled some of the best craftsmen in the fields of stone masonry, stain glass, carpentry, clock works, and iron mongery to construct their new station. Monfort was not an architect in the proper sense as he was an Irish born mechanical engineer whose primary responsibility had been to design and construct bridges for the L&N railroad. Monfort a student of modern architecture chose the neo-Romanesque style of New York designer Henry Hobson Richardson for the new terminal.

Few architects are progressive enough to have an architectural style named after them. Henry Hobson Richardson's interpretation of the massive Romanesque was so innovative it made him one of them. Massive rough stone textures, deeply recessed bands of windows, large round-arched openings, and asymmetrical towers exemplify Richardson Romanesque. Openings were further defined by contrasting color or texture of stone or by short, robust columns. Each of these elements of design can be found somewhere on Union Station.

Monfort had been so inspired by one of Richardson's earlier works, the Allegheny County Pennsylvania Courthouse (1884-6), that he included many of the same details into his vision for the new station. The photo of the courthouse below illustrates the similarity of the two structures.

Pittsburg, Pennsylvania, Allegheny Courthouse and Jail. *-Terry L. Coats Collection*

---

76   The Nashville, Chattanooga & St. Louis Railway Employees Educational Service. Lesson #6. March 1943, page 33.
77   Joe Sherman, *Nashville's Union Station*. 1987.

There was nothing demure or detailed in the design of Union Station, qualities that befit a railroad company trying to demonstrate to its patrons a sense of power and might. The distinctive Union Station soon became the focal point of a bustling, vibrant growing Nashville, something that pleased Major Lewis as well as the Nashville city fathers.

Thousands of tons of Kentucky limestone were mined to fulfill Monfort's design for the exterior of the building. Trains brought the mammoth building stones from Bowing Green, Kentucky to the construction site. As soon as the 150-foot-square foundation had been laid, stone masons began the arduous task of erecting the building using derricks and gin poles. Two years later, the finished station consisted of a track level ground floor, a main floor that served as the passenger depot, and three more floors of office space and storage above the main level.

Rising above the slate covered roofline were two towers, the front one, a clock tower rising to a height of 220 feet and the shorter, arcaded one to the rear of the station. The rear tower with its flying buttresses contained a chimney used for exhaust from the main heat plant in the basement of the depot. The tower also served as a flue for the giant fireplace located in the rear of the main floor waiting room, and ingeniously as an exhaust route for the smoke rising from any steam engines forced to park below the station.

Kayne Avenue Train Yard and Union Station. ca.1915. Seen on the left in this unique wide vision photo of the Nashville skyline is the Tennessee State Capitol and Overton Bush Stables, In the center of the photo can be seen the block-long NC-L&N Freight Depot and the Kayne Avenue Yard office. To the right can be seen a yard tower as well as the original 3-story NC&St.L office building, Union Station and the connected sheds. Of note in the forefront of this photo is a string of former NC&St.L boxcars that were converted by the company into center door cabooses. *-National Archives*

As the massive blocks were lifted into position, stonecutters began carving bas-relief ornamentation into the limestone. The station would be adorned with a multitude of these carvings. Many of the window and door openings were laced with carved lintels or some other decorative embellishment. Hundreds of stones, including stones for several horizontal bands of stone filigree, were added to give an exquisite finishing touch to the exterior of the building.

Nashville Union Station Details. *-Terry L. Coats photographer*

After the major portion of the building was completed, workmen crafted a magnificent brass and wrought-iron porte-cochere to the rear and left side of the station. On the Broadway side of the building was added a low stone entrance portico. The portico contained seven large arches and above the largest of these arches was chiseled "UNION STATION" in three-foot tall letters.

Union Station Entrance. -*Terry L. Coats photographer*

Major Lewis had salvaged the statue of the winged Greek god Mercury from the Commerce Building, demolished after the Tennessee Centennial Exhibition of 1897. Mercury was the mythical god of speed and swiftness, a fitting symbol to convey about trains of the Nashville & Chattanooga Railway. Lewis had the copper statue placed at the apex of the front tower overlooking Broadway. The addition of Mercury brought the height of the terminal to 239 feet above track level. Mercury would stand sentinel over the depot until March 24, 1952 when it was buffeted from it perches by high winds. Crashing to the rail yard below it was so badly damaged it would not return to its lofty post as long as the depot was owned by the railroad.

Mercury statue as it appeared atop the Commerce Building at the Tennessee Centennial. After the fair closed, the statue was stored and then erected as the crowning element above Union Station. -*Tennessee State Library and Archives*

Located below the statue of Mercury was one of the station's most remarkable attributes, the tower's digital clock. This clock was an engineering marvel of its time. Where most buildings would have displayed an analog face on the timepiece, nothing would do Major Lewis but to install a belt driven, gear intensive digital regulator. The clock showed a face to each of the four sides of the tower. Electric motors drove a specially woven canvas belt that had to be imported from France. The clocks kept perfect time until around 1918 when the canvas drive belts became frayed and worn. The damaged canvas began to hang and would eventually burn-up the clock motors. When the railroad could no longer obtain replacement belts from Europe, the clocks were abandoned. The digital displays were replaced with an analog display and the drive mechanism was removed in the 1940s.[78]

Other memories were of the magnificent appointment of the interior of the building. Enamored with Greek myths and all things Egyptian, Major Lewis seemingly spared no expense in composing just the right details for the eye of the traveler as he or she passed under the magnificent stain-glassed expanses overhead.

---

78   *Speaking of Union Station.* Union Station Trust Fund, Nashville Tennessee. 1977, page 38.

Clock Tower at Union Station Nashville. Long gone are the original digital clock face and the original Mercury that once adorned the top of the tower. The digital clock was replaced in 1918 and the original Mercury fell 220 feet to the tracks below in 1952. The clock face was covered with plywood in the declining years of the station. When the terminal was remodeled into a hotel the new owners replaced the clock and erected a non-relief simulation of Mercury. -*Terry L. Coats Collection*

The station was replete with Tennessee marble floors, massive oak benches, a roaring fire in the fireplace, and the hustle and bustle of the train caller announcing the trains every fifteen minutes. The barreled three-story high ceiling was painted pale pink and blue, with green clouds, and angels on wing. This painted ceiling was removed during World War II when the NC&St.L placed offices on the third level of the station.[79]

A huge clock was placed on the second floor balcony over the massive fireplace. Flanking the clock were two female figurines dressed as Greek maidens ... one representing the city of Louisville and the other the city of Nashville. The models for these figurines were none other than Major Lewis' daughter Louise (Nashville) and the daughter of L&N's chief executive officer Milton Smith (Louisville).

Above the main floor and away from the passengers, the NC&St.L maintained offices on floors two and three. The unheated, fourth floor was reserved for the storage of NC

---

79   *Speaking of Union Station*. Union Station Trust Fund, Nashville, Tennessee. 1977, page 14.

railroad records. A catwalk ran from east to west sixty feet off the main floor below and just under the stained glass skylights.[80] The extensive use of and the heavy reliance on a powerful yet simplistic design fulfilled the masterful intent placed in motion by Lewis and Monfort.

The first departure from Union Station occurred on October 3, 1900 when the Chattanooga No. 5, an NC&St.L train, departed Nashville without ceremony. A short time later, the station saw its first arrival when the L&N accommodation arrived from Gallatin, Tennessee. The official opening ceremony would occur a few days later. The date of the dedication for Union Station was October 9th. The depot opened with great fanfare that included a huge parade up Broadway. A report in the *Nashville American* said the parade featured numerous bands, Confederate veterans, horsemen, policemen, firemen, and social ladies riding in victorias, landaus, closed carriages, and open traps.

Union Station interior. *-Tennessee State Library and Archives*

Young ladies from Ward's Seminary personified the Romanesque *angels of commerce* from the interior of the stations grand hall. The twenty young ladies carried, as did their relief statues plaster counterparts, Tennessee-raised products of wheat, vegetables, corn, livestock, cotton, whiskey, books, tobacco, lumber, coal, general merchandise, etc. In a report of the opening, the *Nashville American* the following day called the station a, "Gem of Beauty" and went on to say that the decorations of the station were, "Second to none."

First NC&St.L train out of Nashville Union Station September 3, 1900. Chattanooga bound #5 departs Union Station from the shed to the south of the terminal. Note that the shed still displays what appears to be scaffolding indicating that final touches to the station may not have been completed at the time this photo was taken. *-Nashville, Chattanooga & St. Louis Railway*

Whether you were a passenger on the train or a local Nashville resident, Union Station would be noted for its wonderful restaurants. From its opening in 1900 until about World War I, the formal dining room at Union Station was one of Nashville's finest eating establishments. Known for its elegance and good food, the dining room attracted locals as well as those in travel. Local businessmen met on a regular basis at the restaurant to conduct their business affairs and to socialize with Nashville's finest. Breakfast in the dining room was something quite special. White tablecloths and white

---

80   Ibid, page 13.

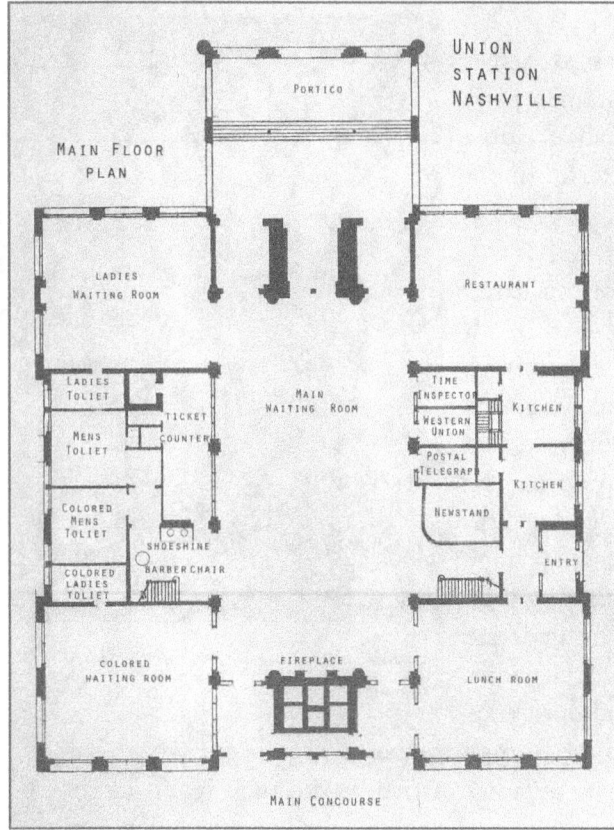

Union Station First Floor Plan

uniformed waiters gave great ambiance to the meals served there. Another attraction to the Union Station dining room was that it was open twenty-four hours a day.

A formal sit-down meal was not always the choice for many of the busy travelers or for those on a more limited budget. If they were in the market for a lighter fare, there was the lunch counter located on the left of the waiting area past the formal dining room, the newsstand, and the telegraph office. This was the place where most of the employees of the station would eat and the train traveler rushing to make a train schedule could grab a sandwich on the fly. An additional change of pace could be found at the Hartman Hotel located next door to Union Station.

Union Station was just one element of a huge campus of railroad structures. Attached directly behind the 150 foot square station was a shed, the country's longest single spanned, gable-roofed structure. Its steel and pine timber trusses were 250 feet wide topped by a 500 foot-long clerestory. Its original slate roof extended over tracks that could accommodate eight, stub-end, and two through tracks.

To the east side of the shed bordering the main building stood the mail, baggage, and express terminal. Constructed of the same mammoth Kentucky building stone from which the station was built, it mirrored the station in much of its features.

Not only were the tracks next to the station utilized for passenger trains, but the main Nashville freight yards were located in the *gulch* as well. Kayne Avenue Yards, on the west side of Union Station had been a fixture of the NC&St.L Railway since the roads inception in 1850. In its prime, the yard was .8 mile long; there was a small turntable and a four-stall engine house used for repairs on terminal

Nashville, Tennessee Hartman Hotel. The Hartman Hotel complex was located on Broadway next to Union Station at the present site of the Frist Center for the Visual Arts. The complex consisted of the hotel, a barbershop, a couple of saloons, a café, and some other facilities. For those laying over between trains the Hartman was a place for lodging, relaxation, and refreshment. -*Tennessee State Library and Archives*

Union Station Nashville Trainsheds Built in 1899 as part of the Union Station project the shed spanned a 200 foot x 500 foot area making it the largest single truss structure in the world. All of the attention shown to the station during the 1980s and 1990s was not shown to the shed and over the years it continued to decline. A fire set apparently by some homeless persons destroyed the wood roof and weakened the metal trusses to a point that the city condemned the structure. Though a gallant fight was waged to save the sheds, in 2001, the 101 year old structure was dismantled. -*Tennessee State Library and Archives*

Nashville Union Station Baggage Depot. This depot was built as part of the Nashville Union Station in 1900 and today is occupied by entertainment facilities. This portion of the station is said to be haunted. -*Terry L. Coats photographer*

Kayne Avenue, Nashville, Tennessee, 1952. -*Metropolitan Nashville Archives; -Bainbridge Collection*

engines as well as light repairs on road engines. The yards served both the NC&St.L and the L&N until main operations for both railroads were moved in 1954 to Radnor Yard south of Nashville. Still in limited service today, Kayne Avenue serves as a crew change facility for the men of the CSX.

With the completion of the new terminal, the L&N and the NC&St.L turned their attentions to capturing a larger percentage of the freight business that had belonged to the steamboats navigating the Cumberland River. Since the mid 1800s, warehouses along Front Street (now 1st Avenue North) had been the main storehouses for materials coming into Nashville. In 1907, a group of businessmen completed the construction of Cummins Station directly behind Union Station. This four-million cubic foot warehouse was, at that time, the largest concrete re-enforced storehouse in the world. Cummins Station helped tip the balance of business away from boats and to the railroads.

The station and the railroads it served were at their apex in business in the 1920 era. In July of 1920, Union Station was serving 54 trains daily. Calling on the depot were such nationally known trains as the *Dixie Flyer*, the *Dixie Flagler*, the *Dixie Limited*, the *Dixie Mail*, the *Pan-American*, and the *Hummingbird*.

The busiest time for the station was certainly the War years of 1941 to 1945. Hustling by the station were troop trains, armament and equipment trains, prisoner-of-war trains, as well as the standard civilian consists.

Present during the war was the Red Cross, who established a canteen in the station serving sandwiches and hot coffee twenty-four hours a day, seven days a week. Pearl Harbor was bombed on a Sunday and by Wednesday of that week the Red Cross had established what came to be the first war-time canteen in America.

Aerial photograph of Union Station and the adjoining Kayne Avenue Yards. -*Tennessee State Library and Archives*

During the war, volunteers from the Red Cross made a point to meet each and every troop train with cigarettes and sandwiches as it traveled through Nashville ... and travel through they did. Sixty-nine miles south of Nashville lay Tullahoma, Tennessee and Camp Forrest. Forty-five miles north of Nashville was Camp Campbell. Troop strengths at these two training facilities stayed around 115,000 to 120,000 personnel after they were established; and almost without exception, every one of those troops came through Nashville. Additionally, since the rolling hills of the area resembled those in much of Europe, the Second Army chose to use Middle Tennessee for maneuvers and training. Nashville also became a recruiting center for the Army's Air Corp. Screening for every pilot, navigator, bombardier, and for several other positions for the entire Corp was done in Nashville. The Second Army and the Air Corp added anywhere from 20,000 to 40,000 more personnel to the bustling crowds the station was already handling.

In 1942, Nashville's Travelers Aid, YMCA, and Salvation Army teamed together to established a United Service Organization ... better known as the *USO*. The railroads donated one of the front rooms of the station to the USO for their use in aiding the soldiers passing through Union Station.

The station was certainly a lively place. It was said that most of the time soldiers and civilians were packed into the station like sardines. The station was never closed and tickets could be bought from one of the ten ticket windows at any hour of the day.

One of the strangest uses of the station occurred during the War when a portion of the depot was used to temporarily house prisoners-of-war until they could be transferred to other locations, like Camp Campbell or Camp Forrest.

As the war finally came to a close, the station slowly got back to a more regular pace. Equipment, locomotives, and cars that had been rescued from the scrap heap in 1942 and pressed into service for the war effort were again returned to the bone yards. Servicemen returned to civilian

Cummins Station, ca. 1907. At the time, this was the largest freight warehouse in the world and was built in an attempt to divert traffic to the railroads from the boats on the Cumberland River. The structure still stands next to Nashville's Union Station and today is occupied by specialty shops, offices, and restaurants. -*Terry L. Coats Collection*

life, factories retooled from making war materials. America returned to normal, but it was never the same.

By the 1950s passenger cars and airplanes were taking their toll on the ridership of the NC&St.L. By 1954, the railroads in America were struggling to maintain the twelve percent of all passenger business they still mustered in the country.[81]

Kayne Avenue Yards as seen from Broadway and the front entrance to Union Station. *-Tennessee State Library and Archives*

With the movement of the freight operations from Kayne Avenue to Radnor in 1954, the offices on the third floor of the station were gradually phased out and the operations moved to Radnor as well. The NC&St.L had actually invested over a million dollars to move their facilities and switching to Radnor in 1917 to 1918, but the plan never came to fruition until Radnor was expanded in the early 1950s.[82]

By the time of the merger in 1957, the glory of passenger train travel on the NC&St.L had faded far from the days of splendor it had once known. Gone were the *Dixie Limited* and the *Dixie Flagler*. The *City of Memphis,* a coach only train, was but a shadow of its former self. Gone were the lounge, diner, and observation car. By 1960 the L&N had scrapped the entire train from its schedule.

The 1960s saw even more decline in the use of the station. By that time the building had fallen into terrible disrepair and a major portion of the interior had to be roped off because of falling plaster and leaking roofs. So badly had the station deteriorated that a short time after the introduction of the *National Railroad Passenger Corporation*, better known as *Amtrak,* in 1971, the station's main waiting room had to be closed completely. In April 1975, the old building was deemed unsafe and ordered closed by Nashville's Codes Department. Amtrak remodeled a portion of the building that had once been used as the station's baggage terminal. The ticket office and waiting room were moved into that building.

Amtrak discontinued the *Floridian,* the last passenger train to serve Nashville, in October 1979. With the discontinuance of this service, the station ceased a seventy-nine year run as Nashville's primary train depot and for the first time since the Nashville & Chattanooga inaugurated service in 1851, there were no longer passenger trains serving the city.

---

81 David P. Morgan, *How To Keep It If We Can't Kill It*. Trains Magazine. February 1956.
82 *Speaking of Union Station*. Union Station Trust Fund, Nashville, Tennessee. 1977, page 120.

1952 Chevrolet Advertisement. The automobile industry advertised heavily for buyers in the post-war era in the early 1950s. -Terry L. Coats Collection

The station became the property of the United States Government's General Services Administration in 1977. That same year, the station was designated a National Historic Landmark and the GSA initiated a plan to turn the station into office space. The elation of 1977 that the dilapidated old station had gotten a reprieve turned to gloom as problems began to beset the project. The venture languished for a number of years as setback upon setback plagued the endeavor.

Upset over the lack of movement on the part of the government, in the mid 1980s, the city of Nashville gained control of the building from the GSA. The city immediately set to find a private developer to rejuvenate the structure. Finally, in the late fall of 1985, the city inked a 99-year lease with Gulf Coast Properties to develop a 128-room luxury suites hotel. Work began in May 1986 to restore the depot to even greater glory than it had held in 1900.

The hotel was granted an occupancy permit on January 1, 1987, after undergoing an $8,000,000 renovation. In 2007, the hotel received yet another renovation.

In 1996, a devastating fire engulfed the train shed behind the station. Quick action by the Nashville Fire Department saved the hotel from major damage, but the shed was not so lucky. The intense heat did major damage to the iron beams. After the fire, the owners of the shed stripped off the roof leaving only the frame and trusses. For a while the area under the shed was used as an open-air parking lot. Building inspectors from the city found the remains to be structurally unsound in late 2002 and the one-hundred year old structure was demolished from January to February 2003.

BATS AND GHOSTS IN THE BELFRY...

During the years the terminal was used for travel, hundreds of thousand of passengers passed through the station. It is said that at least one of those passengers may not yet have made a connection with his appointed train. Today, a portion of the annex that once served as the baggage area is now a pub called the *Flying Saucer*. It has been reported that on several occasions employees have seen an ethereal image in one of the huge mirrors and that those who have seen the image describe a man dressed in 1920s or 1930s clothing replete with a top hat. Others have reported the television in the bar area suddenly turning on at full volume and the coin slot in the per-play pool table sliding in-and-out for no explainable reason.

Hotel patrons have also reported strange happenings and unexplainable visions on the upper floors of the terminal itself. Maybe these apparitions are lost passengers, displaced persons who were forced to move from the shantytown that once occupied the station site, or maybe they are the ghosts of one of the 130 persons killed in the great wreck on Dutchman's Curve in 1918. Whoever they are, they have helped place Nashville's Union Station on several lists as one of the most haunted hotels in America.

Chattanooga

When the Western & Atlantic Railroad steamed into the city of Chattanooga on December 1, 1849, it was to a temporary station … a wooden shed near Railroad Avenue (now Broadway). The first freight depot, also a wooden structure, stood across Ninth Street from the passenger depot. Though there was passenger service by December 1849, the first five months of train service on the W&A was under peculiar circumstances. The tunnel at Chetoogetta Mountain between Atlanta and Chattanooga was still not completed and all train traffic between the cities had to be freighted around the mountain by wagon. The first passage through the tunnel would not occur until May 9, 1850.

The Nashville & Chattanooga rail from the east reached Bridgeport, Alabama in May 1853. From that date until the rails could be completed into the city, passengers were transported on the last leg to Chattanooga by steamboat. The first through N&C train would not arrive in the city until February 11, 1854. Within the next decade, three more railroads would call on Chattanooga.

Chattanooga, Tennessee Passenger Depot, built by the W&A Railroad. -*National Archives*

On March 28, 1857, the first Memphis and Charleston Railroad Company train arrived in Chattanooga. The M&C connected to the N&C at Stevenson, Alabama, then used N&C crews and locomotives for access over Nashville & Chattanooga rails. The M&C would use this arrangement until 1880 when they would obtain track rights over the NC&St.L.[83]

The East Tennessee and Georgia Railroad would be the fourth railroad to enter the city. Not having faith that Chattanooga would develop into a major rail center, the ET&G bypassed the city when building their mainline from Knoxville, Tennessee to Dalton, Georgia. The ET&G entered the city in late 1858 via a branch line from the closest connection point to that line in Cleveland Tennessee.[84]

First Combination Depot...

In 1851, the Western & Atlantic built a permanent small two-story brick combination passenger and freight depot. The first floor was used for both passenger and freight service. The second floor was dedicated to office space for the passenger department.

---

83   Richard E. Prince, *Nashville, Chattanooga & St. Louis Railway, History and Steam Engines.* 1967.
84   David H. Steinberg, *The Next Station Stop will be Chattanooga! The Development of Passenger Train Facilities in Chattanooga.* 1976.

This first depot (located between the present Broad Street and Market Street at East 9th Street) had been built before the arrival of the Nashville & Chattanooga, the Memphis & Charleston, or the East Tennessee & Georgia Railroad. This small structure served the 4,000 inhabitants of the city well when the W&A was the only railroad company serving Chattanooga. With the additional traffic generated by the three new lines, a larger terminal was needed.

1859 Union Station...

Three passenger railroads, the Nashville & Chattanooga, the Western & Atlantic and the Memphis & Charleston Railroads entered into a contract to build a union station. The original structure, the Car Shed as it was called, was begun in 1857 after an agreement was struck between J. M. Spurlock, superintendent of the W&A and the N&C Railroad to build a union station. The depot was completed in 1859 at a cost estimated to be a little less than $38,000.85

Chattanooga, Tennessee Train Sheds, ca. 1860.
-National Archives

This station was located at Ninth and Broad one block west from the site of the smaller 1851 depot. The Car Shed was the creation of Eugene LeHardy, chief engineer for the Western & Atlantic, and was built by the W&A's master mason. Because of the W&A influence, the building closely resembled the car shed depot that had been constructed in Atlanta by the W&A in 1853.

The Car Shed was a large structure. Because of the large expanse of the structure, it was used during the War first as a Confederate and then as a Federal hospital. After the battle of Murfreesboro in January 1863, wounded and dying soldiers were transferred from the battlefield and were placed under the shed. This gave the shed historical significance as it was one of only a few train facilities to be used as a hospital.

Chattanooga, Tennessee Mile Marker 151.0, ca. 1966. The Western & Atlantic Railroad and the NC&St.L used this station built in 1882 jointly. It was razed in 1975.
-National Archives

The W&A was owned by the state of Georgia. To get their tracks into the station the W&A had to cross into Tennessee to lay 15.2 miles of track. Since the land under the tracks was owned by the railroad it can be said that there was a very narrow sliver of Georgia property lying within the bounds

---

85   James Houston Johnston, *Western & Atlantic Railroad of Georgia.* 1931.

of Tennessee. This strange condition did not stop with the 15 miles of track. Union Station itself was an extension of this Georgia owned railroad within the bounds of Tennessee. The centerline of the sheds was a dividing line between the property of the W&A and the N&C and it was the dividing line between the state of Tennessee and Georgia.

The building of handmade brick and stone had a 100 foot arched width and a run of 304 feet. There were two entrances, each covering two arrival/departure tracks as well as railroad offices and ticket facilities. The tracks extended 100 feet north of the sheds toward Ninth Street. This allowed an engine to pull through the shed and not fill the shed with the dense exhaust of wood smoke. Waiting facilities for the depot were not located under the long expanse, but instead were located a short distance away in a small hotel named the Burns House. The Burns House stood at the corner of present day Ninth and Carter Streets. This arrangement of combining the waiting area with a lodge would remain in effect until 1882, when the Burns House was razed and the Nashville, Chattanooga & St. Louis Railway erected a new passenger station and a freight depot in close proximity of the Burns site.

1882 VICTORIAN PASSENGER DEPOT...

The depot to replace the Burns House was a two-story brick building of Gothic Revival design. The first floor of the Richardsonian Romanesque station had arches of rough-faced stone above the windows, and a roof ridge made up of spires and pointed arches. The roof was of West Virginia slate. Begun in 1881, the structure known as the *Head Station* was attached to the old 1859 Car Shed and occupied the 100-foot setback that had previously been left between the old shed and 9th Street. With the completion of the new station, passenger trains no longer headed into the terminal; they were then backed into the shed.

Chattanooga, Tennessee Union Station Interior.
-Tennessee State Library and Archives

Adjacent to the new passenger depot and directly across 9th Street was built a freight station. Both buildings, the design of Nashville architect Colonel W. C. Smith, were completed in 1882 and both opened for business on July 1st of that year.[86] From the time of the building of the first Union Station in 1859 until the construction of this new freight building in 1882, freight traffic was handled by the Western & Atlantic in the original two-story W&A Combination Depot (1851) and by the Nashville & Chattanooga at a brick freight house located near Boyce Street.[87] These two older structures were razed with the building of the new freight house.

---

86   John Wilson, *Chattanooga's Story*. 1980, page 202.
87   John Wilson, *Chattanooga's Story*. 1980, page 58.

The passenger depot displayed an elaborate interior. Passengers making their way to a waiting train would have entered through a double set of walnut doors and then would have walked down a 65 foot long mosaic tile floor to a 20 foot by 40 foot waiting room. In addition, on the main floor of this building, one would find a dining room as well as the baggage room, a men's smoking room, a separate waiting room for the gentler sex, and a number of offices for the railroads. These rooms were appointed with lavish walls of walnut, ash, and white pine. It was said that the new depot was the, *talk of the town*. NC&St.L business offices occupied the remainder of the main floor as well as most of the second floor.[88]

Baggage cart beside NC&St.L rail post office car. *-Terry L. Coats photographer*

In 1900, renovations were made to Union Station. Elaborate filigree was added to the ladies' waiting room, and a new Georgia marble floor was installed though out the first level.

A long simmering legal feud erupted in 1905 between the inhabitants of Chattanooga's Union Station over the station's ownership. Over the years of litigation the courts had always sided with the State of Georgia and the NC&St.L in their contention that the depot was shared property between the two railroads, and that the other lines sharing the depot with the NC did not have a legal right to the station. Unhappy with that ruling, the three lines under the control of the Southern Railroad system, the Southern Railroad Company, the Cincinnati, New Orleans & Texas Pacific Railway Company, and the Alabama Great Southern Railway Company, along with the Central of Georgia Railroad organized the Chattanooga Station Company and built Terminal Station. Upon the completion of the station and tracks facilities, the roads along with the East Tennessee Virginia & Georgia and the Memphis & Charleston, that had merged into the Southern Railroad discontinued the use of the W&A and NC depot and moved all operations to the new facilities. The 1905 Terminal Station survives today as the Chattanooga Choo Choo Hotel.

In 1911, the old NC&St.L car shed sustained a fire and was heavily damaged. The damaged portion of the shed was soon rebuilt and at that time the NC&St.L decided to add to the structure. With the addition of the new construction, the sheds reached a length of 425 feet.

In 1926, after a realignment of Broad Street, the tracks to the depot were rearranged and a greater part of the old car sheds that had stood for 68 years were demolished.[89] Of the

---

88　David H. Steinberg, *The Next Station Stop will be Chattanooga! The Development of Passenger Train Facilities in Chattanooga*. 1976.
89　James Houston Johnson, *Western & Atlantic Railroad of Georgia*, 1931.

aforementioned 425 feet of shed, only 125 feet were left standing. With the loss of the cover of the old brick building, three new butterfly sheds were erected along the platforms. The rearrangement of the tracks also effected the movement of the trains into the station as well. After this time, all southbound trains had to head into the depot and all northbound traffic had to back into the depot.

Union Station underwent a second extensive renovation and redecoration in the years 1926-9. This wonderful old station struggled on through the demise of the NC&St.L and the eventual passing of passenger train service to and from Chattanooga. On May 1, 1971, the last passenger train *(Georgian)* passed south through Chattanooga on its way to Atlanta. A short time later, the State of Georgia announced plans to sell the old depot. Late in 1972, the state owned half of the depot was sold at auction and shortly afterward the L&N sold its half.

Chattanooga, Tennessee. Krystal Building located at Broadway and 9th Street. -*Terry L. Coats photographer*

A late, last-ditch effort was made by preservationists to save the depot and to develop it for retail purposes; but it was to no avail. Being on the National Register of Historic Places was not enough to save the depot from the wrecking ball. In April 1973, the 116 year old structure that included part of the original 1857 train shed made way for new construction. At the time of its destruction, the train sheds were the only surviving pre Civil War buildings in downtown Chattanooga. Today, the Krystal Headquarters and the Tallan office building occupy the site of the original passenger station. The downtown library, Tennessee American Water Company office, and the TVA complex are on the site of the Car Shed.

Atlanta

In December 1836, Georgia Governor William Schley signed an act authorizing the "Construction of a railroad from the Tennessee line, near the Tennessee River, to the southwest bank of the Chattahoochee River." The following year, Colonel Stephen Harriman Long, government engineer, while surveying for the Western & Atlantic Railroad found the banks of the Chattahoochee River to be an unsuitable terminus on which to build. He moved seven miles away from the river, finding in the foothills of that area a natural roadbed for the projected railroad. Long drove a wooden stake in the red Georgia clay and in doing so marked the southern terminus for the state railroad. This location would become one of the greatest rail centers in America.[90]

---

90   The location at which Colonel Long drove the stake is today known as the W&A Railroad. Milepost "0." It can be found in present day Underground Atlanta.

Colonel Long first designated this location as Terminus; the name would change in 1843 to Marthasville, then in 1847 finally to Atlanta. It may have been Colonel Long who gave Atlanta its first name, but he apparently did not have much faith in that exact location becoming anything other than a wood supply station. When given an opportunity to invest in land at Terminus, he placed all his monetary investment in land near Marietta instead.

Sometime after February 1842, the Western & Atlantic constructed in Terminus a board and plank structure and used it as their general purpose offices and as the city's first depot. This small depot, a saw mill, and two stores became the town of Terminus.

For a number of years there were no other buildings and very few people living in the community. The inhabitants of the hamlet were not numerous enough to warrant the building of a church. Additionally, in no way could the small number of people in Terminus remotely come close to supporting the salary of a minister to fill a pulpit. Though small in number, the people in this near wilderness area still had spiritual needs. On occasion, when a minister did visit the area, the folks of Terminus put the small W&A clapboard train station to work as the first church in the area. In 1843, there did not seem to be a problem with the separation of church and state, and thus the little state owned railroad building served both quite adequately.

With the arrival in Terminus of the Georgia Railroad in 1845, the Macon & Western Railroad in 1846, and the Atlanta & West Point in 1847, the little W&A station would be used by all four railroads and would become not only the city's first train station, but also its first Union Depot. This depot would serve from 1842 until 1853 when this rudimentary wood depot was replaced with a new wood and brick structure.

1853 TRAIN SHED...

The second Atlanta depot would be built at the same location as its predecessor, the board and plank building. This depot, Atlanta's first true *Union Station* was located on the square of land now bordered by the modern day Pryor, Alabama, Central, and Wall Streets.

Samuel Mitchell, the man who donated this five-acre parcel to the city, specified that it could only be used for railroad purposes.[91] As it turned out, Mr. Mitchell's act of benevolence was only slightly overshadowed by the fact that at the time of his gift, it could not be proved whether or not he was the lawful owner of the property.

Samuel Mitchell was a citizen of Zebulon, Georgia in the 1820s. Zebulon was located about 50 miles south of the future site of Atlanta. One night a stranger named Benjamin Beckman appeared at the door of the Mitchell house seeking lodging. Sam took him in

---

91 Atlanta Journal Constitution. April 6, 1930.

for what was to be a one-night stay. Unfortunately, Mr. Beckman took ill and the stay was extended for a much longer time.

Last train out of the 1871 Atlanta depot. -*Terry L. Coats Collection*

During the stay, Beckman took a fancy to one of Sam's horses and tried to do a little horse-trading with his host. Mitchell refused an even swap of his horses for the one Beckman was riding and insisted that Beckman sweeten the deal if they were to do business. Beckman reveled that he had been the recent winner of a piece of property made available after the forcible evacuation of the Cherokees during the Trail of Tears removal. Beckman valued the land at $41.00, and convinced Mitchell that the land and his horse would be an honest price for the Mitchell stallion. Mitchell agreed to the deal and the exchange was made.

As Benjamin Beckman rode off, Samuel Mitchell was left holding the deed to Land Lot No. 77 in a far off part of the Georgia wilderness. Little did Sam know that he was now the owner of a piece of property that would one day become the very heart of Atlanta, Georgia?

A hitch developed when the official copy of the property deed was consumed in a fire at the Pike County, Georgia courthouse. About the same time as the courthouse fire, Mr. Beckman died. A protracted legal fight ensued between Mr. Beckman's heirs and Mr. Mitchell. After some legal negotiations, it was determined that Samuel Mitchell had lawfully purchased the property and that the donation of the land was proper.

This brick 1853 structure made famous in the David O. Selznick movie production of *Gone with the Wind* came to be known as the *train shed*. This structure, one of the first train sheds built in America, served Atlanta from 1854 until November 15, 1864. On that date, at the beginning of his march to the sea, Yankee General William T. Sherman burned this beautiful old depot to the ground as part of his torching of Atlanta.

Atlanta, Georgia, ca. 1911. -*Terry L. Coats Collection*

The two photographs on this page are both of the train shed. These photographs were captured by George N. Barnard, official photographer of the Chief Engineer's Office and were shot during the Federal occupation of Atlanta from September to November 1864. The photograph on the left shows the depot during occupation, the one of the right shows the building immediately after General Sherman torched the city, leaving the station in ruins.

Atlanta, Georgia Depot, ca. 1864. -*Library of Congress*

Atlanta, Georgia Depot. This photo was made a short time after Federal forces destroyed the depot. -*Library of Congress*

Records indicate that a temporary wooden structure was built in 1866 to succeed the destroyed *Car Shed* depot. This wood structure served the people of Atlanta from 1866 to 1871 when the W&A built a substantial brick structure. Although no photographs of this wooden depot exist, it can be assured that this station more than likely resembled the simple log cabin depot that served Terminus from 1842 until the 1853 structure was built.

1871 UNION STATION...

By 1871 a Union Station was built as a replacement for the destroyed *pre-war train shed*. This station erected at the intersection of Pryor and Wall Streets, the present day site of *Underground Atlanta* would serve the growing population of Atlanta in the boom years following the War.

This beautiful Victorian Gothic brick facade station measured 369 feet by 119 feet. Most of the area under roof was composed of the iron-arched sheds over the multitude of tracks serving the facility. Designer Max Corput incorporated six towers around the perimeter of the Mansard roofed structure. All of the towers were unique and no two were alike.

On the main floor of this two-story depot were segregated waiting rooms, ticket offices, baggage facilities and a lunch room. Storage rooms, conductor's offices, and a telegraph office were located on the second story.

All rail traffic entering the city used this station for its passenger service. Described in the *Atlanta Constitution* as, "The handsomest, largest, and commodious iron depot in the country," the station in its prime served the NC&St.L, L&N, Atlanta, Birmingham & Coast (an Atlantic Coast Line subsidiary), Seaboard, Southern, Central of Georgia, and the Western Point Route Railroads.

Atlanta Terminal Station During the time the railroads were under the control of the USRA. The 1871 Atlanta Union Station was temporary closed and all rail traffic through the city was diverted to Terminal Station. *-Dain L. Schult Collection*

It would be to this depot that the Dixie Flyer and its sister Dixie trains would report. These crack Chicago and St. Louis to Jacksonville trains were the pride of the southern railroad system.

The NC&St.L was the bridge railroad for the IC, L&N, Mopac, and C&EI to the north and the Central of Georgia, Georgia Southern & Florida and Florida East Coast to the south. On the track parallel to the Dixie's, would have sat the Southland and the Flamingo operated by the L&N, the other major road to occupy the depot.

The first train in the United States to be given a name was the Dixie Flyer. So popular was the Dixie Flyer that the NC&St.L would develop an entire set of *Dixie* trains. The N&C named almost everyone of their Chicago to Florida trains in some *Dixie* flavor. At one point or another, there was the Dixie Flyer (1892), Dixie Limited (1913), Dixie Express (1925), Dixieland (1936), Dixie Flagler (1940), Dixie Mail (1943), and in 1942 the short lived Dixiana that only made five runs before it was discontinued. During its time, no finer train could be found than the Dixie Limited. This train was replete with deluxe lounge cars, maid service for the ladies and valet service for the men.

By the late 1890s, the 1871 depot was showing its age and was grossly undersized for the operations of the seven railroads that were sharing its space. Plans were put forward to replace the old depot with a facility of a size and character in keeping of a growing and prospering Atlanta. In 1902, the Georgia legislature passed a bill to divert surplus state funds to build a new station for the state owned line but the attorney general ruled that the use of those funds was unconstitutional. Some of the overcrowding would be alleviated when the city built the new Terminal Station. However, it would not be until 1930 before this old station would be replaced.

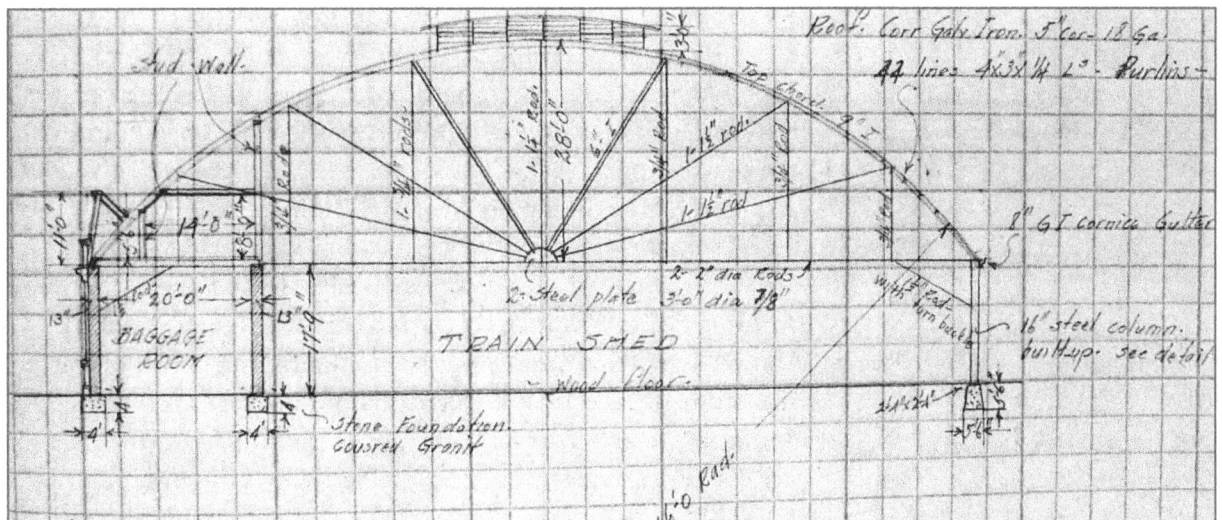

Atlanta, Georgia Union Station Cross section-1871 Atlanta Union Station. -*National Archives*

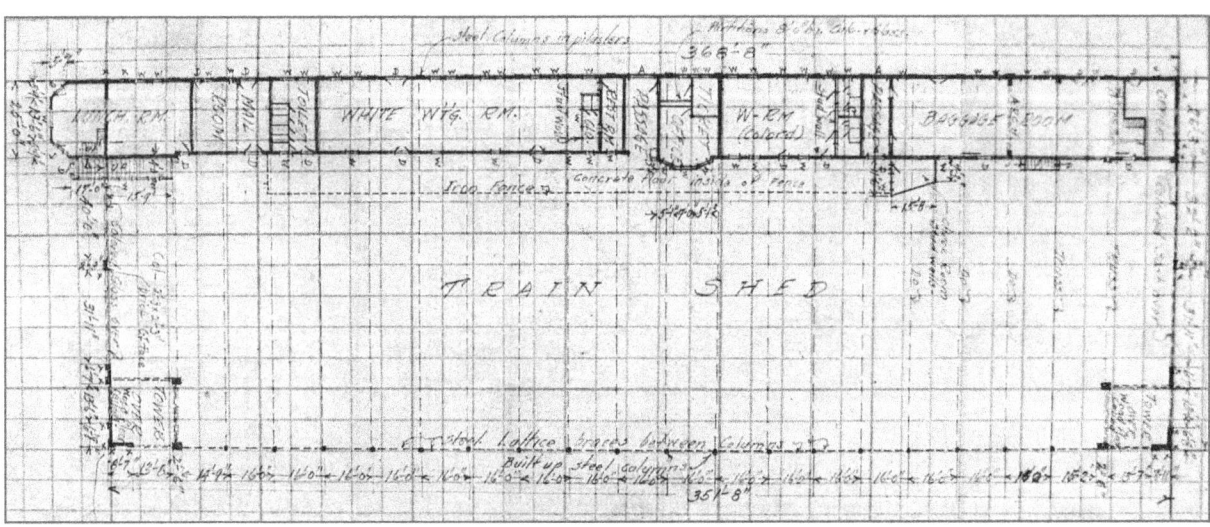

Atlanta Union Station First Floor Plan, 1871. -*National Archives*

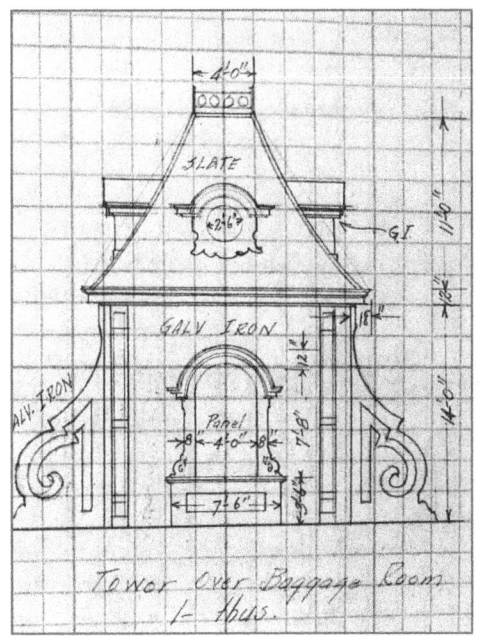
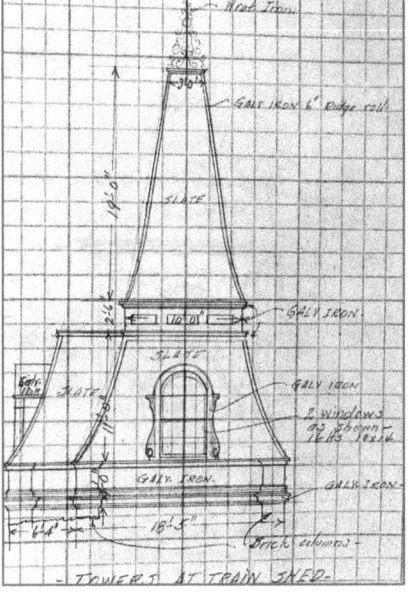

Atlanta Union Station Roof Towers, 1871. -*National Archives*

Atlanta, Georgia Mile Marker 289.0 Union Station, ca.1946. Opened in 1930 this terminal served the Georgia Railroad the Atlantic Coast Line and the NC&St.L. It saw its last train arrival the day before Amtrak service started and was razed in 1972. -*Library of Congress*

Atlanta Freighthouse and Roundhouse. -*National Archives*

Atlanta, Georgia Terminal Interior. This is an interior photograph showing the main waiting room of this terminal. -*Terry L. Coats Collection*

The new *Terminal Station* was built in Atlanta in 1905. At that point the Southern, Central of Georgia, and the Western Point Route Railroads moved their operations to the new facilities. A few years later, the Seaboard would also abandon Union Station in favor of Terminal Station.[92]

During the period of control by the USRA administration operations of the NC&St.L shifted to Terminal Station as well. In an attempt to economize the operations of the railroads, the USRA closed many duplicate train routes and consolidated the use of train terminals. Moving the NC&St.L's operations to Terminal Station was an example.

1930 Union Station...

Construction began in 1928 on a new Union Station as a replacement for the 1871 structure of the same name. The location chosen for the new station would be the site of what had once been the old roundhouse and shops of the Western & Atlantic Railroad. General Sherman destroyed the roundhouse, shops, and all the associated buildings of the W&A during the burning of Atlanta.

Built at a cost of $600,000 including viaducts, sheds, and approaches, this new depot opened in 1930. It stood at Forsyth and Spring Streets four blocks distance from its 1871 predecessor. The main structure was elevated to street level above the railroad *gulch* with a series of viaducts spanning the tracks of the NC, L&N, and Georgia Railroads below. These three companies shared the terminal at its opening. In 1933, the AB&C Railroad moved into Union Station. When the AB&C was absorbed into the Atlantic Coast Line in 1946, the ACL also moved their operations to Union Station as well.[93]

Built of cut limestone, eight massive round columns held the portico to a second story height. The massive waiting

---

92   Richard E. Prince, *Nashville, Chattanooga & St. Louis Railway, History and Steam Locomotives.* 1967, page 66.
93   Ibid.

room just inside the portico included a side room set aside specifically for female travelers, so they could wait in additional comfort.

Built in a time of segregation, the station contained a ticket booth that separated the colored and white waiting rooms. From each Terrazzo floored waiting room was a corridor leading to a tiled concourse at the head of a stairway. A baggage, check, and parcel room also opened to this concourse. All baggage and parcels were lowered to track level via freight elevator.[94]

Atlanta, Georgia Union Station Sheds. -*Terry L. Coats Collection*

At ground level, a 1,350 foot umbrella shed sheltered five double tracks. To expedite the movement of passengers, the NC&St.L erected a viaduct connecting the station plaza to the Spring Street and Forsyth Street viaduct affording additional access to the station as well as facilitating an interchange with the Atlanta Terminal Station two blocks away.

The station was razed in 1972. Today, all that remains of this beautiful station are some concrete pads over which stood the umbrella sheds at track level.

MEMPHIS

EARLY NC&ST.L TERMINALS...

Rail service to and from Memphis began with the building of the Memphis & Charleston Railroad in 1852. By 1854, the M&C had built the first depot on Charleston Street. In the coming years other railroads including the Memphis & Little Rock, Mississippi & Tennessee, Memphis & Ohio, Memphis, Clarksville & Louisville, Louisville & Nashville, Tennessee Midland, the Kansas City, Ft. Scott & Memphis, and the Kansas City, Memphis & Birmingham had joined the M&C. With all these railroads calling on the city, there was a need for depots to serve the lines. It was impractical for all these companies to build separate structures, thus, the idea for union depots developed. There were five depots in Memphis at the turn of the century.

The L&N Railroad bought the Tennessee Midland Railroad when the TMRR defaulted on their loans in December 1895. The L&N then turned around and leased that road for a 99-year period to the NC&St.L. The Nashville, Chattanooga & St. Louis Railway entered Memphis in 1896 with the absorption of the Tennessee Midland Railroad and began operating one train from Memphis through Lexington to Paducah. Additionally, the NC operated a

---

94   The Western Railroad of Alabama and the Georgia Railroad. The Courier Magazine Publication of the A&WP Railroad, Volume 7, No. 4. April 1930.

daily second train Memphis to Lexington only. The Memphis to Paducah train connected to the NC&St.L Nashville Division at Hollow Rock Junction. A secondary connection could be made to the River City by a connection to the L&N trains at McKenzie.

Before the acquisition of the Tennessee Midland Railway the McKenzie connection had been the only way NC&St.L passengers could have traveled to Memphis. The NC&St.L did not handle Pullman service over the Memphis to Paducah route. For passengers wanting sleeping accommodations, the NC&St.L would handle the fare to McKenzie with a transfer to the L&N for the remainder of the travel.

The first depot in Memphis used by the NC&St.L was the station at Main and Broadway. They shared this facility with the Kansas City, Memphis & Birmingham Railroad (Frisco), and the Kansas City, Ft. Scott & Memphis Railroads (Frisco).

In March 1900, primarily at the request of the Illinois Central Railroad, a meeting was held with officials of the city of Memphis to discuss whether the railroads should refurbish the several stations they then occupied or whether there was a need to build a Union Station for all the companies to use jointly. After a two-month discussion on the topic, nothing was resolved and all parties involved continued at their present locations.

Curtailed but not quashed, the movement for a true Union Station persisted. About March 1901, the NC&St.L moved from its facilities at Main and Broadway to the Calhoun Street Depot (Central Depot) at Calhoun and Main Streets. The Illinois Central Railroad originally built the two-story building in 1888. Along the track level of the depot was also located a one-story building that was constructed in 1874 as part of the shops complex of the Mississippi & Tennessee Railroad.

Memphis, Calhoun Street Station ca.1907 built 1888. Calhoun St. Station was located at Calhoun and Main the location of the current Central Station Amtrak Station. The NC&St.L as well as others used it before the NC moved their operations to the new Union Station. *-Robert Tomb Collection*

In April 1901, the L&N moved their operations from the north Memphis stations at Action Street and Main Street to the same Central Depot on Calhoun Street and began using the *cut-off* tracks from the L&N to the NC&St.L to access the Calhoun Street station. L&N cars and locomotives operating to Calhoun Street station were stored in the nearby NC&St.L yards and used the NC&St.L roundhouse turntable for turning their locomotives. With the move, the L&N, the NC&St.L, and six other railroads, were calling at this depot. Memphis finally had a semblance of a *Union Station*. During this time there were a total of three train depots serving the Memphis area.

In October 1908, the Memphis City Council took the first steps toward the approval and construction of a new $2,000,000 Union Station to serve all railroads calling on the city. The council opened talks with a newly formed company, the *Memphis Railroad Terminal Company* (a company made up of ten different railroad companies), for the construction of the new terminal. A site for the new terminal was purchased and over two hundred houses were demolished to make room on the property.

This was a grand gesture by the city and the *Memphis Railroad Terminal Company* to centralize and combine rail service, but it was not to be. The year 1909 would see the undoing of the company. By February, Southern Railroad, a partner in the terminal project withdrew from the organization. It became apparent that with the demise of the Southern Railroad's participation each of the other members would have to contribute an additional ten percent to pay for the building of the new terminal. By July, the company was rapidly falling apart as each railroad began looking toward their self-interests and not as a member of the whole. A major complaint was that some of the railroads would be paying a disproportionate amount toward the cost of the station in relation to the amount of rail traffic they did in the city. By September, the leadership of the company conceded defeat and the idea of a combined union station was dead. This failure to establish a single union station would only be resolved in the construction of two major stations in the city in 1912 (Union) and 1914 (Central).

Down but not out, some members of the old Memphis terminal company reorganized and on September 25, 1909, the *Memphis Union Station Company* chartered with the goal of building a new passenger station, power house, and a car and locomotive servicing facility. Five railroads … the Missouri Pacific, St. Louis Southwestern, the Southern, the Louisville & Nashville, and the Nashville, Chattanooga & St. Louis bought equal amounts of $100,000 in capital stock and signed an agreement to make the new proposed union station their exclusive Memphis terminal for a period of fifty years. Each of the five companies would also pay a portion of operating the new station in proportion to the amount of car traffic each company generated through the facility. This time the group was successful. Construction began on the new Union Station on April 1, 1910.

On April 1, 1912, two years to the day from the start of construction, the station

Memphis Union Station Mile Marker 237.0, built 1912, ca. 1940s. *-Mike Condren Collection*

opened for business. The day before, on March 30th, an open house was held with over 10,000 persons in attendance of the grand opening. Memphis finally had the Union Station it had been talking about building since just after the Civil War.

As the largest stone building in Memphis, the new terminal made quite an impression. The early Italian Renaissance style building of Bedford limestone and Vermont granite was a massive building (285 feet by 84 feet) consuming almost the entire block at the corner of 2nd and Calhoun Streets. As one approached the depot, an eye was immediately drawn to the twin towers and the three grand staircases to the front of the building. The building by architect John A. Galvin was four-storied. A crescent shaped center stairs rose above a Calhoun Street level porte-cochere to a large balcony. Resting on the balcony were six massive Ionic order columns of solid Indiana limestone that reached skyward to the roofline in accent of three large circular windows replete with carved filigree. The center stairs led to the main waiting area, while the stairs on the northwest front of the building led to the separate Colored waiting room.

The main waiting room for the station was seventy-six feet by one hundred feet in length. This room was tiled on the walls and the ceiling in a harmonious design. All floors were Italian marble. On both sides of the waiting room ran a balcony the entire length of the room. Travelers on these second story balconies had a clear view over the train sheds and the terminal yards to the south and over the cityscape of Memphis to the north. The main waiting room as well as the Colored and the ladies waiting rooms were all appointed with heavy mahogany settees. The ladies room was also equipped with wicker rockers. Adjacent to the main waiting room were the ticket offices, luggage checkrooms, parcel checkroom, telegraph room, Pullman and information rooms, telephones, drinking fountains, newsstand, and toilets.

Conveniently bordering the common areas of the station was located a marble-clad very large lunchroom. All counters were white marble accented by polished mahogany seating. For those who wanted a more formal cuisine, the station offered a dining room. The meals and service in this Italian Sienna marble clad dining room was said to have been the equivalent to any of the first-class hotels in the city. The general offices for the rail companies and the officials using the station were located on the upper floor of the station.

Down the stairs to the ground floor, the level for the platforms of the trains was located a *rest room*. This was not a restroom in the preverbal sense as we call a toilet today, this was a room removed from the more public waiting areas on the main floor of the station. It also included a ladies' retiring room, a barbershop, a billiards parlor, and a well-equipped drugstore. This area was supplied for the comfort of those travelers who would be spending several hours in the station between trains. Also located on this ground floor were a railway mailroom, Southern Express Company offices and three large baggage rooms, and crew facilities for trainmen that included lockers, showers, and toilets.

Exiting on the ground floor from the terminal, passengers walked through a concourse where the tracks that served the station ended. Immediately behind the concourse stood four butterfly sheds that provided shelter for eight tracks. An innovative feature built into the platforms was a subway system at each track that allowed for the automated handling of baggage and parcels from the express cars. When a train arrived, the express cars were spotted next to a hatchway over an elevator to the subway below. The parcels were then shuttled to baggage and express rooms in the basement of the station, at which point another elevator would raise or lower luggage to the main waiting room on the main floor.

By 1943 the station was beginning to show its age and was in need of expansion, primarily brought on by the increased business of World War II. Thirty-one trains were calling on the station daily. Ticket sales and the handling of baggage were up three-hundred percent from pre-War statistics.

In March 1943, it was announced by the president of the Memphis Union Station Company that $100,000 would be expended to bring the station up to needed standards. The exterior of the building was steam cleaned and extensive remodeling was preformed on the interior. Several of the existing platform tracks were lengthened to accommodate longer trains and two new platform tracks were created from storage tracks. Two new storage tracks were built in the yards to replace the ones taken at the terminal. To help ease congestion, new tracks were built from the station through the yards and connected to the main lines of Memphis known as "Broadway." Also built at this time were new servicing shops for diesel locomotives and passenger coaches.

The inaugural run from Union Station of the *City of Memphis* occurred on May 17, 1947. The train left the station at 8:05 AM each morning, arriving in Nashville in the early afternoon, and returning to Memphis at 7:40 PM each day. The last run of the *City* would occur out of Memphis as a nameless all coach train No. 5-105 on September 1, 1958. The last semblance of a former NC&St.L train operating out of Memphis would be L&N train No. 106-107. This train departed Union Station for Nashville on May 22, 1967.

Records indicate that as early as 1954 there were overtures by the Memphis rail companies at Union Station to consolidate operations to the Central Station two blocks west on Calhoun Street. Built in 1914, Central Station was the only other depot in the city. In 1939, the only other station to serve Memphis, Poplar Street Station, had finally closed leaving only Union Station and Central Station to serve the trains. The Illinois Central had used the Poplar Street station up until 1939 on a very limited basis. Passengers were allowed to board and depart from that station, but no tickets were sold there. Opposition to the closing of Union Station appeared to have been heavy. Ten years later in 1964, the newspapers were still carrying articles calling for the closure of the station.

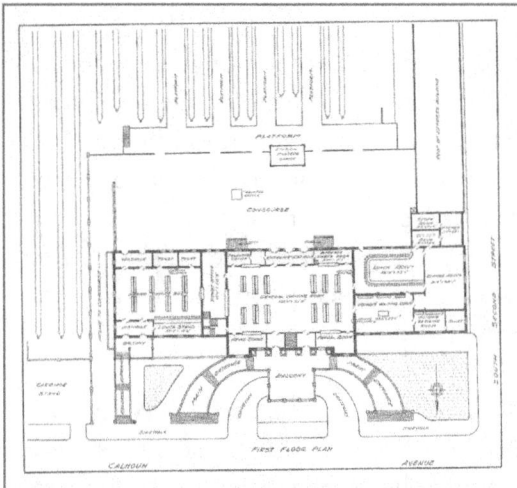
Memphis First Floor Plan.
-From www.cbu.edu/~mcondren

Memphis Main Waiting Room Photograph.
-From www.cbu.edu/~mcondren

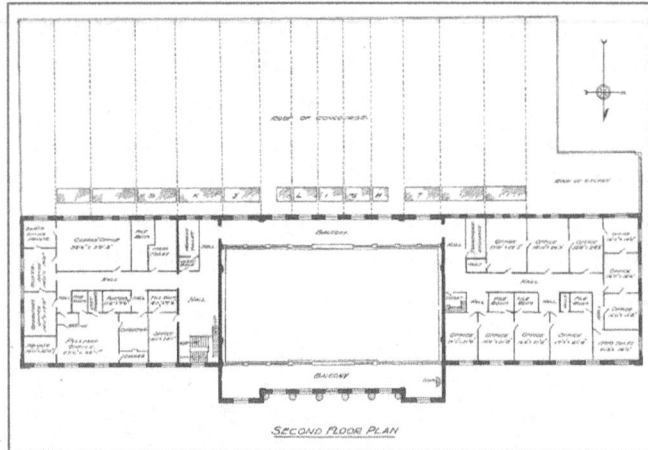
Memphis Second Floor Plan. *-From www.cbu.edu/~mcondren*

Memphis Black Waiting Room Photograph. *-From www.cbu.edu/~mcondren*

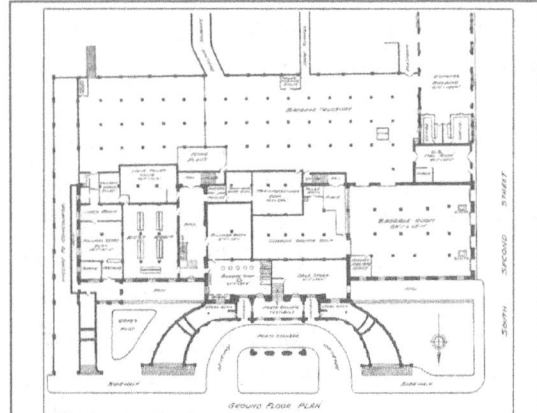
Memphis Ground Floor Plan.
-From www.cbu.edu/~mcondren

Memphis Main Dining Photograph.
-From www.cbu.edu/~mcondren

On April 1, 1964, the lease was up for renewal at Union Station. The three tenant railroads and several support companies occupying the station decided to not renew and to instead find other facilities.

The Missouri Pacific moved to the old St. Louis, Iron Mountain & Southern station in the Georgia Street Yards. This was the small depot they had moved from when they moved to Union Station in 1912. The Southern moved to the old Memphis & Charleston Railroad station on Lauderdale Street (basically a glorified freight station) and the L&N negotiated a lease with the IC for terminal privileges at Central Station. The other tenants, the Railway Express Agency, the Pullman Company, and Western Weighing & Inspection Bureau all found other offices about the city.

All these moves had been done without the blessings of the Tennessee Public Service Commission. The Memphis City Council voted on March 31st to impose a $50.00 per day fine on each of the roads until they returned to their former home. By May, the Interstate Commerce Commission got into the act as well. They stated that neither the Southern, L&N, nor MoPac had gotten approval for the abandonment. On October 14, 1964 a Federal judge filed an injunction against the three roads to force them back into the station. All three railroads immediately filed appeals to the judge's order and the issue was delayed. The matter was battled until March 1965 when the United States Sixth Circuit Court of Appeals upheld the lower court's ruling that the railroads had violated the ICC's regulations relating to the abandonment. The railroads continued to keep the case tied up on appeal until October 1966, when the United States Supreme Court refused to hear the case. Their refusal to hear the case allowed the Sixth Circuit ruling to stand.

On December 1, 1966, two-and-a-half years after they had abandoned the Union Station, the L&N and the Southern, were forced to re-establish service there. That day, a total of four trains, two L&N and two Southern that called on the station. The following day, the station saw a grand total of ten passengers arrive into Memphis on both railroads. It had been a long arduous fight and at least for a while the U. S. Government and the City of Memphis had the upper hand.

Under the court mandate, the station reopened, but this time to a much smaller operation. When it closed in 1964, Union Station employed between 115 and 120 people. At its re-emergence, there were a mere 25 people manning the station. The huge main waiting room that had served tens of thousands of passengers would not reopen. Gone were all eating facilities and no longer needed was the drugstore, the barbershop, the 200-foot long express room on the ground floor, the huge baggage rooms, and the offices of the railroad companies. The old station was but a ghost of its old grandeur. Instead of the grand waiting room, a smaller room that had once served as the ladies lounge had been remodeled and would now suffice. Passengers entering the station would no longer climb the grand granite staircase on Calhoun Street instead, they would enter at street level on that side of the building, and would walk though the old cobweb filled main waiting room to a newly built ticket office.

Politics and business are fickle animals. From April 1964 until December 1966, the city of Memphis and the U. S. Government had fought all the way to the Supreme Court to keep the three railroads from vacating the station. In April 1967, a meeting was held in the Memphis Mayor's office. Present at this meeting were officials of the railroad, representatives from the Union Station Company and members of the Mayor's staff. The subject of the meeting was again talk of abandoning the terminal. This time a new player had entered the game. The United States Postal Service was in need of a downtown location for a new regional distribution center and the station property was a prime location for this new structure. A proposal was made by those in attendance to raze the 1912 station, build a new post office on two-thirds of the site, and then to build a small cinder block building on the southeast corner of the property as a replacement.

The old terminal struggled on into 1968 with the last passenger train, a remnant of the Southern Railroad's *Tennessean* departing the station on March 30, 1968. A short time later, the terminal closed permanently. By winter, wrecking balls had demolished the station; the tracks and ties were removed, and it was gone.[95]

With the complete withdrawal of train service to the terminal, the post office was free to use the entire property for the needed distribution center. The new center was erected on the footprint of the old station and its yards. The station had fronted Calhoun Street and the post office now faces Third Street.

---

95   My thanks to Michael Condren and others who created and maintain the Memphis Stations Evolution to 1970 website at www.cbu.edu/~mcondren. This site was most helpful in telling the story of Memphis Union Station and the other stations used by the NC&St.L during its tenure in Memphis.

Chattanooga Division

Pardon me boy is this the Chattanooga Choo-Choo?
... Irving Berlin

The original Nashville & Chattanooga Railroad between the named cities became the Chattanooga Division of the NC&St.L Railway. Chartered by the state of Tennessee in 1845, construction began on the Nashville & Chattanooga Railroad in 1848. Businessmen and farmers in the Tennessee capitol city wanted an outlet for Middle Tennessee products. The mid-state was a major producer of livestock, spirits, non-food products, as well as an abundance of metallurgy mined between Middle Tennessee and the southeast part of the state just outside of Chattanooga.

By the 1840s railroads were under construction from Pennsylvania through the Mid-Atlantic States of the Carolinas and into Georgia. If a rail line could be built to Chattanooga a connection could be made to the railroad pushing north from Georgia and from there a connection to the Atlantic would be shortly forthcoming. This rail line from Middle Tennessee would be a much shorter and quicker route to the ocean than had been the inland waterways. To reach the ocean by water, a boat had to transverse first northwest up the Cumberland River to the Ohio and then to the Mississippi River to New Orleans around the state of Florida and finally up the east coast. A rail line would cut thousands of miles and weeks of travel off the delivery time to the coast.

Engine No. 1, Tennessee, arrives in Nashville, 1851.
-Terry L. Coats Collection

In 1848, Vernon K. Stevenson, principal stockowner of the N&C, was named as the railroad's first president. One of his first acts as president was to contact J. Edgar Thomson Chief engineer of the Georgia Railroad & Banking Company. Stevenson asked Thomson to scout the terrain for a proposed route for the N&C between Nashville and Chattanooga. After Thomson settled on a proposed route, he and Stevenson personally rode by horseback over the terrain to scout the future course the N&C would take. Later that same year, contracts were let to start the grading of the line from Nashville.

Nashville, Tennessee Cherry Street Tower and Watchman's Shack. This 1911 photograph was made at 4th Avenue South (now Cherry Street). The Nashville & Chattanooga Railroad placed its first locomotive, Tennessee, in service in 1850 at this location. *-Tennessee State Library and Archives*

On December 13, 1850 the steamboat *Beauty* docked at the wharfs on the Cumberland River in Nashville. Aboard the boat was the

Tennessee, a small 20-ton, 4-4-0 locomotive built by the A. Harkness and Sons Manufacturing Company of Cincinnati, Ohio. Accompanying the locomotive were thirteen freight cars and one passenger car built by the Keck and Davenport Company, also of Cincinnati. A few days later the locomotive and the cars were transported by mule team though the streets of Nashville and placed on the tracks of the N&C Railroad at Cherry Street (4th Avenue South).

By April 1851, the line was completed as far as Antioch, 8 miles south of Nashville. On April 13, 1851, the first train ran on the Nashville & Chattanooga. By July 4, the line had been completed to Murfreesboro, a distance of 45 miles from the capitol city. In Murfreesboro, it was reported that as many as 10,000 people witnessed the arrival of the first train into that town.[96]

Cumberland Mountain

Eighty-five miles south of Nashville is located Cumberland Mountain a formidable obstacle along the proposed route to the terminus at Chattanooga. Realizing that making a bore through the mountain would be a long and laborious task, it was concluded that construction would have to start the same year the grading for the mainline began. By starting the bore at the same time construction started from Nashville, the tunnel could be completed by the time tracks were completed to that point. The N&C engineers made a five-fold attack on cutting through the mountain. In addition to the bores made at the two track entrances, the railroad also drilled three 170-foot deep vertical shafts. The shafts allowed workmen to be lowered to track level and to drill toward both entrances from the center of the mountain. After the completion of the drill, the three shafts served as exhaust stacks for the smoke generated by the steam engines passing through the tunnel. By 1852, using Irishmen and company owned slaves; the tunnel had been hammered, picked, and black powdered through the mountain. At an elevation of 1,147 feet above sea level, the Cumberland Tunnel would be the highest point on the entire system. Completed on February 22, 1852, the 2,228-foot tunnel broke through the saddle of the mountain and allowed access for the railroad to descend to the other side from the Elk River watershed to Tantallon, Sherwood and finally to Stevenson, Alabama. It was at Stevenson, that in 1857 the tracks of the Memphis & Charleston Railroad joined those of the N&C. The M&C would then use the N&C Bridge across the Tennessee River and N&C tracks for egress into Chattanooga.

Cumberland Tunnel operated unabated from 1852 until 1960 when finally the L&N Railroad was forced to enlarge the size of the tunnel to accommodate the larger autoracks and piggyback cars being carried through the area. On October 4, 1961, the L&N ran its first piggyback train from Radnor to Tilford Yards via Cowan. At the head of the train were

---

96   The Nashville, Chattanooga & St. Louis Railway 1845-1945. The Railroad Journal, Volume 9, No. 8. April 1945.

an ex-NC&St.L F3A and a F3B for power. Though now both painted in L&N Dulux solid black with the red ball nose emblem, No. 1801 (801) and the B unit was still NC&St.L at heart. The 150 miles of track from Nashville to Chattanooga was completed as far as the Tennessee River at Bridgeport, Alabama by May 1853. From that date to February 11, 1854, all transport from Bridgeport to the terminus at Chattanooga was made by steamboat. On the latter date the first through train of two passenger cars and four to five freight cars finally entered Chattanooga, but it was not until after they built across the deep ravine at Whiteside, Tennessee, climbed Raccoon Mountain, and making a dip into northern Georgia. Initial thoughts were to cross the Tennessee River in Chattanooga in lieu of climbing Raccoon Mountain then dropping down to cross the river at Bridgeport. This route would have been easier to construct, but would have extended the track distance by some 14 miles. The idea of following this route was considered, but soon abandoned.

ARRIVE AT UNION DEPOT
F.H. DOWLER, Agent.

Nashville, Chattanooga & St. Louis Railway
No. 1 .... 2 35 pm
"   2 .... 2 50 pm
"   5 .... 9 35 pm
*No." 99 ....10 18 pm

Western & Atlantic Railway
No. 2 ....1 00 pm
" 4 ....1 00 pm
" 70 ....9 30 pm

Chattanooga Southern R. R.

No. 2 ....4 22 pm

Do not run Sunday
**Runs also into Union Station

One must marvel at the genius of engineer Edgar Thomson. Although he chose a circuitous route to gain access to Chattanooga, still today the modern rails of the CSX railroad follow this exact route to and from Chattanooga.

In 1859, Vernon Stevenson made a motion at a board meeting to move the headquarters of the N&C Railroad to Chattanooga, citing the fact that the city was fast becoming a centralized rail hub and that the general offices of the company would be better suited there. The motion was apparently tabled and no other actions were ever taken to make the move.[97]

As originally operated by the N&C Railroad, the Chattanooga to Nashville line was broken into three divisions. The first division, the Nashville Division stretched 60.33 miles from Nashville to the Duck River in Bedford County, the second, the Winchester Division consisted of the 62.33 miles from the Duck River to the Tennessee River near Bridgeport, and the third, the Chattanooga Division was the remaining 27.5 miles from the Tennessee River to Chattanooga.[98] After the N&C acquired other lines, this section of track simply became known as the Chattanooga Division.

Cowan, Tennessee, 1863, from a sketch by Civil War soldier N. B. Abbott. -*Drawn by Terry L. Coats from the Abbott sketch*

Locomotive #365 waiting at Wartrace, Tennessee. -*Jerry Fox Collection*

Mail train running as an extra, Sherwood, Tennessee, March 1946. -*Marietta Museum of History*

---

97   Jesse C. Burt, *The Nashville & Chattanooga Railroad, 1854-1872*. Manuscript, Tennessee State Library and Archives. 1951.
98   J. W. Arbuckle, *Cowan Pusher District and Tunnel*. The Herald-Chronicle, Winchester, Tennessee. No copyright, page 21.

During World War II, the Chattanooga Division of the NC&St.L was pivotal in the war efforts, handling some of the heaviest military, and supply traffic in America. By 1944, the railroad had extended CTC from Stevenson, Alabama to Nashville to help expedite the movement of these trains. At that time the CTC tower in Cowan was built and controlled of signaling on this division was handled from that location.

The original Nashville & Chattanooga is today the Nashville Division, Chattanooga Subdivision of CSX Railroad. There is still a heavy demand for the pusher engines at Cowan and since Tennessee is located geographically in about the center of the CSX system, today it is one of the heaviest traveled routes in America.

SHELBYVILLE BRANCH

When Vernon Stevenson and surveyor John E. Thomson were plotting the route for the line between Nashville and Chattanooga, it was decided to skirt the center of Bedford County. It was said that landowners did not want the smoke and noise of the mainline through the center of the county. A portion of the east side of the county was chosen for the route instead. Some citizens of Shelbyville, not wanting to be excluded from having rail service, approached Stevenson and proposed that a spur line be built from Shelbyville to a point on the to be built mainline. The most convenient point for a connection was Wartrace and it was decided to build to that point. The 8 mile branch was laid on very light 35 pound rail between the two cities. It was started in 1851 and was completed the following year. This would be the first branch on the N&C. The Shelbyville Branch was unique in that it would be built entirely by the N&C and not purchased as a supplemental line as were all of the later acquisitions made by the railroad.

Today, the Walking Horse & Eastern Railroad operates the original Shelbyville branch from Shelbyville to Wartrace as a short line. The primary commodities carried by the WH&W are plastic resins, recyclable aluminum and paper, and LP gas. For a few years in the early 2000s, an excursion train was run on this line using a F-unit painted in NC&St.L colors and a couple of ex-Reading Railroad passenger cars.

COWAN AND PUSHER DISTRICT

Helper Engine on Cumberland Mountain. -*Nashville, Chattanooga & St. Louis Railway*

Cowan, Tennessee and the long run to the top of Cumberland Mountain remains today a place to view a unique phenomenon in railroading. One hundred and forty five years after its opening, the four and one-half mile long, 2.43 percent grade south of the mountain and the 2.5 mile long, 2.5 percent grade between Cowan and the tunnel's north portal still requires pusher locomotives to help heave the trains approaching from both directions over the mountain.

Cowan, Tennessee Pushers. Note that this is a passenger train and it is being pulled up the mountain by the helper engine. For safety reasons, passenger trains were pulled not pushed, as were the freights. -*Nashville, Chattanooga & St. Louis Railway*

It is not known when the first helpers were used on this section of the Chattanooga Division to push longer trains up from Cowan going south or up from Sherwood heading north. Perhaps it just happened one day when the two little Rogers engines normally assigned to a train on this division had more than together they could handle. A third engine probably was called upon to help push and a dynasty was created. As the years progressed and trains grew longer, the tiny Rogers 4-4-0 and 4-6-0 engines that were first used as helpers were supplanted by heavier Consolidations. In 1915, the NC purchased three 2-8-8-2 Mallets to handle the job. The Mallets were supplanted during WWII when it was not deemed financially prudent to spend the money to do a major overhaul on the locomotives. The NC substituted their Mikados after the Mallets were retired. When the diesels arrival in 1950, the Maroon and Yellow GP-7s were placed into service and the steam engines were retired from the pusher district forever. An interesting note concerning the pusher district was that on freight trains, the pushers were assigned to the rear of the trains to push but on passenger trains, the action was reversed and the helpers were placed in front of the lead engine and they helped by pulling the entire train to the crest of the mountain.

Tracy City Branch
"The Mountain Goat"

Just after the N&C reached the base of the Cumberland Mountain at Cowan, two speculators, Leslie Kennedy, an Irishman from the future Tracy City area, and his Nashville attorney, William N. Bilbo, realized the potential of extracting the coal reserves north of Monteagle. To raise the capitol needed to form a coal company, Kennedy and Bilbo approached several prospective investors in Nashville but their solicitations fell on ears. Undeterred by the negative response he received in Nashville, Bilbo looked further for a field for investors. Bilbo was so convinced in this venture he turned his attentions to investors in New York. One of a group of New York investors was a man by the name of Samuel F. Tracy. Tracy traveled to Tennessee to see for himself the richness of the coalfields. Another of this group of New York investors was a civil engineer by the name of Major A. E. Barney. Barney was asked to survey the terrain between Cowan and the top of the mountain to see if it would be feasible to build a railroad up the mountain to extract the coal. After Barney gave a positive report on building a railroad, this group of New York investors was so convinced of the prospects of the coal and

mineral reserves they bought the William Bilbo's interest in the project. Shortly afterward, they incorporated as the Sewanee Mining Company under a state of Tennessee charter. This charter gave the Sewanee Mining Company powers to mine coal and other minerals, and to connect by rail the Upper Cumberland region to the existing Nashville & Chattanooga Railroad at Cowan.[99]

Construction began in 1853 on the line that would one day become the Tracy City Branch of the NC&St.L. The first portion of this branch was built as far as the Lower Coal Banks, *Midway* in 1856. The first coal from the Sewanee Mines at Midway was brought down to the interchange at the NC main line on November 8th of that year. By 1858, the branch had been extended through Sewanee, Monteagle, and into Tracy City. Eventually, depots were built at all three towns.

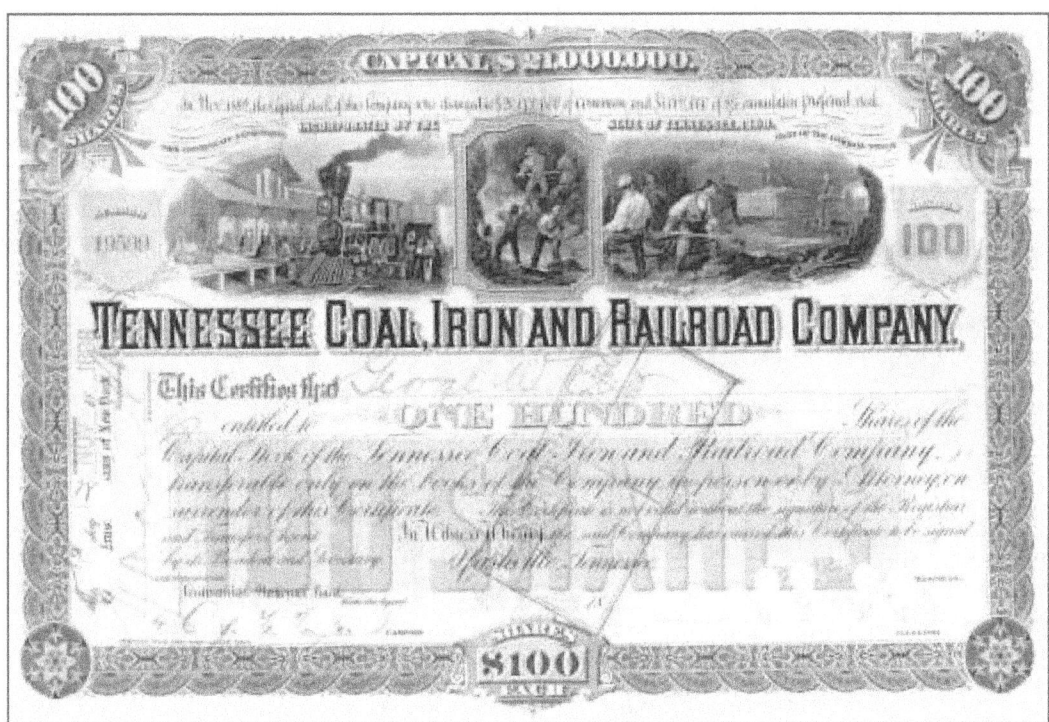

Tennessee Coal, Iron and Railroad Company Stock Certificate. -*Terry L. Coats Collection*

The climb up the mountain from Cowan was a steep and arduous one. To get to the summit, the tracks had to ascend at approximately a 100 foot rise per mile. Major Barney was able to ply the rails up the mountain while keeping the climb to an average of 2.0 percent for the first few miles and 2.5 percent after that. He was also able to lay out the line to accommodate equilibrium between the number of empty cars going up the mountain and the same amount of loaded cars coming down. The grueling climb was said to be so steep that

---

99   J. W. Arbuckle and Alan C. Shook, *The Mountain Goat*. 1992, page 4.

only a *Mountain Goat* could make it. The moniker stuck and from that point on this branch of the NC was referred to by that name.

Just before the War Between the States, the economically strapped Sewanee Mining Company reorganized and changed its name to the Tennessee Coal & Railroad Company. This new company had only gained a minimal foothold when the War brought a halt to the extraction of coal from the Sewanee area. Disrupted in 1863, the mines would not resume production until 1868.

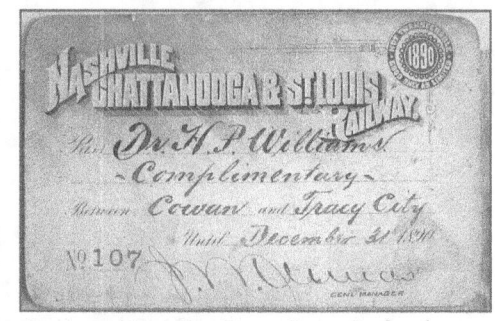
Cowan to Tracy City Pass. -*Cowan Railroad Museum*

On January 1, 1887, the Nashville, Chattanooga & St. Louis Railway for the amount of $601,000 purchased the rail line and all its franchises from the TCI&RR. This was the second acquisition by the NC of properties previously owned by the TCI. In 1883, the company had also purchased from the TCI the 5 mile Inman Branch. The Inman Branch connected to the NC&St.L at Victoria, Tennessee on the Sequatchie Valley Branch. The NC would operate this Inman Branch until 1903 when the mines closed.[100]

Tracy City Branch Train Crew. -*William Turner Collection*

Coal mining on Sewanee Mountain would ebb and flow over time, but mostly there was a positive flow of materials off the mountain. Advancements in manufacturing brought about an increased demand for coal needed to fire the furnaces of industry. Advancements in extraction methods also made it easier to obtain and in doing so made coal a valuable commodity. The abundance of the coal reserves on the mountain allowed this branch to become one of the most profitable lines in Tennessee. The economic boom brought economic and cultural development for the railroad and those on the mountain as well.

From time-to-time the company suffered setbacks. The coal in the Tracy City area was found to be of limited quantity and the mine near the town was finally worked-out. This mandated that the tentacles of the line be extended to places with deeper veins of coal. The 20 mile long branch was extended north through Coalmont to Palmer in 1918 when the Tennessee Consolidated Coal Company opened new mines in that area. From this main line, the rails branched again to eight smaller spurs emanating from Coalmont and Tracy City.

Coal mining from this area lasted for many decades, but by the 1920s American families were slowly moving away from heating their houses with coal. Even the continued

---

100   Dain L Schult, *Nashville, Chattanooga & St. Louis: A History of "The Dixie Line."* 2001, page 65.
Richard E. Prince, *Nashville, Chattanooga & St. Louis Railway: History and Steam Locomotives.* 1967, page 31.

Mountain Goat at Prior Ridge Mine
-*Nashville, Chattanooga & St. Louis Railway*

use of coal by industrial plants was not enough to warrant the cost of extracting the coal from these Grundy County, Tennessee mines. Competition from areas such as those in the Appalachian Mountains with their larger deposits also had a devastating effect. Soon, less and less coal was being withdrawn from the mountain and business faded away.

By 1930, the deposits on Pryor Ridge, Nunnley Ridge, Freemont, and five other small runs dried up or were becoming too expensive to mine. These short-spur branches were abandoned by the railroad and within a short while coal mining on the mountain was almost non-existent.

UNIVERSITY OF THE SOUTH

The history of Tracy City Branch of the NC&St.L was dominated by coal mining, but that history was not limited by any means to the extraction and transportation of coal; there was the University of the South as well.

A short time after the Sewanee Mining Company started to lay tracks up the mountain, delegates of the Episcopal Church met in Chattanooga to seek a site for the establishment of a denominational college in the region. This Chattanooga meeting took place in 1857. The following year, the owners of the Sewanee Mining Company donated 15,000 acres of land in Sewanee for the establishment of a seat of higher education. On October 10, 1860 the cornerstone of the University of the South was laid. The college flourished until 1863 when Yankee soldiers overran the area and burned the college to the ground. After rebuilding, the college reopened in 1866 and graduated its first class in 1868. Since that time, Sewanee has produced twenty-five Rhodes Scholars, garnering the distinction of the most Rhodes Scholars per capita of any school in the country.[101] Of note, is the fact that after the War General Robert E. Lee was offered the position of president of the college, but he declined. Instead, he accepted the same position at Washington College in Lexington, Virginia.[102]

NC&ST.L MOTOR TRANSIT COMPANY

For many years, coal and passenger traffic on the branch flourished, but by 1926 passenger traffic on the Tracy City Branch had been in a severe decline. The emergence of the private passenger car and the improvement of the highway system in Tennessee cut severely into the passenger traffic on the branch. That year, an application of abandonment was presented to the Railroad and Public Utilities Commission of Tennessee. The commission

---

101 Sewanee, The University of the South. Wikipedia, the free encyclopedia, http://en.wikipedia.org.
102 Ibid.

Tracy City, Tennessee branch bus service. -*Nashville, Chattanooga & St. Louis Railway*

granted the abandonment with the stipulation that the NC&St.L replace the passenger cars on the train with bus service from Cowan to Coalmont.

The NC&St.L agreed to the stipulation. They purchased a fleet of three 29-passenger busses and two trucks to be used for the transportation of luggage and baggage. On July 1, 1926, the NC&St.L entered the motor carrier business. The company contended that through the use of busses they could save $31,000 annually over the running of the train cars while maintaining the same quality service for which the NC had come to be known.

The bus-truck service was put into place to supplant what had been the four round trip daily trains between Cowan and Tracy City. This was a distance of twenty miles, with two of those round trips extended beyond Tracy City to Coalmont, an additional six miles. The busses ran on approximately the same schedule as had the steam trains they replaced. The morning bus left Cowan at 7:40 AM and arrived in Coalmont at 9:25 AM. A second run was made between 11:50 AM and 1:35 PM. Evening runs were made between 3:40 PM and 5:00 PM, with a 6:35 PM and 7:55 PM run to Tracy City only. Service in the opposite direction followed the former train schedule in a like manner.

Unfortunately the life of the NC&St.L Motor Transit Company was short lived. By 1930, the Nashville, Chattanooga & St. Louis Railway was back in the same offices of the Railroad and Public Utilities Commission of Tennessee with an application for abandonment, this time it would be for the abolition of the bus and truck service they had started a mere four years earlier.

After the abandonment of the bus service the railroad returned to passenger train service. In 1926 there were three daily trains in each direction between Cowan and Coalmont. In 1930 passenger service was reduced to one round trip daily by a mixed train.[103] Ironically, as hard as the NC&St.L tried to discontinue passenger trains in the 1920s on the Tracy City Branch, the L&N was still running passenger trains over this line through the fall of 1971.[104]

All the coal mines on Cumberland Mountain and the Tracy City branch would eventually either play out or become too expensive to mine but for various reasons, the Tracy

---

103 Terry L. Coats, *Tracy City Bus Service, 1926-1930*, The Dixie Flyer, NC&St.L Preservation Society Newsletter, Volume 4, Issue 4. November 2006.
104 J. W. Arbuckle and Alan C. Shook, *The Mountain Goat*. 1992, Introduction.

City branch was able to outlast many of its sister NC branches. The branch lasted through the demise of the NC&St.L, the L&N, and the Seaboard System. It was under the ownership of the CSX system that the line finally closed. The last cars were removed from siding of the branch on April 30, 1985.

Eventually the ties and rails were removed leaving just the old right-of-way. Today, this right-of-way has been preserved as a *Rails to Trails* conservation project and is now a multi-use recreational corridor known as the *Mountain Goat Trail*.

SEQUATCHIE VALLEY BRANCH

The Sequatchie Branch was constructed in three segments; 1) Bridgeport to Jasper, 2) Jasper to Pikeville, and 3) The branch from Victoria to the mines at Inman.

A Tennessee legislative act of 1857-8 granted a charter to the Memphis & Charleston Railroad for the purpose of extending their railroad from Bridgeport to Chattanooga on the north side of the Tennessee River. The same act granted permission to the N&C Railroad to build from the Memphis & Charleston's extension to a point not to extend past Jasper, Tennessee. An act of the State of Alabama legislature dated 1859-60 authorized construction for the portion of this line that lay in Alabama.

The Sequatchie Coal & Iron Company Stock Certificate. -*Dain L. Schult Collection*

The Sequatchie Valley Railroad was chartered by the State of Tennessee in 1868 to extend from the previous terminal of the line at Jasper 45 miles to Pikeville. Between 1876 and 1879, the Sequatchie Valley Railroad built 9.5 miles of track between Jasper and Victoria. It was the NC&St.L that actually built the railroad for the Sequatchie Valley Railroad.[105] The NC&St.L purchased the railroad in 1887 and afterward extended the line to Pikeville under the charter granted to the Sequatchie Valley. The tracks were extended to Whitwell in 1887, to Dunlap in 1888, and finally to Pikeville in 1891.

In 1882 the Tennessee Coal Iron and Railroad Company, the same company to develop the coalfields on the Tracy City Branch, built a 5 mile branch from Victoria to the company's coalfields at Inman, Tennessee. Immediately after the completion of the line in January 1883, the NC&St.L purchased this short branch.

During its tenure as a branch of the NC&St.L, thousands of tons of coal were transported to coal burning plants including the area TVA power plants. Furthermore, this area was rich in native hardwood that produced thousands of carloads of logs, crossties, and timber. Lesser commodities shipped off this branch included livestock, cement, minerals, and cast iron cookware.

Today the Sequatchie Valley Railroad operates a short line over a portion of this former branch. The Sequatchie Valley hauls lumber and plastics. The rails are still in operation from Bridgeport, Alabama to Kimball, Tennessee. All rails north of Kimball have been removed.

The Orme Branch

Built in 1904 by the Campbell Coal and Coke Company and the Needmore Company, the 10.5 mile long Orme Branch served until 1942 when the coal supply was exhausted. This branch diverts from the Sequatchie Branch of the NC&St.L approximately 1 mile north of Bridgeport, Alabama. Tracks to the mines at Orme were so steep that locomotives were unable to make the grade under a load, so the cars were winched up the mountain to the mines. Other industries along this branch included a large rock crushing plant and ballast quarry at Cumberland, Alabama.

There were only two depots on this branch, one at Montague that was a simple passenger-freight shelter and one at Orme, a combination station that is still standing.[106] Two section houses on this branch still stand as well. They are now private residences. The abandoned right-of-way has been paved and is today Alabama Highway 98, the only road into Orme.

105   Dain L. Schult, *Nashville, Chattanooga & St. Louis: A History of "The Dixie Line."* 2001, page 65.
106   Elmer G. Sulzer, *Ghost Railroads of Tennessee*. 1975, page 248.

Lebanon Branch

In 1866, the first trans-continental railroad was still three years away from completion when a group of Southern businessmen envisioned a railroad from the Atlantic Ocean passing through Tennessee and then on to the Pacific Ocean. A bill in the Tennessee legislature was passed on May 24, 1866 that chartered the Tennessee & Pacific Railroad Company. The charter provided for a railroad between Knoxville and Jackson, Mississippi, to pass through Nashville and Memphis. The T&P was to be a bridge between an existing railroad in Norfolk, Virginia and to other railroads in Mississippi leading to the Pacific.[107]

The T&P grandiose plan to build to the Pacific fell somewhat short in that only 31 miles of track from Lebanon to Nashville was ever completed. The first train between those cities ran on September 20, 1870, just in time for the Wilson County Fair of that fall.

The area around Lebanon and Wilson County was known for its abundance of cedar trees. With the invention of barbed wire in 1873, the demand for a rot resistant fence post became a premium. Additionally, many roads in America were macadamized, a process that called for an abundant supply of resilient timber. To fill the needs for posts, lumber, and other forest products, the T&P shipped tens of millions of board feet of red cedar lumber from its Lebanon lumber yard.

The Tennessee & Pacific entered Nashville over 1.5 miles of NC&St.L trackage and called at a depot located at Cherry Street (4th Avenue South) and Hart Street. This depot was built by the T&P in 1872.

The T&P struggled through financial difficulties for eleven years. By 1877, the company's debts were too overwhelming for them to overcome. After the T&P defaulted on its bonds, the state of Tennessee revoked the T&P charter and took control of the company. In October, the NC&St.L seized upon the opportunity to expand its holding and purchased the T&P from the state. The NC&St.L allowed the railroad to operate under its original name until 1888 when it became known as the Lebanon Branch of the NC.

Last Accommodation Run on the Lebanon Branch, Monday, November 3, 1930. -*Nashville, Chattanooga & St. Louis Railway*

In 1887 the NC&St.L was joined in Lebanon by the start of construction of the Nashville and Knoxville Railroad. Chartered as a coal carrying railroad, it was its founder Alexander Crawford's hopes that he could mine coal in the Middle Tennessee area and ship that coal north over connecting railroads to fuel iron rolling mills he owned in Pennsylvania.

---

107 *The Iron Horse Comes to Lebanon, Tennessee.* Tennessee Historical Quarterly. Winter 1972, page 360.

Crawford's initial idea was to build his railroad between the existing CNO&TP Railway out of Chattanooga and the town of Carthage, Tennessee on the Cumberland River. This route turned out to be unobtainable so Crawford revised his plans and decided to instead build from the NC&St.L connection at Lebanon east toward Standing Stone, Tennessee (later named Monterey) which was the site of the coal fields. The charter for the railroad was amended and construction started. By July 1890 the railway was completed from Lebanon to Cookeville.

Alexander Crawford died in April 1890 and the reins of the Nashville & Knoxville were passed to his two sons. The sons were not as proficient at empire building as had been their father and within a short time the railroad was experiencing severe financial difficulties. Despite the difficulties, the N&K continued to build and by 1893 the line extended to Standing Stone.[108]

About this time, the Tennessee Central Railroad under the direction of former Memphis & Charleston Railroad president Jere Baxter was granted a charter. The company started construction at Emory Gap, Tennessee with the intent of building to an intersection with the N&K at Standing Stone. A short time later, as a measure to benefit the companies, Baxter and the Crawford brothers struck an agreement that would allow the Nashville & Knoxville and Tennessee Central to interchange freight at Standing Stone. The freight would then be transported by the N&K to Lebanon and at that point it would be transported over the NC&St.L into Nashville.

Unfortunately, the creation of the TC did not go exactly as planned and by 1895 the company was experiencing financial difficulties of its own. The stockholders lost faith in Jere Baxter and he was banished from his position as president of the TC. By 1897, with the help of investor friends in St. Louis, Baxter reappeared and was able to right the ship, and was able to re-charter the railroad as the Tennessee Central Railway. With a new company at his control, Baxter resumed his vision of completing the TC through Middle Tennessee. Over the next few years, the TC was extended from Emory Gap across the Emory River to Harriman. The Crawford's sold the N&K in 1902, and later that year the line was extended from Lebanon to Nashville. By 1904, the Tennessee Central was able to combine the old and new TC's, the N&K, and by purchasing the Nashville & Clarksville Railroad west of Nashville, was operating a system of rail from Harriman through Nashville to Hopkinsville, Kentucky.

During the boom years around 1915, the NC&St.L ran a morning train to Nashville, a late evening accommodation, and four other regularly scheduled passenger trains as well as several freight trains daily. The years took a toll on this line and by 1930

---

108 Cliff Downey, *Tennessee Central Railway: History, Locomotives and Cars.* 2005, page 3.

all passenger trains had been discontinued. The line struggled until 1935 when the NC was granted permission to abandon the Lebanon Branch.

Jere Baxter and the Tennessee Central battled the NC&St.L throughout the time the two railroads had parallel tracks from Lebanon to Nashville. Though Baxter did not live to see it, the Tennessee Central would win the war of attrition and would see the NC&St.L run its last train over the Lebanon Branch on July 13, 1935.[109]

Train Depots in Lebanon

The T&P maintained its headquarters in Lebanon. In 1869, the railroad built a two-story Victorian-style combination general office building, passenger and freight station. It displayed ornamental iron balconies and a Mansard roofed four-story tower at one end and a single-story freight room at the other. This depot would serve the T&P and later the NC&St.L Railway until 1916 when a new depot was built by the NC. The old depot was located approximately .75 mile from the town square. Its location was a far distance to commute for those passengers conducting business in the merchant district. Persons departing the trains were either forced to walk or to hire some public conveyance to make their way to or from the city square. This situation was exasperated some years later when the Tennessee Central Railway came to town. The NC&St.L certainly lost passengers to the TC because of the location of the old station. The TC depot was located very near the square. If a NC passenger who had made his way as far as Lebanon wanted to travel on to the east on the TC, he or she would have to detrain at the NC depot then transfer back to the TC depot to continue on toward Harriman and Knoxville. Because both the Tennessee Central and the NC&St.L operated parallel tracks from Lebanon to Nashville, the prudent traveler going further east of Lebanon would choose to travel on the TC rather than have to change trains in the middle of their trip.

It was this competition from the Tennessee Central that caused the NC&St.L to build the new depot in 1916. This depot was a short three blocks from the city square and one and a half blocks from the TC depot. With the construction of the new depot, the old 1869 Victorian station was relegated to use as a freight house. It later was sold and became part of the Barry Carter Milling Company's plant. The building served several other functions before being abandoned. On the night of May 23, 1971, the old building caught fire and was destroyed. Today, the 1916 NC&St.L depot still stands and is part of a flour milling operation in Lebanon.

---

109   Cliff Downey, *Tennessee Central Railway: History, Locomotives and Cars*. 2005, page 44.

Old Hickory Powder Plant Branch

On April 2, 1917, President Woodrow Wilson delivered an address to a joint session of Congress and called for a declaration of war against Germany. The resulting congressional vote brought the United States into World War I.

Two years before the president's declaration, the prospect that this country would enter into a world war was looming heavy over the United States. At the time, the United States was sadly deficient of defense and war manufacturing. To remedy this situation, three sites ... Bell, West Virginia, Louisville, Kentucky, and a site in Tennessee ... were chosen as possible locations for the building of a munitions plant.

Old Hickory Branch Water Tower and Engine #1.
-Metropolitan Nashville Public Library

The location finally chosen for the erection of what would become the largest smokeless powder plant in the world was the semi-isolated small farming area of Hadley's Bend in Middle Tennessee. The site chosen for this plant was ideal in almost every respect. Located in a remote area away from cities and towns there would be less concern of collateral damage in the case of an explosion, *Jacksonville* or *Old Hickory*,[110] as the site would be called, was nestled in the bend of the Cumberland River about twelve miles upstream from Nashville. The location on the river gave it access to water for both the building of the plant and its operations; moreover it was located in close proximity to the coalfields of Tennessee and Kentucky, giving it ample access to fuel.

The federal government approached the E. I. DuPont Company in the fall of 1917 to start construction of the plant. DuPont and the government signed contracts in January 1918 and construction began on March 8th.

The contracts called for the building of a plant along with a sprawling worker's village as support. Since America was at war by this time, the expedited construction of the plant and village would be no small task. The old country lane that had previously served the small hamlet of Hadley's Bend was widened and heavily macadamized in order to accommodate the massive trucks delivering materials and men at the site. In short order, materials were being delivered up this road as well as being ferried up the river by barge from Nashville. To facilitate construction and to eventually transport from the plant the anticipated one million pounds of powder the plant would produce daily, it was necessary to construct a railroad.

---

110 The community of Old Hickory was located a short distance from the ancestral home of President Andrew Jackson, the Hermitage, and had taken on Jackson's nickname of *Old Hickory*.

Understanding the urgency of the matter, officials of the NC&St.L caused a survey to be completed to map out a right-of-way from the mainline on the Lebanon Branch. The survey would provide for a railroad to be constructed from the plant reservation 7.5 miles back to a connection to the NC&St.L and the Tennessee Central mainlines at Hermitage Station.

Construction on the railroad spur began on February 10, 1918, approximately one month ahead of the ground breaking for the plant. Immediately, two hundred men and fifty mules were placed on the project. Thirty days later, trains were operating over the line. The work had involved the moving of thousands of cubic feet of earth, rock and barrow, the clearing of trees and stumps off ten acres of right-of-way, and the building of culverts, runoffs, and drainage ditches. Thus, was established a world's record in railroad construction.[111]

Subsequent to the opening of the first line to the plant, a second track was also started. A second main to the plant as well as a large interchange yard near the mainline at Stones River were completed within five months of the start of construction. The double main railroad would be needed to facilitate movement of thousands of carloads of materials going to the building site. In addition to the plant itself a village capable of housing 30,000 to 35,000 people was created out of the rural setting. By the latter part of 1918 there were over 10,000 men working at the site unloading materials and erecting structures. So much building was under way that at times construction outpaced the delivery of materials. A transportation department employing over two hundred men had to be set up to disseminate the needed materials to the proper job sites. As the first main of the NC tracks was being laid, a loading platform was constructed four miles from the plant to shorten the delivery distance of needed materials. After the railroad was completed, a large warehouse was erected as a receiving depot for the material. So much construction was underway that Mason and Hanger Company, the main contractor for the project, leased the Ezell Quarry on the tracks of the NC&St.L in Newsom Station, Tennessee. This quarry and another ran day and night to supply stone and gravel for the project. Before the project was completed, the NC Railway delivered a total of 2,402 carloads of stone and gravel. At the peak of operations, the NC&St.L was operating thirty-two trains daily carrying together 17,000 workers and an average of 275 freight cars.[112] It was reported that out of the tens of thousands of carloads of materials that were transported to the DuPont facility, the NC&St.L Railway only misplaced two carloads.

One of the most unique trains to run on the NC&St.L was an employees train reserved exclusively for ladies. The *Powder Puff Special,* as the train was called, left Nashville's Union Station each morning at 7:00 AM. During the 45 minute commute to the powder plant each day the women would chat, play cards, and knit clothing for soldiers, the Red Cross, and their family members. After construction on the plant was finished, the train retained its feminine character and was used to transport female passengers from Old Hickory to Nashville to shop.

---

111   Dixon Merritt, *Sons of Martha*. From the chapter titled *Old Hickory*. 1928.
112   Old Hickory News. December 7, 1918, page 15.

The influx of personnel was so heavy going to the plant each day that trains on the L&N system also brought passengers from Nashville to Edenwald, Tennessee. They were then transported to the north side of the Cumberland River opposite the plant where they crossed the river by means of a ferry.

At the signing of the Armistice on November 11, 1918, the construction project had been under way for eight months and one day. On the site where there once had been only farmland and cornfields, now stood over 2,600 major structures and over 1,200 smaller ones. Of this number there were 1,125 six-room bungalows, 348 supervisor's houses, 251 one- or two-story apartments, 2 hotels, 4 YMCA buildings, 2 banks, 2 drug stores, a theater, a fire department building, and two train stations. Completing the town had involved the construction of miles of streets, sanitary sewers, a pumping and filtering plant for the water brought up from the Cumberland River, and a city park.

Old Hickory, Tennessee Mile Marker 17.0 This station was on the grounds of the Old Hickory E. I. DuPont plant and served as a station for the employees. -Dr. W. O. Greene Collection

In their haste to complete the plant and to start production, the federal government underestimated the effect United States forces entering the war would have on bringing it to a quick finale. Though the plant and village was built at a supersonic pace, the war in Europe ended just as workmen were putting the final touches on the facilities.

The signing of the Armistice brought production to an immediate halt. Production at that point had reached 700,000 pounds powder of a projected 1,000,000 pounds per day. The plant had been producing powder for less than four months when production stopped. After January 1919, those workers not needed for the security of the stored powder were furloughed and the plant was closed.

The U. S. Government decided to sell the plant in 1920. A group of businessmen formed the Nashville Industrial Corporation for the purpose of purchasing the site, dismantling the factory, and selling the machinery and material. The corporation purchased the $85,000,000 plant and surrounding village for pennies on the dollar of its actual value. The government owned the Old Hickory branch, but it was run by the NC&St.L while the plant was producing powder for the military. The government offered to sell the branch to the NC in 1923, but the railroad declined the offer despite the rumors that DuPont might reopen the plant. That year, the DuPont Company did in fact look for a site where they could open a plant for the manufacturing of Rayon. After a countrywide search for suitable sites, DuPont settled on the abandoned Old Hickory plant. A short four years after they had sold the plant to the Nashville Industrial Corporation the company was back, hat-in-hand to repurchase the defunct facility. When the NC&St.L declined the offer to purchase the branch line, the Tennessee Central Railway wasted little time in making the purchase instead. The TC operated the branch until the demise of the railway in 1968.

In the 1930s DuPont added a production line to include moisture-proof cellophane and yarn. The war years of the 1940s brought on additional expansion. DuPont sold a portion of its on-site operations to Reemay, Inc. in December 1986. Today the Nashville & Eastern Railroad serves the two plants over the old 7.5 mile NC&St.L branch. Though no longer operated as a double main, the N&E still transports an average of five trains per week to the plants.

Map of the Chattanooga Division

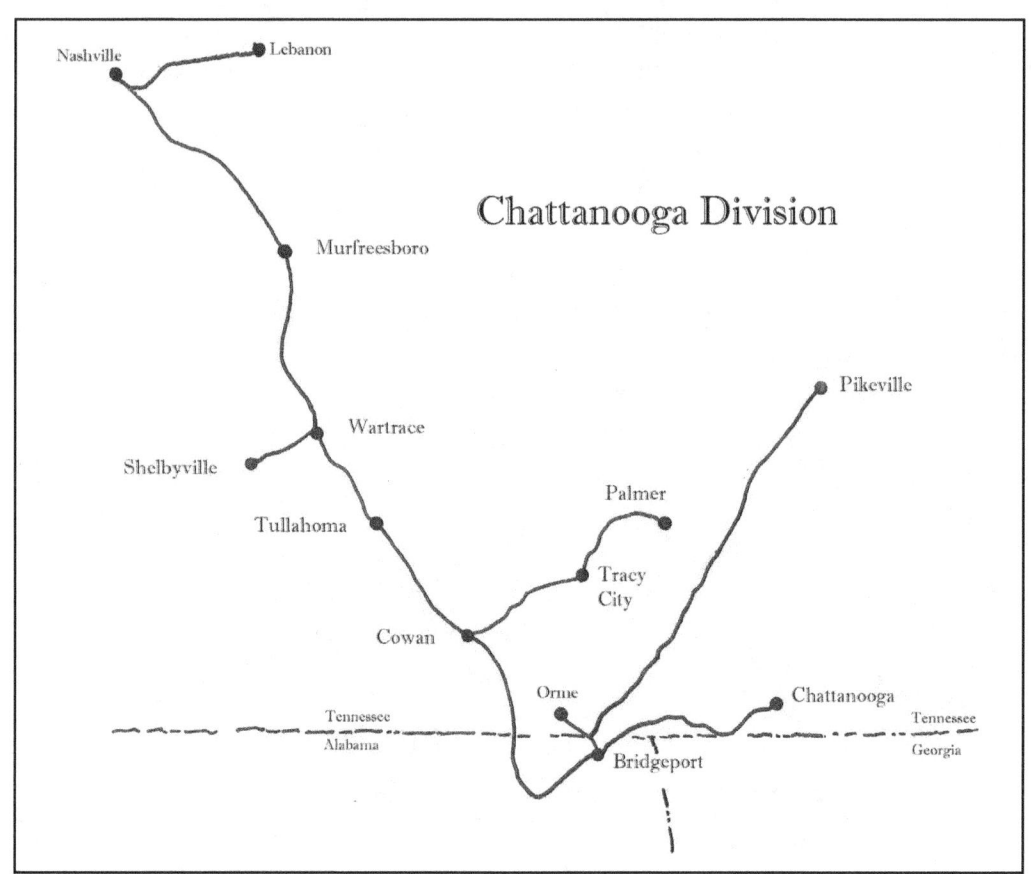

CHATTANOOGA DIVISION MAIN LINE

Antioch, Tennessee Mile Marker 10.0. -*National Archives*

Anderson, Tennessee Mile Marker 101.0. -*University of Louisville Collection*

Bell Buckle, Tennessee Mile Marker 51.0 Passenger Station. -*National Archives*

Bell Buckle, Tennessee Mile Marker 51.0. Shown are both the passenger, built 1888, and the brick freight depot, built 1878. Also located near the station was a stockyard and several section houses. -*Mark Womack Collection*

Bridgeport, Alabama Mile Marker 112.0, ca. 1909 and built 1891. The train to the left of this photo is about to depart north along the Pikeville Branch of the NC&St.L while the one to the right is eastbound on the mainline toward Chattanooga. This building was razed in 1966. -*Photo by C. J. Wyatt, Sr.; -Dennis Lambert Collection*

Bridgeport, Alabama Mile Marker 112.0, built 1917. This Spanish Mission style station opened for service in 1918. This station served the dual purpose of passenger station on the ground floor and the branch office of the Sequatchie Valley Branch located on the second floor. The offices for the SVRR were moved from the small office building seen in the photograph on page 149. It was razed in 1917 to make way for the freight depot section of this station. The Bridgeport depot was refurbished in 1998 and then suffered a fire in 1999. It was refurbished once again and today serves as a museum. -*Nashville, Chattanooga & St. Louis Railway, H. C. Hill photographer*

Bridgeport, Alabama. Seen in this photograph is the Carpenter Gothic depot used by the NC&St.L as a combination station until the railroad constructed a Queen Anne station in 1891. At that time this structure became the freight depot. Freight service moved to the Spanish Mission station in 1918. Also seen in this photograph is the two-story tower that controlled the switch directing traffic from the double main line to the single line across the bridge. The tower was razed in 1969. *-Photo by Mrs. George Alexander Dawson; -Dennis Lambert Collection*

Bridgeport, Alabama, built 1901. This small building served as the branch office for the Pikeville (Sequatchie) Branch of the NC&St.L. This building was razed in 1916 to make way for the current Spanish Mission style depot. *-Photo by Bradley Crawford Jones, Jr.; -Dennis Lambert Collection*

Chattanooga, Tennessee Headhouse and Sheds. To the right in this 1960s photo can be seen the present day Read House Hotel and below the Greyhound bus station. A portion of the shed dates to before the War Between the States. *-Warren Stephens Collection*

Chattanooga, Tennessee Mile Marker 151.0, ca. 1966. The Western & Atlantic Railroad and the NC&St.L used this station built in 1882 jointly. It was razed in 1975. *-National Archives*

Chattanooga, Tennessee Motorcar Sheds. *-Nashville, Chattanooga & St. Louis Railway*

Chattanooga, Tennessee Mile Marker 148.9. Maintenance of Way Shacks at Moccasin Bend. -*Bob Bell, Jr. photographer*

Chattanooga, Tennessee Mile Marker 149.2 Roundhouse. -*Bob Bell, Jr. Collection*

Christiana, Tennessee Mile Marker 42.0. This combination depot was built in 1882 and served the NC&St.L until 1942. The railroad retired several depots on the Chattanooga Division during WWII. -*Tennessee State Library and Archives*

Cortner, Tennessee Mile Marker 61.0, built 1889. -*Bob Bell, Jr. Collection*

Cowan, Tennessee C.T.C. Tower. -*Terry L. Coats photographer*

Cowan, Tennessee Mile Marker 86.9. Freight Depot ca. 1947. -*Cowan Railroad Museum*

Cowan, Tennessee Mile Marker 87.0. Cowan depot, built 1904. This 1½ story Carpenter Gothic Revival station replaced the original N&C depot built in 1852. This station was distinctive in its use of several styles and textures of siding as well as the original bay window on the second floor.
-*Tennessee State Library and Archives*

This photo made in 1916 depicts the three-story building that served as the main yard office for Cravens Yards in Chattanooga. -*National Archives*

Decherd, Tennessee Mile Marker 82.0. -*Bob Bell, Jr. photographer; -Terry L. Coats Collection*

LaVergne, Tennessee Mile Marker 16.0, built 1896. -*Tennessee State Library and Archives*

Estill Springs, Tennessee Mile Marker 77.0. *-Bob Bell, Jr. photographer; -Terry L. Coats Collection*

Florence, Tennessee Mile Marker 26.0, built 1873. This 50 ft. x 25 ft. brick structure was built at a cost of $2,647.00 and served the people of Rutherford County, Tennessee until it was retired by the railroad in 1927. *-National Archives*

Haley, Tennessee Mile Marker 58.0, built 1882. *-Bob Bell, Jr., Jr. photographer; -Terry L. Coats Collection*

Florence, Tennessee. This shelter Station replaced the nineteenth century station that had served the town. *-Bob Bell, Jr., photographer; -Terry L. Coats Collection*

Fosterville, Tennessee Mile Marker 45.0, built 1890. This was the second station on this site. The original depot was destroyed by a cyclone in March 1890. This station served the NC&St.L until 1942 when it was privately purchased. An arsonist destroyed the building in March 1977. *-Rutherford County Historical Society; -Terry L. Coats Collection*

Haley, Tennessee. *-Terry L. Coats Collection*

Murfreesboro, Tennessee Mile Marker 32.0, built 1898. This contemporary photograph of Murfreesboro shows that the station has retained many of its 1898 features. Some changes have been made in the roofline, as several dormers on the roof are missing from its original design. -*Kenton Dickerson Collection*

Murfreesboro, Tennessee. This turn of the century photograph shows the original eyebrow and large center dormers conspicuously missing in the modern photograph at left. Also missing is the matching freight and baggage depot that was built to the south (left in this photo) of the main station. -*Nashville, Chattanooga & St. Louis Railway*

Murfreesboro, Tennessee Freight Station This brick freighthouse was constructed in 1867 at the Salem Pike crossing of the railroad. This structure replaced the original depot constructed in 1851 as the N&C was first pushing through the area. The L&N Railroad razed this wonderful old station about 1972-3. -*National Archives*

Normandy, Tennessee Mile Marker 62.0, built 1889. -*Bob Bell, Jr. Collection*

Rucker, Tennessee Mile Marker 38.0, built 1889. This structure cost just over $2,100 to construct and was abandoned by the NC&St.L in 1942. -*National Archives*

Shellmound, Tennessee Mile Marker 129.0. -Nashville, Chattanooga & St. Louis Railway; -*H. C. Hill photographer*

Smyrna, Tennessee Mile Marker 20.0, ca. 1916. Built in 1873, this station is still standing and as of 2009 is undergoing renovation. The original station has been expanded over the years. A severe derailment in 1950 sent a diesel engine through a portion of the station that was never rebuilt. -*National Archives*

Chattanooga, Tennessee Mile Marker 149.2. Cravens Yard Sand Tower. -*National Archives*

Sherwood, Tennessee Mile Marker 96.0, ca. 1925. The people in this photograph were waiting for the train to take them to a Fourth of July picnic. -*John Lynch Collection*

Sherwood, Tennessee Interlocking Tower, ca. 1916. -*National Archives*

Stevenson, Alabama Mile Marker 112.0. Depot and hotel, built 1872. This depot served as a union station for the Nashville & Chattanooga and the Memphis & Charleston Railroads. Today CSX and Norfolk Southern trains still pass the station. Attached to the north side of the station is a railroad hotel. The depot is now a railroad museum. -*Terry L. Coats photographer*

Stevenson, Alabama. Double water towers. -*National Archives*

Tullahoma, Tennessee Mile Marker 69.0. Passenger station, ca. 1916. This station still stands today and is used by CSX RR as a signal maintenance warehouse. The station has been moved and added onto several times. During WWII this station saw overwhelming business when nearby Camp Forrest was used as a training camp for U. S. soldiers and as a POW camp for German soldiers. Today, on the Camp Forrest property, Arnold Engineering and Development Center serves the military and NASA as a test facility. -*National Archives*

Tullahoma, Tennessee Freight Depot. -*Bob Bell, Jr. photographer*

Wade, Tennessee Mile Marker 24.0. This small 14 ft. x 16 ft. shelter was built in 1905 at a cost of $632. It is very similar to many other shelters on the NC&St.L line and was retired from service in 1936. -*Tommy Johns Collection*

Wartrace, Tennessee Mile Marker 55.0. The passenger depot with the brick freighthouse can be seen to the left in this 1916 photograph. -*National Archives*

Lebanon Branch of the Chattanooga Division

Donelson, Tennessee Mile Marker 8.0. -*National Archives*

Lebanon, Tennessee Mile Marker 31.0. The NC&St.L built this depot in 1916 to replace the old Tennessee & Pacific depot shown in the photo below. This structure still stands and is currently being used as the office for a flour milling company. -*National Archives*

Hermitage, Tennessee Mile Marker 11.0. -*National Archives*

Lebanon, Tennessee Freighthouse. -*National Archives*

Easton, Tennessee Mile Marker 3.0. -*National Archives*

Lebanon, Tennessee. The NC&St.L and the Nashville & Knoxville RR used this Mansard roof station jointly until 1902 when the Nashville & Knoxville reorganized as the Tennessee Central Railway. At that time the TC built their own depot just off the town square and this building became the sole property of the NC&St.L. A number of years later the NC&St.L abandoned this structure as its passenger station and built the stucco station (shown on page) near the city square. At that time, this building reverted to use as a freight depot. It burned in 1972. -*National Archives*

Leesville, Tennessee Mile Marker 23.0. This station was closed after the abandonment of the Lebanon Branch of the NC. Some years later it was turned 90 degrees from its original location and was moved across the tracks to its present location. It was used as a gas station and general store for a number of years. It is still standing next to the old right of way on Old Roadbed Road and is currently used as a storage facility. *-Terry L. Coats photographer*

Tate's Crossing, Tennessee Mile Marker 17.0. Mr. Tate built this small passenger shelter on his farm. His daughter, who was attending school at Peabody College in Nashville used the structure to wait for the local Lebanon to Nashville train. It has been rebuilt and moved to the Wilson County Fairgrounds in Lebanon, Tennessee. *-Terry L. Coats photographer*

Mount Juliet, Tennessee Mile Marker 17.0. Pictured is the NC&St.L depot on the right of the photograph and the Tennessee Central depot to the left. *-Tennessee State Library and Archives*

Mud Tavern, Tennessee Mile Marker 6.0. *-National Archives*

Tuckers Gap, Tennessee Mile Marker 25.0. This depot was moved to the Wilson County, Tennessee fairgrounds in 2005 and was refurbished and contains a small museum and a model railroad. The depot is open to the public during the annual fair and on special occasions. *-Terry L. Coats photographer*

Silver Springs, Tennessee Water Tower Mile Marker 21.0. *-National Archives*

Old Hickory Branch of the Chattanooga Division

Old Hickory, Tennessee Mile Marker 17.0. This station was on the grounds of the Old Hickory E. I. DuPont plant and served as a station for the employees. *-Dr. W. O. Greene Collection*

Orme Branch of the Chattanooga Division

Orme, Tennessee Mile Marker 135.0. This station was used from 1904 until the abandonment of the Orme Branch in 1942. It is now in private ownership and is used for storage. *-Terry L. Coats photographer*

SEQUATCHIE BRANCH OF THE CHATTANOOGA DIVISION

Cartwright, Tennessee Mile Marker 153.0. Shelter built 1920. -*Tennessee State Library and Archives*

College, Tennessee Mile Marker 172.0, ca. 1920s. -*Tennessee State Library and Archives*

Copenhagen, Tennessee Mile Marker 126.0. -*Tennessee State Library and Archives; -Allen Hicks Collection*

Dunlap, Tennessee Mile Marker 161.0. -*Tennessee State Library and Archives*

Daus, Tennessee Mile Marker 153.0. Two unidentified men standing in front of the Daus depot at the turn of the century. The shelter shown at right would eventually replace this station. -*Tennessee State Library and Archives*

Daus, Tennessee Shelter. -*Allen Hicks Collection*

Jasper, Tennessee. Gothic combination depot destroyed by fire in 1921 and the present station was built as its replacement. *-Dennis Lambert Collection*

Lees, Tennessee Mile Marker 140.0, built 1891. Combination Station, ca. 1917. Left to Right: Vollie Summers, Charlie Womack, Morgan Summers, Luther Hurd, Sebern Holland, Jessie Shoemate, unknown, unknown, Claude Allison, John Ryan, George Akeman, unknown, Harry Rankin, unknown, Walter Rankin. *-Bledsoe County, Tennessee Historical and Genealogical Society's Photograph Collection*

Jasper, Tennessee Mile Marker 135.0, built 1923. This Queen Anne station replaced an interim depot built after the destruction of the Gothic station seen above. Today, this depot serves as the Jasper City Hall. *-Terry L. Coats photographer*

Mt. Airy, Tennessee Mile Marker 166.0 Shelter. *-Tennessee State Library and Archives*

Pikeville, Tennessee. *-Tennessee State Library and Archives*

Pikeville, Tennessee Mile Marker 180.0. Original Sequatchie Valley Railroad Depot. *-Tennessee State Library and Archives*

Richard City, Tennessee Mile Marker 126.0 (Copenhagen). This photo depicts the first of two Carpenter Gothic stations to serve this community. The second station was much larger than was this one. -*Bob Hookey Collection*

Sequatchie Branch Mile Marker 17.5 and Water Tower at Mile Marker 138.5. -*National Archives*

Sequatchie, Tennessee Mile Marker 138.0. Shelter. -*Tennessee State Library and Archives*

South Pittsburg, Tennessee Freighthouse, ca.1971. -*Tom R. Knowles photographer*

South Pittsburg, Tennessee Mile Marker 129.0. This Freighthouse served as a passenger and freight station until 1888. After that time, it served only as a freight facility. -*Nashville, Chattanooga & St. Louis Railway*

Sweetwater, Tennessee Mile Marker 147.0. -*Tennessee State Library and Archives*

Victoria, Tennessee Mile Marker 142.0. The station was built as part of the original Sequatchie Valley RR. Today it is a beautifully restored private residence and was previously a feed store. -*Terry L. Coats photographer*

Whitwell, Tennessee Mile Marker 146.0, built 1911. -*Tennessee State Library and Archives*

SHELBYVILLE BRANCH OF THE CHATTANOOGA DIVISION

Shelbyville, Tennessee Mile Marker 63.0, built 1908. This depot replaced the 1891 Gothic Revival depot that was moved to another location. The 1908 station still stands and has been extensively remodeled and is currently an adult education center. -*Bob Bell, Jr. Collection*

Greeley, Tennessee Mile Marker 56.5. This small shelter still stands and is used for storage on private property. -*Terry L. Coats Photographer*

TRACY CITY BRANCH OF THE CHATTANOOGA DIVISION

Coalmont, Tennessee Mile Marker 115.0, built 1904. *-Tennessee State Library and Archives*

Fairmont, Tennessee Mile Marker 102.0, ca. 1916. *-National Archives*

Monteagle, Tennessee Freight Depot. *-National Archives*

Monteagle, Tennessee Mile Marker 101.0. Passenger Depot, built 1905. *-National Archives*

Sewanee, Tennessee. Built in 1959 by the L&N Railroad, this depot served the line until it closed in 1985. Clad in stone, its architectural details fits into the theme of other buildings of nearby University of the South. The depot is currently used as office space. *-Terry L. Coats photographer*

Sewanee, Tennessee Mile Marker 95.0. *-Tennessee State Library and Archives*

St. Marys, Tennessee
Mile Marker 93.0.
-*William Turner Collection*

Palmer, Tennessee Mile Marker 126.0. Depot and Consolidated Coal Commission Office, built 1919. -*William Turner Collection*

Tracy City, Tennessee Mile Marker 107.0. Depot area showing downtown Tracy City. The NC&St.L roundhouse is to the left of the photo. The tall building to the right with the bell tower is a private school. Both the depot and the school burned under suspicious circumstances. -*Tennessee State Library and Archives*

Aerial view of the depot, engine facilities, and roundhouse area in Tracy City, Tennessee. -*William Turner Collection*

Nashville Division
"The Windy"

I was born in Dixie in a boomer shack, just a little shanty by the railroad track.
The humming of the drivers was my lullaby, and a freight train whistle taught me how to cry.
... Freight Train Blues – John Lair

Nashville & Northwestern Railroad

At about the same time the Nashville & Chattanooga Railroad was building from Nashville eastward toward Chattanooga; the Hickman & Obion Railroad began construction of tracks from Hickman, Kentucky to the southeast toward Union City, Tennessee. Incorporated in 1852, the Hickman & Obion began to grade a right-of-way from Hickman that year.

Memphis & Ohio and the Nashville & Northwestern Railroads were constructing lines through this northwest corner of Tennessee at the same time. Both companies had intentions of passing either though or near the vicinity of Union City, Tennessee. Hickman & Obion Railroad president, George Washington Gibbs, realized that if he could construct his railroad south from the Mississippi River landing at Hickman, he would be able to connect to one or maybe even both of these lines. This connection would be a great windfall for his venture and would allow him to connect the river landing at Hickman to points south and east.

President Gibbs was able to talk local farmers into doing the bulk of the grading for the right-of-way in exchange for stock in the company. By 1855, the H&O had completed grading 14.1 miles of right-of-way south toward Union City.

Unfortunately, money ran short for the H&O just after the grading was completed and Gibbs was forced to abandon the project. The Hickman & Obion never accomplished the laying of any rail before the company was forced into selling the railroad to the Nashville & Northwestern Railroad in November 1855.

Union City, Tennessee NC&St.L/GM&O Passenger Station Mile Marker 154.0, built 1900. *-Terry L. Coats photographer*

Like the H&O, the Nashville & Northwestern had incorporated in 1852. The company's charter allowed the N&NW to construct a railroad from Nashville to Hickman and there establish a Mississippi River landing.

After incorporating, the N&NW chose Colonel John A. Gardner, a local Weakley County, Tennessee attorney and statesman as its first president. Colonel Gardner, the company's major stockholder was able to obtain from the city of Nashville and from the state of Tennessee $27,000 of financing toward the construction of the railroad.

Matson Station, Kentucky (aka State Line) Mile Marker 161.0, built 1915. A depot built in 1902 was replaced in 1914, but burned and was replaced with this station in 1915. This depot still stands and is in bad condition, but is scheduled for renovation. -*Terry L. Coats photographer*

When the financially strapped Hickman & Obion Railroad was unable to complete the line to Union City, the Nashville & Northwestern seized upon the opportunity to purchase the unfinished H&O right-of-way. This windfall allowed the N&NW to complete the last 17 miles track from Union City to a Mississippi River landing. The N&NW had originally intended on building a competitive track from Union City to the river paralleling those of the Hickman & Obion. By purchasing the H&O the need for head-to-head duplication was alleviated.

The railroad was met with great anticipation in west Tennessee. The citizens of Weakley County, Tennessee were not lost on the advantage a railroad connecting McKenzie and Union City would be to the county's economy and elected to raise capital by private subscription for the grading of a right of way through the county. When the subscriptions failed to raise the needed funds, the county went so far as to raise taxes to appropriate the money.[113] By the mid 1860s, the combined efforts of the Nashville & Northwestern Railroad and the citizens of Weakley County allowed the railroad to complete an additional 37 miles from Union City south through northwest Tennessee to McKenzie, Tennessee and a connection with the Memphis & Ohio Railroad.

In 1856, Vernon K. Stevenson was elected as the second president of the Nashville & Northwestern Railroad. Stevenson would be the first of three Nashville & Chattanooga presidents to hold a dual presidency of both railroads. It was under Stevenson's direction that the N&NW completed the still unfinished Hickman & Obion Railroad right-of-way and then extended the railroad to McKenzie. Just as he had done to build the line from Nashville to Chattanooga, Stevenson procured bonds from the state of Tennessee to build this western section of the N&NW.

By the outbreak of the War for Southern Independence, the N&NW had not only completed building the section of track in northwest Tennessee, but had built tracks in middle Tennessee as well. In an attempt to fulfill its charter mission of connecting Nashville with the Mississippi River, the N&NW had under construction three sections of track at the

---

113 Virginia C. Vaughn, *People and Places of Downtown Martin*. 1997.

same time. In middle Tennessee they completed laying 24 miles of track west from Nashville to the Harpeth River at Kingston Springs and east from the Tennessee River at Knott's Landing[114] back 6 miles toward that western expanse. When added together, the Hickman to McKenzie, Nashville to Kingston Springs, and Tennessee River toward Nashville rights-of-way amounted to 82 miles of trackage for the N&NW.

Union City Freighthouse. -Bob Bell, Jr. photographer

Confederate Fort Donelson on the Cumberland River fell to Federal forces on February 16, 1862. With the fall of this stronghold, the Confederates were forced to abandon the capitol city of Nashville. The capitulation of Donelson threw panic into the citizenry of the city. In an attempt to flee Nashville ahead of the advancing Federal Army, people flocked to Nashville's N&C Union Station and fought to gain passage on any train leading away from the city. Every available car of the Nashville & Chattanooga Railroad was utilized in the evacuation. Every car that is except the ones held in a special train by Major Vernon K. Stevenson, Confederate Quartermaster for the supplies in Nashville and president of the Nashville & Chattanooga Railroad. As pandemonium broke out in the streets of Nashville, Stevenson abandoned his post as quartermaster and hurried to the special train he had waiting on the south side of the city. Stevenson loaded onto this train his family, servants, some of the finest of his home furnishings, and a multitude of his horses and carriages. Stevenson never gave any thought to his responsibilities as a Confederate officer. Because of his actions, hundreds of thousands of dollars worth of war materials belonging to the Confederacy was lost.[115]

Stevenson reestablished himself in Atlanta while securing the company books and records of both the N&C and N&NW Railroads in nearby Augusta, Georgia. The shameful abandonment of his Quartermaster job in Nashville must not have given much rise to the Confederate government, because shortly after arriving in Atlanta he was appointed to the same positioning within the Confederate government.[116]

Even with the mass abandonment of Nashville, the Federals made a cautious approach toward the city. The Yankees mistook the massive amount of traffic in and out of the Nashville N&C depot as a Confederate fortification of the city rather than what it really was … a mass exit. It was not until February 24, 1862, a full week after the fall of Fort Donelson, that the

---

114   During the War, Knott's Landing would be renamed Johnsonville by the occupying Federal army. Johnsonville was named for Gov. Andrew Johnson, military governor of Tennessee and later President of the United States.
115   Robert C. Black, III, *Railroads of the Confederacy*. The University of North Carolina Press, 1952.
116   Dain L. Schult, *Nashville, Chattanooga & St. Louis: A History of "The Dixie Line."* 2001, page 38.

Federal Army marched into Nashville. Shortly afterward, they began a conversion of the city into a supply depot from which they would distribute food, ammunition and other supplies in support of their armies in the western theater. Nashville was turned into a massive Federal supply center. To fill the storehouses, the Federals would have to transport a vast quantity of materials from the north. The Yankees had two options by which they could efficiently move these supplies. They could either bring them by rail over the L&N Railroad via Louisville, or they could float them down the Cumberland River from the Ohio River and Mississippi River.

The L&N railroad running south from Louisville, Kentucky to Nashville had been completed in 1856; it would be the Federals' most commanding rail link into the city. Up until the coming of the railroad the Cumberland had been the main supply line, however, the river was undependable as a year-round transportation route. Ice in the winter months and low water flow at other times of the year often made the Cumberland an unpredictable and unreliable source of transportation.

Disruption of the Federal supply lines of the Cumberland River and the L&N Railroad was of utmost importance to the Confederates. The Rebels knowing of the variability of the river route made the decision to concentrate on the rails of the L&N Railroad and to make them variable as well. Over the course of eighteen months, repeated raids made by Generals John Hunt Morgan and Nathan Bedford Forrest wreaked havoc on this rail line. On Morgan's Christmas raid of 1862, he captured 1,800 prisoners, killed 150, burned 2,300 feet of trestles, tore up 35 miles of L&N tracks, burned three depots, three water stations, and destroyed a large quantity of Federal stores. This raid closed down the L&N for five weeks.

Relief was needed from these kinds of losses and disruptions. The North needed an additional supply line to supplement the river and rail supply lines already in existence. The Yankees turned their attentions to the unfinished Nashville & Northwestern Railroad landing on the Tennessee River. By order of Edwin M. Stanton, Secretary of War, the N&NW was to be completed from the Federal wharfs and Knott's Landing onward to connect to the line already finished from Nashville to Kingston Springs.

Gardner, Tennessee Laborers House -*National Archives*

The Federal occupation of Nashville brought about many changes to the city; tens of thousands of refugees, many of them runaway slaves known as contraband, poured into the city. By the summer of 1863, the population of Nashville soared from its pre-War 17,000 inhabitants to well over 80,000. A boom town sprang up between the *gulch* and 17th Avenue North. Seemingly overnight, thousands of homes, saloons, and tent businesses appeared. In order to alleviate some of the overcrowding, and to develop a much needed workforce, the United States Military Railroad (USMRR) turned to runaway slaves and free-blacks as a source of construction labor. Secretary Stanton's order to complete the yet unfinished link of the Nashville & Northwestern Railroad and a need to get thousands of runaway slaves off the public dole was a win-win proposition for the Federals. These men were hired to grade the right-of-way and to complete the unfinished N&NW. It is estimated that 10,000 laborers were pressed into service to build this line. A short time into the construction processes, the USMRR seized on a way of exploiting these men by talking them into enlisting in the army as Federal soldiers. As soldiers, their wages dropped from the $20.00 they had been hired at as construction workers to $11.00 per month soldier's wages. All along, they were doing the same work, but now the government was paying them about half as much. The line that had been started by Dutch and Irish laborers working for the N&NW was completed by Black troops in the service of the USMRR. Work began on February 7, 1864. During the time of construction, 115 miles of track was laid including the construction of five to eight car length sidings at every 8 mile interval. Additionally, forty-five new water tanks were constructed and firewood stops were established.[117] The line opened for service on May 10, 1864.

The topography between Nashville and Johnsonville contains many low lands, dips and valleys. To gap this uneven terrain, a multitude of wooden bridges and trestles had to be constructed. These wooden trestles and bridges soon became prime targets for Confederate raiders. As a means of protecting these vulnerable structures field fortifications, guard houses had to be constructed at strategic locations overlooking the facilities. The responsibility of guarding these trestles and bridges would fall to the same Black troops, whom only months earlier had labored and sweated to build the railroad. Assigned to the task of manning these fortifications were the 12th and 14th U. S. Colored Troops Infantry Regiment.

Trestles and bridge #2 over Sullivan's Branch on the Nashville & Northwestern Railroad. The train in the picture is a photographic train used to document the tracks of the USMRR during the Civil War. -*National Archives*

---

117   Thomas Weber, *The Northern Railroads in the Civil War 1861-1865*. 1952, page 196.

During the short tenure between its completion in May 1864 and the end of the War, the 56 miles of rail line would garner a great deal of history. Despite the aforementioned guard emplacements, several successful raids were carried out on the bridges and trestles along the line. The structures were quickly repaired.

The most historic event to occur along this line took place on November 4, 1864 when a dramatic assault was made on the Federal supply depot at Johnsonville. General Nathan Bedford Forrest and his cavalry engaged in a pitched battle against nine Federal gunboats on the Tennessee River. These boats had been sent down from Paducah in support of the depot. During the battle, Forrest was able to capture and sink four of the gunboats. Additionally, he and his men destroyed 14 transports, 17 barges, 33 pieces of artillery and seized or destroyed between two and six million dollars worth of military goods. Forrest also took 150 prisoners of war. Thinking that the garrison was going to be overtaken by Forrest's superior force, Commander Colonel C. R. Thompson ordered the entire stores at Johnsonville burned. Destroyed was millions of dollars worth of supplies as well as the entire warehouse facilities. Forrest's capture of the gunboats is the only recorded time in world military history that a cavalry unit has been able to defeat naval units in an armed conflict.

On November 30th, the day of the Battle of Franklin, this rail line was abandoned and all rolling stock was moved to safety. In December during the Battle of Nashville, General John Bell Hood ordered all the trestles on this line destroyed to prevent the Yankees from sending supplies and reinforcements into battle from the west. By late winter the trestles were rebuilt, but when heavy spring rains came they washed away again.

In September 1865, the USMRR returned control of the railroad to the Nashville & Northwestern. Immediately, N&NW president Michael Burns set to the task of completing the railroad that the coming of the War had disrupted. With the appropriation of additional loans from the state, the Tennessee River was bridged at Johnsonville and shortly thereafter, the company was pushing the railroad toward the company's western expanses at McKenzie. During the War approximately 16 miles of track between Hickman and Union City had been removed and carried away by Federal troops. This track was restored after the War. Much of the grading work between the Tennessee River and McKenzie had been completed before the War erupted; it was now a matter of completing the construction by laying rails. This work was finally completed and in 1867 there was a connection from Nashville to the Mississippi River at Hickman, Kentucky. In 1866, the New Orleans & Ohio Railroad from Mayfield, Kentucky completed a connection to the N&NW right-of-way at Paducah Junction (Gibbs, Tennessee). This connection allowed an interchange over the NO&O to the Ohio River at Paducah, Kentucky. A few years later, the NC&St.L would make its own connection to Paducah when it leased the Paducah, Tennessee & Alabama. The PT&A would become a part of the Paducah & Memphis division of the NC.

The Nashville & Northwestern was only able to stay solvent for a couple of years after being returned by the Federals. The War had placed the company in a financial position from which it simply could never recover, which was the case for many railroads in Tennessee. The N&NW defaulted on its loans to the state and on July 1, 1867, making it the property of the loan holder. At that time, M. P. Clark was elected president of the N&NW replacing Michael Burns, the president during the war years. During this time, Burns held dual presidency of the N&C between 1864 and 1868 and the N&NW between 1863 and 1867. Colonel E. W. Cole succeeded M. P. Clark to the presidency in 1869 and would become the third N&C president to hold dual presidency of both railroads.

Nashville & Chattanooga and Nashville & Northwestern Pass 1871. -Terry L. Coats Collection

With the N&NW already under the guidance of an N&C president, the N&C leased the N&NW from the state of Tennessee on July 1, 1870.[118] On August 1, 1872, the N&C purchased the N&NW outright and operated its new acquisition for approximately a year under the name of the Nashville, Memphis & St. Louis Railway. The NM&St.L was absorbed into the N&C system and on the same day, May 30, 1873, the entire railroad was renamed to the Nashville, Chattanooga & St. Louis Railway.

Despite being a port on the Mississippi River, Hickman, Kentucky was smaller than its sister city Columbus, Kentucky twelve miles up the river. Because Columbus was larger and gained railroad access first, Hickman would never enjoy the prominence of the larger hub.

In late 1873, a major change took place on the northern end of the Nashville Division. The majority of the freight traffic that had been handled from Union City to Hickman on the N&C was diverted to the Memphis & Ohio Railroad at Union City for transport to the facilities at Columbus. This diversion would relegate the Union City to Hickman trackage to local branch status.

Further diversions were made in the amount of materials shipped in and out of Hickman over the NC&St.L when, in 1911, the Chicago Memphis & Gulf Railroad, a subsidiary of the Illinois Central, lay tracks from Dyersburg,

Martin, Tennessee Freighthouse This structure was built by the Illinois Central but it was a shared depot with the NC&St.L. This station structure sat parallel the IC. The NC&St.L reached the north end of the depot via a stub-end track. An NC&St.L boxcar in the process of being loaded can be seen under the shed. -Richard Kelly Collection, The Color Shop, Martin, Tennessee

---

118   Richard E. Prince, *Nashville, Chattanooga & St. Louis Railway: History and Steam Engines.* 1967, page 23.

Tennessee into the river city. Eventually the CM&G would reach industries previously served only by the NC&St.L and in doing so became a direct shipping link to West Tennessee and points south.

Despite the fact that this Union City to Hickman portion of the railroad got little use, the NC&St.L, when referring to its main line, would always include all trackage between Chattanooga and Hickman.[119]

The approach to Hickman was a precarious one. Tracks entering town from the east were very often subject to flooding and complete washouts as the Mississippi River was constantly leaving its banks and washing over the tracks. In 1911, it was decided to reroute an entrance into town from the south to loop back into the station from the west. After this rerouting was completed, the old tracks did not have to be relied on during time of high water.

During its time of prime operation, there were two passenger trains as well as a mixed train (freight and passenger) serving Hickman six days a week. This gave the populace in Hickman three trains each day to and from the river city. In October 1942, the primary shipper on this line the Mengel Company, a wood processing plant in Hickman, was the victim a devastating fire. The plant was so damaged that it was never rebuilt. The loss of the plant, the loss of freight business to the Chicago, Memphis & Gulf Railroad and an increase in auto and common carrier traffic over the highways severely cut into freight and passenger traffic on this branch. In 1944, the NC&St.L petitioned the ICC for abandonment of the track from Union City to Hickman. The request was denied. Between 1944 and 1951, conditions only grew worse and the railroad again asked permission to close the line. This time the petition was accepted and the line was finally abandoned on October 15, 1951.

A second diversion on the Nashville Division took place in 1944 when the Tennessee Valley Authority completed a dam at Gilbertsville, Kentucky and created Kentucky Lake. The creation of the new lake radically raised the water table in the Eva and Johnsonville, Tennessee areas south of the dam. Ten miles of the original Nashville & Northwestern line was abandoned and the mainline was relocated six miles south (upstream) of Eva at a point where U. S. Highway 70 crossed the river.

The flooding of Kentucky Lake also precipitated the relocation of the Illinois Central rail line near Gilbertsville, Kentucky. A new routing for this line allowed the IC to cross the lake atop the newly constructed dam. In a measure to recycle and to reuse the old abandoned Gilbertsville drawbridge previously used by the IC was lowered onto river barges and floated intact up river to the location for the new river crossing of the NC&St.L between Waverly and Camden, Tennessee.

---

119   Elmer G. Sulzer, *Ghost Railroads of Tennessee*. 1975, page 70.

The old community of Johnsonville on the abandoned line was re-established as New Johnsonville two miles east of the relocated Illinois Central Bridge. On the west bank of the Tennessee River, the thriving community of Eva, in existence since 1868, was also abandoned. It was not re-established.

Under the control of the NC&St.L, this division of the railway would operate under several names. The NC would refer to the former N&NW as the St. Louis Division, the Northwestern Division, and finally the Nashville Division. The nickname for the division, the name the railroad men would refer to, was the *Windy*. Modern students of railroading debate as to whether the word *wind* was used as a verb because the tracks curved and twisted so much or whether the word was used as a noun denoting that there always seemed to be a strong wind blowing in the vicinity of the trains and tracks.

This part of the railway remained an important part of the NC&St.L system until the merger in 1957. Today the line between Nashville and McKenzie is the mainline for CSX trains running between Nashville and Memphis. Over what was the original N&NW north of McKenzie runs a short line railroad known as the Dresden Branch. The Kentucky & West Tennessee Railroad (KWT) operates this short line and transports shingles, lumber, logs, clay, and brick. The track from just south of Dresden to Union City were abandoned and removed in the late 1980s.

Centerville Branch

The counties of Hickman, Lewis, and Dickson, Tennessee are rich in iron ore, timber, and phosphates. In an attempt to tap these natural resources, the Nashville & Tuscaloosa Railroad Company received a charter from the State of Tennessee in June 1877 to construct a rail line from Burns in Dickson County into Centerville and continuing on through Lawrenceburg and to the Alabama state line pointing toward Florence, Alabama.

Built as a narrow gauge, construction the first 23 miles of track went quickly, but by 1878 problems arose and construction stalled. In July 1880, the Nashville & Tuscaloosa contracted with the Nashville, Chattanooga & St. Louis to complete the railroad from Graham to Centerville and on to Kimmins, Tennessee.

On the northern approach to Centerville, the railroad needed to cross the land of Mrs. Mary Griner as it made its way toward the river. Officials from the NC&St.L contacted Mrs. Griner about gaining egress across her land and she told the men that she wanted to consult with her husband, Robert, to obtain his permission before inking the contract. Mrs. Griner stepped into the parlor discussed the matter with Robert and then returned saying that her husband agreed with one stipulation. He wanted a station built on the property and the station was to bear his name. The odd part of this story was that Robert had given

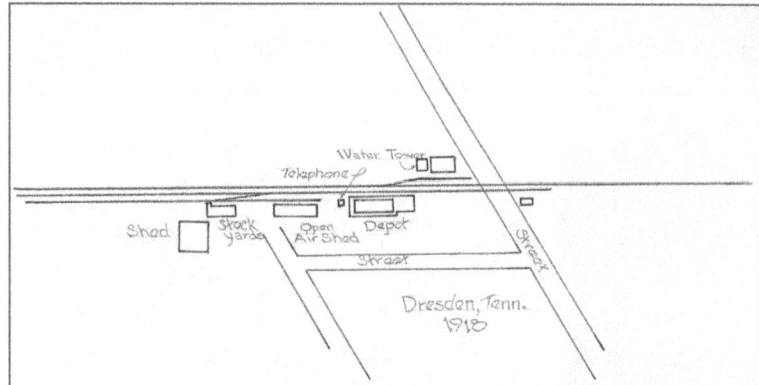

Dresden Track Plan

Dresden Depot

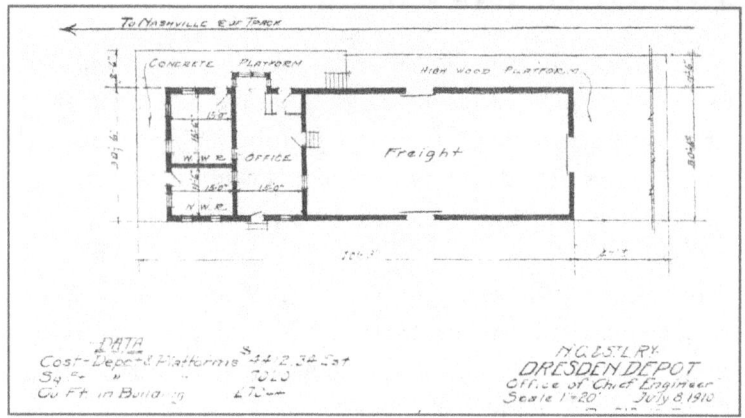

Dresden Depot Floor Plan

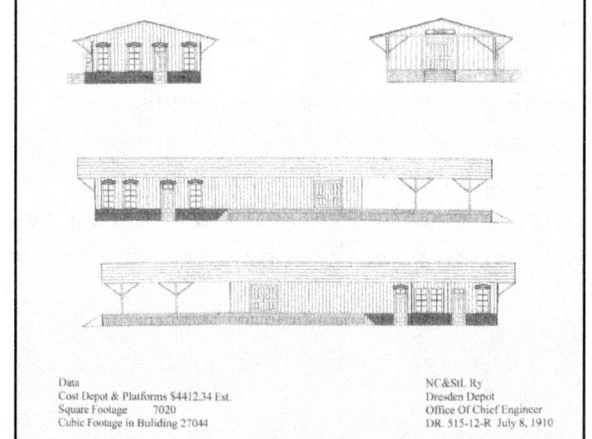

Dresden Depot Elevation Drawing

Centerville, Tennessee Mile Marker 86.0, built 1893.
-*National Archives*

his permission despite the fact that he had departed this world four years before the date of this incident. As the story goes, Mary had gone into the parlor to discuss the matter with her husband's photograph before they both agreed to the deal. This stop along the NC&St.L would be known as Grinder's Switch.

The change in name from Griner to Grinder is probably attributed to the men at the new shops in Nashville. All whistle posts, mile marker and town name signs along the right-of-way were cast in the foundry at the shops. Apparently someone misspelled Griner and added the "d" when they made the casting.

Some decades later, Minnie Pearl, who was actually from Centerville, would put Grinder's Switch on the map by including the little hamlet as part of her act from the stage of the Grand Ole Opry.

The 9.2 mile section of track from Graham Station into Centerville was completed in 1882 and the entire line from Dickson to Centerville was deeded to the Nashville, Chattanooga & St. Louis Railway in March 1883. In 1884 the NC extended this line from Centerville to the Lewis County line near Kimmins. After the NC reached the Lewis County line, the Southern Iron Company of Alabama, owner of large deposits of iron ore in the Mannie (Allens Creek) area saw the approaching extension as a golden opportunity to ship their products by rail and, thus, constructed a 17 mile narrow gauge line to connect to the NC. In 1892, the Southern Iron Company wanted to build two iron furnaces at its Allen Creek facilities. To raise needed capital, the company approached the NC&St.L in hopes of selling them the 17 miles of short line. The NC&St.L eventually bought the line for $125,000 with the stipulation that the iron company had to ship its ore exclusively over the NC. The iron company agreed and the deal was struck.

The railroad inherited by the NC&St.L in this transaction was a narrow gauge line. The transferring of iron ore from the narrow gauge cars to standard gauge ones at Dickson became a tremendous burden to the railroad. To eliminate this situation, the entire line was converted to standard gauge in June 1894. At the same time, the junction point with the main line was moved from Dickson two miles east to Colesburg, Tennessee.

The mines at Allens Creek prospered for a number of years. At their peak of operations, there were several stores, a school, church, and almost 1,200 houses dotting the hillsides above the mines. Unable to compete with an expanding steel industry the mines closed in 1923. The smelting furnaces were dismantled in 1936. The railroad tracks were removed in 1942 and the rail was used in the war effort.

The remainder of the branch from Hohenwald north survived the merger of 1957. Today the South Central Tennessee Railroad Company operates this branch as a 50 mile short line from Colesburg at the CSX mainline south to Hohenwald. They transport LP gas, chemicals, pulpwood, cross ties, newsprint, auto parts, clay, and wire.

Ralston, Tennessee Mile Marker 138.0. *-Sharon Humes Collection*

Ralston, Tennessee Shelter. *-Sharon Humes Collection*

Map of the Nashville Division

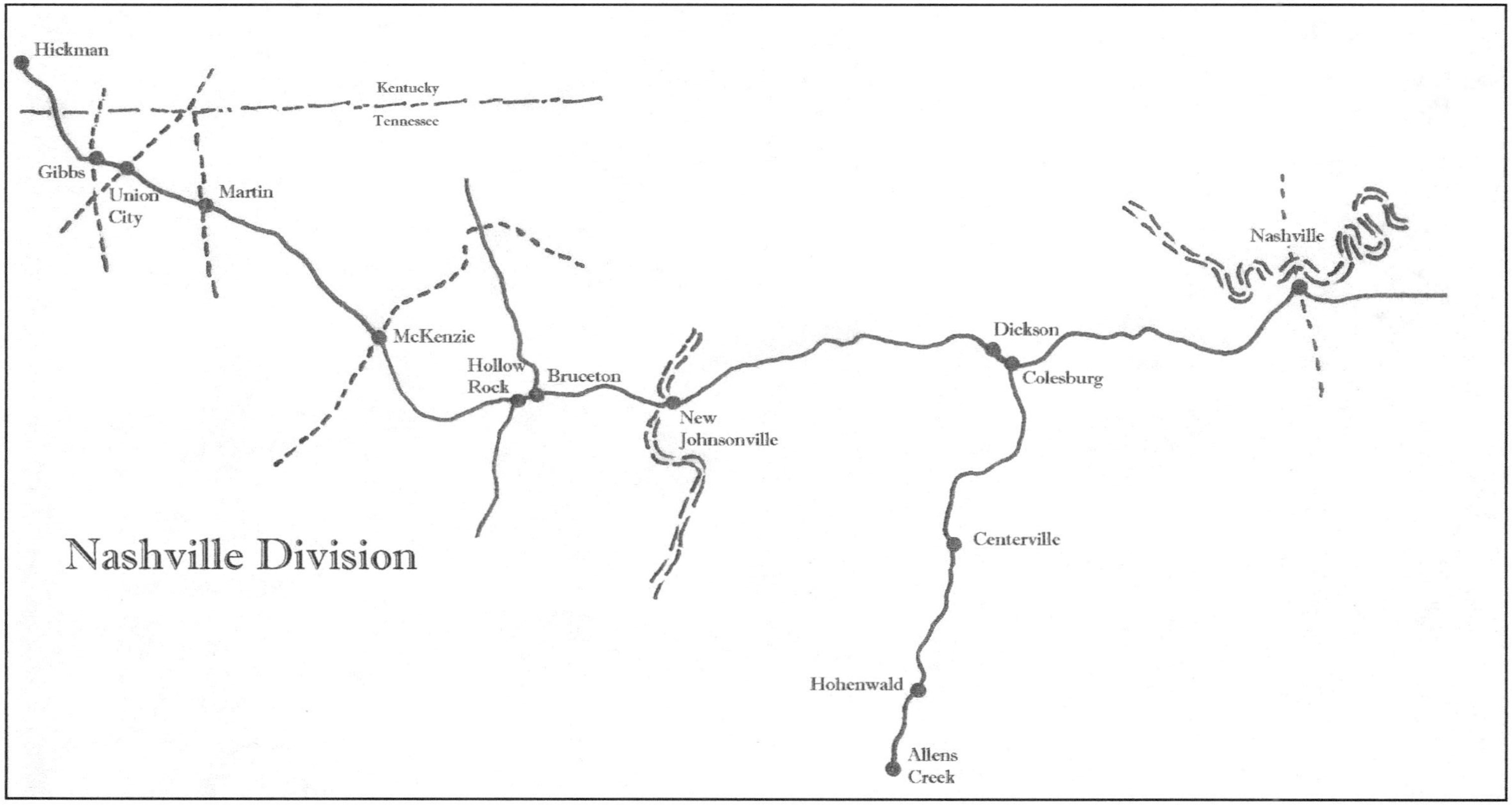

Nashville Division Main Line

Nashville, Tennessee Mile Marker 4.0, Belle Meade Plantation. The Harding family, owners of the Belle Meade Plantation, built this private depot. It was used as a stop for the family as well as the domestics who worked at the farm. *-Tennessee State Library and Archives*

Bellevue, Tennessee Mile Marker 12.0. *-Tennessee State Library and Archives*

Bruceton, Tennessee Mile Marker 94.0. *-Bob Bell, Jr. Collection*

Bruceton, Tennessee CTC Tower. *-Terry L. Coats photographer*

Bruceton, Tennessee Roundhouse. *-Terry L. Coats photographer*

Bruceton Hotel. This hotel was the home away from home for the railroad crews that used Bruceton as a layover point. This photo was made in 1980 shortly before it was abandoned and finally razed. *-Rudy Ross Collection*

Camden, Tennessee Mile Marker 86.0. -*Terry L. Coats Collection*

Craggie Hope, Tennessee Mile Marker 25.0, built 1904. -*National Archives*

Denver, Tennessee (ala Box) Mile Marker 75.0. -*National Archives*

Dickson, Tennessee Mile Marker 42.0, built 1923. This Queen Anne depot replaced the Carpenter Gothic station moved down the track that was used as the freight depot. -*Terry L. Coats photographer*

Dickson, Tennessee Halbrook Railroad Hotel. The Halbrook served as a railroad hotel for railroad workers and travelers alike. Tennessee Governor Frank G. Clement was born in this hotel. -*Terry L. Coats photographer*

Dickson, Tennessee MOW Sheds and 1882 Carpenter Gothic Depot. -*Bob Bell, Jr. photographer*

Dresden, Tennessee Mile Marker 132.0, built 1891. -*L&N Collection, University of Louisville*

Eva, Tennessee Mile Marker 80.0. -*Ken Ingram Collection*

Gardner, Tennessee Laborers House. -*National Archives*

Dresden, Tennessee. This is the Nashville & Northwestern Railroad Depot that the NC&St.L replaced in 1891. -*Terry L. Coats Collection*

Gardner, Tennessee Shelter Mile Marker 144.0. -*Bob Bell, Jr. Collection*

Gibbs, Tennessee Mile Marker 151.0. Gibbs was a junction point between the NC&St.L and Illinois Central Railroads. This station and the one in Martin, Tennessee were similar in appearance. The Illinois Central designed both. -*Tennessee State Library and Archives*

Gleason, Tennessee Mile Marker 125.0, built 1898. -*National Archives*

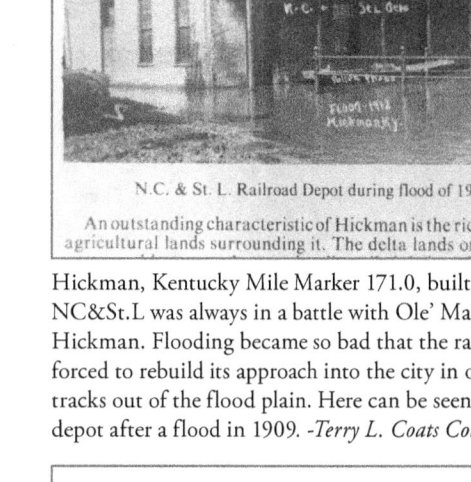
Hickman, Kentucky Mile Marker 171.0, built 1909. The NC&St.L was always in a battle with Ole' Man River in Hickman. Flooding became so bad that the railroad was forced to rebuild its approach into the city in order to run its tracks out of the flood plain. Here can be seen the Hickman depot after a flood in 1909. -*Terry L. Coats Collection*

Hico, Tennessee Mile Marker 113.0, built 1915. This station closed in 1927. -*National Archives*

Huntington, Tennessee Mile Marker 105.0, built 1896. At 138 ft. x 30 ft., this was one of the larger NC&St.L Gothic style depots. The platform around this station was of brick and not the conventional concrete. Note the dormers on the roof of this station. -*L&N Collection, University of Louisville*

New Johnsonville, Tennessee Mile Marker 75.0, built 1945. -*Terry L. Coats photographer*

Johnsonville, Tennessee Mile Marker 77.0, built 1891. -*National Archives*

Johnsonville, Tennessee Bridge Maintainers House. -*National Archives*

Johnsonville, Tennessee Freighthouse. -*National Archives*

Kingston Springs, Tennessee Mile Marker 24.0, built 1928. This depot replaced a depot that burned the year before. -*Terry L. Coats photographer*

Martin, Tennessee Mile Marker 141.0, built 1903. Martin was a junction between the NC&St.L Railway and the Illinois Central Railroad. The "V" shaped passenger depot served both railroads. In the early 1900s it was this depot that was the first to witness the passing of the Dixie Flyer onto NC&St.L tracks on its way to Florida. -*Terry L. Coats Collection*

Martin, Tennessee Freighthouse. This structure was built by the Illinois Central, but was shared with the NC&St.L. In this 1917 photo men and mules are breaking ground for a new United States Post Office. Today the depot is gone and the old post office is now part of the city's library. -*Richard Kelly Collection, The Color Shop, Martin, Tennessee*

McKenzie, Tennessee, ca. 1917. This photo was made by NC&St.L company photographer H. C. Hill as part of a series of photos he made after a train accident in the proximity of the station. *-Nashville, Chattanooga & St. Louis Railway; -H. C. Hill photographer*

McKenzie, Tennessee Freighthouse. *-L&N Collection, University of Louisville*

McKenzie, Tennessee Mile Marker 117.0. This union station was shared by the NC&St.L and the L&N. The station was an L&N design. There was an identical though slightly larger depot to the McKenzie depot located in Milan, Tennessee The McKenzie depot still stands and is owned by the CSX Railroad.

Nashville, Tennessee Mile Marker 0.0. Freighthouse located at 10th Avenue North between Broadway and Church Streets. This structure was 850 feet in length and stood until it was replaced by the Tennessee State University campus. *-Nashville, Chattanooga & St. Louis Railway*

Newsom, Tennessee Mile Marker 16.0. *-National Archives*

Pegram, Tennessee Mile Marker 20.0. *-Bob Bell, Jr. photographer*

Union City, Tennessee NC&St.L/GM&O Passenger Station Mile Marker 154.0, built 1900. -*Terry L. Coats photographer*

Waverly, Tennessee Mile Marker 67.0, ca.1916. -*National Archives*

White Bluff, Tennessee Mile Marker 30.0. -*L&N Collection, University of Louisville*

White Bluff, Tennessee Shelter. -*Bob Bell, Jr. Collection*

CENTERVILLE BRANCH OF THE NASHVILLE DIVISION

Allen's Creek, Tennessee Mile Marker 106.0, built 1899. -*National Archives*

Aetna, Tennessee Mile Marker 85.0. -*National Archives*

Bon Aqua, Tennessee Mile Marker 53.0, ca. 1918. -*National Archives*

Centerville, Tennessee Mile Marker 86.0, built 1893. -*National Archives*

Goodrich, Tennessee Mile Marker 70.0, built 1891. -*National Archives*

Graham, Tennessee Mile Marker 67.0. -*National Archives*

Hohenwald, Tennessee Mile Marker 95.0, built 1896. *-National Archives*

Lyles, Tennessee Mile Marker 59.0. This station still stands. It was moved some miles from its original location and served as a private home for awhile. Today it is part of a rehabilitation center. *-National Archives*

Kimmins, Tennessee. This photo is thought to be a Nashville & Tuscaloosa Railroad station that pre-dated the coming of the NC&St.L. *-Tennessee State Library and Archives*

Kimmins, Tennessee Mile Marker 88.0. This is the NC&St.L depot that replaced the Nashville & Tuscaloosa station shown to the left. *-National Archives*

Nunnelly, Tennessee Mile Marker 69.0, built 1896. *-National Archives*

Riverside, Tennessee Mile Marker 104.0, built 1902. *-National Archives*

Twomey, Tennessee Mile Marker 77.0, built 1896. Site of a small yard as well as a very short wye. -*National Archives*

Tidwell, Tennessee Mile Marker 49.0. -*National Archives*

NASHVILLE BRANCH OF THE NASHVILLE DIVISION

West Nashville, Passenger Station Mile Marker 3.0. -*National Archives*

West Nashville, Freighthouse. -*National Archives*

Huntsville Division

"Lets go down to the River"

O sinners lets go down, Lets go down, come on down
O sinners lets go down Down in the river to pray
As I went down in the river to pray, Studyin about that good ol way
And who shall wear the Robe and crown?
Good Lord show me the way
  ... Allison Krauss

The States of Alabama and Tennessee issued charters upon charters during the 1850s for the building of the railroad segments that would become the Huntsville Division. In many cases, a company was given a charter to build a portion of this line only to later go bankrupt and not be able to complete its intended construction. At some future point, another company received a charter to finish the construction the first company had been unable to complete. In many cases, the second company also failed and it was only after these lines were purchased by the NC&St.L that much of the trackage was ever constructed.

When completed, the Huntsville Division branched off from the main trunk of the NC at Decherd, Tennessee. At Elora, Tennessee, it split again with one branch running northwest though Tennessee toward Fayetteville, Lewisburg, to Columbia and another branch going south into Alabama. The Alabama segment ran through Huntsville, crossed the Tennessee River at Hobbs Island using a 22 mile ferry link, and terminated on the Coosa River in Gadsden.

During the most prosperous days of the NC&St.L, Elora was a very busy junction. On any given day there were eight trains receiving and delivering passengers to and from Huntsville to the south, Decherd to the north, and Columbia to the west. For those having business in town, there was also a railroad hotel in Elora to accommodate those needing an overnight stay.[120]

1882 NC&St.L Pass. -Terry L. Coats Collection

The Alabama portion of the division was composed of three segments. It originated as the Winchester & Alabama, the Huntsville & Elora, and the Tennessee & Coosa Railroads. A forth section from Huntsville to Hobbs Island was developed by a group of private land developers from Huntsville.

---

120   NC&St.L Bulletin, *Lewisburg Branch*. October 1955, page 10.

There were river ports at several locations on the NC&St.L ... Hickman, Perryville, and Paducah, but the Huntsville Division had the distinction of being the only division on the system to not stop at the waters' edge. At Hobbs Island, the line pushed ahead and crossed the river by having its own navy. From the landing at Hobbs Island to the one at Guntersville, a distance of 22 miles, the NC&St.L operated a car-float barge system. Boating operations on the Tennessee River lasted for over sixty-five years. The barges operated from 1893 until a few years after the NC/L&N merger. Though the L&N already had egress to Gadsden, Alabama over their Alabama Mineral subdivision, they continued to run trains on the barges until 1960.

Huntsville, Alabama Mile Marker 130.0 Passenger Station The architect for this station was William C. Smith the same architect who designed the Chattanooga Terminal and many of the structures at the Tennessee Centennial. -*Mark Womack Collection*

Winchester & Alabama Railroad

In 1849, State of Tennessee charters granted permission to the Winchester & Alabama Railroad to construct a road from Winchester, Tennessee southward toward the Alabama state line. A subsequent charter allowed the W&A to modify the charter for a connection to the Nashville & Chattanooga at Decherd, Tennessee. The Alabama Act of 1855-6 authorized an extension to the charter granted in Tennessee allowing the Winchester & Alabama to construct a road from the terminus at the Tennessee/Alabama line on into Huntsville. Though the charter was issued, no construction in the State of Alabama was ever attempted by the W&A. The Winchester & Alabama did complete the building of track from Decherd to Fayetteville and in 1859 the first locomotive made its way into the latter city.

The years of the Civil War were not kind to the W&A. After the fall of Middle Tennessee to Federal forces the USMRR took over control of the railroad. Under Federal operations, the iron rail on this branch became a valued commodity and was ripped up by the Yankees for use on the N&C mainline between Nashville and Chattanooga. No trains ran on this line from the middle of 1863 until after the War, when the railroad was finally returned to its owners.

The W&A received some financial aid from the state of Tennessee to rebuild the war-ravaged line, but it was not enough to keep the railroad from sinking into receivership. The line went into private hands for a short while and then was purchased by the Memphis & Charleston in 1875. The Memphis & Charleston was bent on empire building. The M&C purchased the W&A as well as the McMinnville & Manchester Railroad in hopes of operating them as a cut-off from their mainline north through Sparta, Tennessee and then into Cincinnati on the future Cincinnati Southern Railway. When it became apparent that the Cincinnati Southern would be built further east through Harriman, Tennessee, plans to develop the W&A and the line to Sparta were abandoned.[121]

Additionally, the M&C's control of these Middle Tennessee railroads was met with stiff opposition; the M&C reconsidered their business options. Two years later, on July 28, 1877, the NC&St.L, who was also doing some empire building of their own, purchased from the M&C the Winchester & Alabama and the McMinnville & Manchester Railroad as a package deal. The McMinnville & Manchester would be added to the Southwestern Railroad and the Bon Air Railway to become the Sparta Branch of the NC&St.L, while the Winchester & Alabama would become a part of the 99 mile long Elora to Gadsden, Huntsville Division.[122]

Huntsville & Elora Railroad

In 1886-7, a charter was issued by the State of Alabama to the newly formed Huntsville & Elora Railroad. The H&E was granted permission to build from where the Winchester & Alabama terminated at the Tennessee-Alabama line on south to Huntsville. This was the same route that the State of Tennessee had previously issued a charter to the Winchester & Alabama Railroad to build in 1855-6. The H&E established a route and started construction, but only a small amount of grading had been done by the time the railroad was sold. The NC&St.L purchased the H&E on October 28. 1887. At the time of the purchase, no rail had been laid and only a small amount of grading had been done. It was under NC&St.L control that any construction was brought to fruition and any track was laid.[123]

Tennessee & Coosa Railroad

The Tennessee & Coosa Railroad was chartered by the Alabama Act of 1844-5 for the purpose of building a road between a point near Gunter's Landing (later Guntersville) on the Tennessee River to the most eligible point on the Coosa River. In 1872, an act refined the charter to state that the road was to be built from Gunter's Landing north to a point on the Alabama-Tennessee state line and south from the Tennessee River to a point at or near Attalla or Gadsden, Alabama.[124] The original T&C charter would have allowed the road to build as far south as Montgomery, but an extension south of Gadsden never materialized.

---

121   Richard E. Prince, *Nashville, Chattanooga & St. Louis Railway: History and Steam Locomotives.* 1967, page 26.
122   NC&St.L Bulletin, *Lewisburg Branch.* October 1955, page 4.
123   NC&St.L Bulletin, *Huntsville Branch.* April 1956, page 4.
124   Ibid, page 5.

The T&C was purchased by the NC&St.L on April 6, 1891. At the time of the purchase, about 30 miles of track had been built northward from Gadsden. The NC&St.L completed the unfinished 7.6 miles of trackage linking Gadsden and Guntersville.

Along with financial considerations as part of the purchase contract, the NC&St.L agreed to cross the Tennessee River and construct a line north to connect to the rail line coming south through Huntsville from Elora, Tennessee.

HUNTSVILLE TO HOBBS ISLAND

After the railroad reached Huntsville in the early 1890s, it was a natural step for the line to be advanced toward the Tennessee River. A river outlet would allow the merchants in Huntsville an outlet not only north by rail, but also to the south via boat.

In 1892, a group consisting of Huntsville businessmen and northern capitalists came together to form the *Northwestern Land Association*. Over the following years, this group opened businesses and banks, secured cotton mills, developed property, and, in 1893, built a 15.5 mile railroad to Hobbs Island.

For whatever reason, these men did not coordinate with the Tennessee & Coosa Railroad Company building north from Gadsden in finding a common meeting point at the Tennessee River. Neither group ever intended to build a connecting road to the other; thus, each one built a different landing. The T&C built to Gunter's Landing some 22 miles upstream from Hobbs Island, the terminal chosen by the Huntsville group. Obviously, neither group ever anticipated that the NC&St.L would eventually purchase these two assets and that at that time the NC would have two rail sections landing miles apart. The NC&St.L had a problem. They now owned two pieces of track separated by miles of water and they needed to connect them.

It would not be practical to shift the tracks approaching from Gadsden and reroute them toward Hobbs Island. To move them toward Hobbs would eradicate the business already established at the busy river terminal of Gunter's Landing.

The answer would be to move the track north of the Tennessee River to connect Huntsville to Gunter's. However, this was not as simple a solution as it would seem on the surface. There were several obstacles to be overcome, included but were not limited to, having to purchase approximately 25 miles of new right-of-way to the river and then the 25 miles of track would have had to be rebuilt. On the north bank of the river, there were high bluffs. Extending off the bluffs to a bridge would be a simple act, but doing the same from the Gunter's side was not such a simple matter. In order to reach a point where a bridge could be erected a very long expanse of near 1.5 miles of trestles would have to be built. Additionally, building a bridge with sufficient height to clear marine traffic beneath it would be a very expensive and cumbersome endeavor.

In lieu of building a direct crossing at the river, the NC elected to create a boat-barge transfer operation to connect the two railheads. For the next 67 years, up through the time the L&N took over the NC, a water taxi system was used to ferry trains across the river.

Hobbs Island to Guntersville Barge Transfers The "NC&St.L Navy"

It is said that this 22 mile crossing had the distinction of being the longest railroad ferry in the world. To facilitate operations two stern-wheel steam-powered boats were purchased by the NC&St.L. in 1893. The 89-ton *Huntsville* was built new. The second boat, the *Hattie McDaniel* was bought second-hand by the NC. Both boats were placed into service in 1893 and were used to tow railroad barges and to carry passengers until just after the turn of the century.

Guntersville paddle wheeler with barge at Hobbs Island, Alabama. The NC&St.L carried passengers on this transport until 1928.
-*Nashville, Chattanooga & St. Louis Railway*

These two old river veterans were replaced with much larger stern-wheelers in 1903. These two boats, the *Guntersville* and a second Huntsville, stayed in service until after WWII. In 1946, the *Guntersville* was replaced with a modern diesel powered tugboat that carried the same name. The old *Huntsville* was not retired until 1951, but saw very limited service in its later years.

Guntersville tug boat with barge, ca.1947.
-*Nashville, Chattanooga & St. Louis Railway*

Over the years, the car floats in service at Hobbs Island increased in size. The original barges held two tracks with a capacity of three cars each. These barges were replaced with ones with a capacity of eight cars and finally in 1938, the NC had constructed in Nashville, much larger ten car barges. These two vessels served the NC and the L&N until the end of service.

Passenger service aboard the boats was abandoned in 1928. Up until that time, passengers were carried on the upper decks of the boats while the train cars were carried aboard the floats. Shortly after the abandonment of the carrying of passenger cars on the barges, the train was also abandoned.[125] [126]

Huntsville paddle wheeler. This paddle wheeler was used from 1893 until 1946 when it was replaced by a new diesel tugboat.
-*Nashville, Chattanooga & St. Louis Railway*

---

125   NC&St.L Bulletin, *NC&St.L Navy*. August 1952, page 5.
126   NC&St.L Bulletin, *MS. Guntersville*. August 1946, page 3.

Sparta Branch

The area from Tullahoma northeast to Ravenscroft, Tennessee was rich with coal, lumber, mineral ores, and other raw materials. Additionally, good grazing lands produced an abundance of livestock in this area. Meandering through this area and flowing northward until it united with the Cumberland River was the Caney Fork River. The waterways running west to Nashville afforded the inhabitants of the plateau an avenue over which they could transport these raw materials to market. Raw materials were also carried out in small loads by wagon and livestock was driven overland by drovers. Carrying the materials out by wagon and packet boat was a slow and arduous means of transporting the materials to market. The prospect of bringing a fast moving railroad to the area certainly came as welcome news to the citizenry of the Cumberland Valley. Seeing the benefits that railroads could bring, they were among the first in the state to charter a railroad.

The Sparta Branch, also know as the McMinnville Branch of the NC&St.L, was composed of three precursors, the McMinnville & Manchester Railroad, the Southwestern Railroad, and the Bon Air Railway.

The McMinnville & Manchester began building at a junction with the Nashville & Chattanooga Railroad at Tullahoma. They built in a northern direction through Manchester with construction culminating for the company at McMinnville. Construction began in 1855 and continued through the following year. This line was leased by the N&C from its beginnings and through 1862 was operated as a branch of that railroad. During the War, this line changed hands several times up to June 30, 1863 when Braxton Bragg's Confederate Army of Tennessee abandoned Tullahoma and crossed the Tennessee River to Chattanooga. Within a month, the line was in control of the Federal Army and was thereafter operated by them. The northern portion of this line between McMinnville and Manchester was abandoned in 1864 and the rails stripped for use for repairs on the Nashville to Chattanooga main lines as well as other needs on the USMRR.

Bon Air, Tennessee. Hopper car. -*Bondecroft History Center*

Rebuilt to operating standards after the War, the line operated until 1871 when the company was sold in foreclosure after it was unable to repay construction loans to the state. The Memphis & Charleston Railroad purchased the railroad from the State of Tennessee. As indicated before, the M&C purchased this line in anticipation of using it and the Winchester & Alabama Railroad in southern Tennessee as a cut-off from the M&C mainline north to Cincinnati, Ohio. When those plans fell through, the M&C placed both railroads up for sale. In a package deal, the NC&St.L purchased the 35 mile McMinnville & Manchester Railroad as well as the 39 mile Winchester & Alabama Railroad.

For the next eighty years, the NC&St.L ran this McMinnville to Manchester line as its Sparta Branch … hauling coal, lumber, ore, and other natural material. Though parts of this branch were shut down in the Depression of the 1930s, the line struggled until the 1957 takeover.

In 1983, to prevent the loss of current rail traffic as well as to attract new industry to Coffee, Warren, and White Counties, the Tri-County Railroad Association formed and bought the Sparta Branch. Operated as the Caney Fork & Western Railroad, today the railroad still operates trains from Tullahoma to Sparta carrying carbon black to a tire plant, steel, grain, and fertilizer, while exporting wood, lumber, and wood chips to the CSX interchange at Tullahoma.

COLUMBIA BRANCH
DUCK RIVER VALLEY RAILROAD

Hellfire and Damnation - Petersburg to Talley Station
… Local Lincoln County refrain quoted in anger and frustration in lieu of something stronger

It was 86 miles from the division point at Decherd to the terminus of this branch at Columbia, Tennessee. On November 4, 1872, the State of Tennessee granted a charter to the Duck River Valley Narrow Gauge Railroad. The Duck River Valley was to build a road from Johnsonville, Tennessee through the heart of southern middle Tennessee to the town of Fayetteville. Written into the charter was also an option to build past Fayetteville to the Nashville & Chattanooga Railroad at Decherd, Tennessee.

The actual railroad built was a much shorter 36 mile long section of narrow gauge track (3-feet, 0-inch width) from Columbia to Petersburg, Tennessee. Whether any attempt was ever made to construct the intended line from Columbia to Johnsonville is not known.[127] In 1879, this narrow gauge railroad was leased by the NC&St.L for a period of forty years. As a stipulation to the lease, the NC had to extend the line an additional 14 miles from Petersburg to Fayetteville.[128]

---

127 NC&St.L Bulletin, *Lewisburg Branch*. October 1955, page 4.
128 Thomas E. Bailey, *Engine and Iron: A Story of Branchline Railroading in Middle Tennessee.* Tennessee Historic Quarterly, Volume XXVIII, Number 3. Fall 1969, page 260.

The NC completed the track to Fayetteville on March 16, 1882, and after completing some repairs on a couple of inherited locomotives, opened the line to traffic in May 1882. The NC&St.L continued to operate the railroad as a narrow gauge until May 31, 1886, a date that would make history in American railroading. The preceding February, a convention was held at the Kimble House in Atlanta, Georgia. At the convention, the attendees, a group of southern railroad representatives, voted to standardize the gauge of their railroads from the 5-foot, 0-inch that most of the railroads used as standard, to a 4-foot, 9-inch gauge. The 4-foot, 9-inch was chosen because that was the gauge used by the Pennsylvania Railroad, a company with whom many southern roads wanted to interchange.

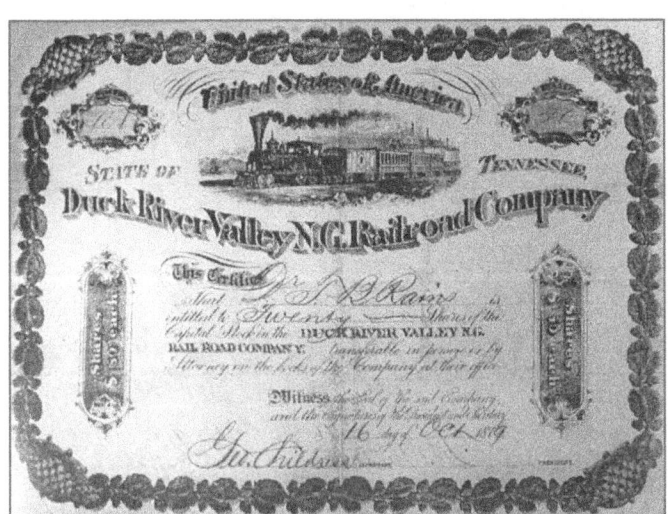

1879 Duck River Valley Narrow Gage Railroad Company Stock Certificate. -*Nashville, Chattanooga & St. Louis Railway*

The monumental task of making all of the changes on the same day was set for Monday, May 31 and Tuesday, June 1, 1886. Starting at 3:00 AM on the morning of the 31st and continuing for a period of 36 hours, hundreds of crews worked diligently across thousands of miles of track to un-spike, move, and then re-spike one of the two rails along the mainlines. Additionally, rolling stock and locomotives had to be converted to the new standard. Other crews were assigned the task of pulling wheels, lathing axles, and then replacing the wheels to the new gauge. In the case of the NC&St.L, the narrow gauge tracks on the Duck River branch were converted to the 4-foot, 9-inch gauge. Up until that time, there was an exchange track next to the Fayetteville depot and a bottleneck in the transfer of freight from the narrow gauge to the standard gauge cars. The re-gauging of the tracks alleviated this situation.[129]

The NC&St.L ran the Duck River under a lease until November 23, 1887 when it purchased the line outright from the railroad's stockholders. With the purchase in 1877 of the Winchester & Alabama Railroad from Decherd to Fayetteville, the NC&St.L had a branch line from the Nashville to Chattanooga main line at Decherd to Columbia, Tennessee. This segment labored on until 1945 when from lack of patronage, the Lewisburg to Columbia segment of the trackage was abandoned. The remainder of this line was abandoned in 1961.

---

[129] At one time, 23 different track spacings were being used in this country, a condition that created a logistical and economic nightmare. In 1892, the NC&St.L purchased the narrow gauge tracks between Aetna and Allens Creek on their Centerville Branch. In 1894, the NC widened this track to standard gauge.

Harms, Tennessee Mile Marker 127.0. The station agent and other railroad personnel pose for this early 1900s photograph. Note the young lad peering out the window at the camera. *-Jack Towry Collection*

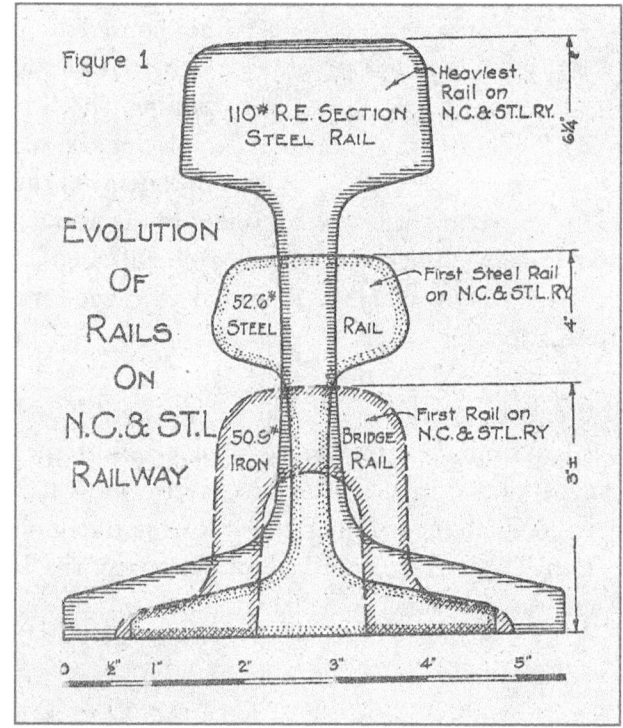
Evolution of Rails

Middle Tennessee & Alabama Railway

The Middle Tennessee & Alabama Railway was a short line from Fayetteville, Tennessee running 36.5-miles to Capshaw, Alabama, a suburb in the western limits of Huntsville. This branch of the Huntsville Division was originally planned as the Decatur, Chesapeake & New Orleans Railroad. Under its charter, the route would start in Gallatin, Tennessee north of Nashville and continue south through Shelbyville and Fayetteville, Tennessee to a terminus in Decatur, Alabama.

The DC&NO Railroad chartered on July 20, 1887. That year, a subscription of $150,000 in bonds was pledged by Lincoln County as backing for the DC&NO and for the Cincinnati & Birmingham Railroad. The investment had been made in hopes that the DC&NO or the C&B would build through Fayetteville and that either line would enter into direct competition with the NC&St.L for freight business in the county. It was thought that competition between the two railroads would lower freight costs for the county's shippers.[130]

The Cincinnati & Birmingham restructured to become the Cincinnati, Alabama & Atlantic Railroad, but the reconstruction died before it could rise to its feet. From the outset, the DC&NO too had trouble starting. It did, however, manage to build from the Alabama-Tennessee state line northward as well as from the N&C's Columbia Branch southward, arriving at a meeting point at the Duck River near Coldwater, Tennessee. The railroad never approached its proposed goal of building all the way from Gallatin to Decatur.

The DC&NO failed to meet several construction deadlines and in doing so failed to procure much of the $150,000 subscribed to it. Without this financial backing, the railroad was forced into bankruptcy and was sold at public auction in 1893. That same year, the DC&NO was re-chartered as the Middle Tennessee & Alabama Railway. The MT&A had little more success in making this line profitable than had the DC&NO. It too was foreclosed upon in 1897. The NC&St.L purchased the line in the spring and proceeded to extend the line from Jeff to Capshaw, Alabama. Additionally, the NC had to rebuild most of the MT&A trackage. Because it had been so shoddily laid, the MT&A was practically of no use as constructed.

The people of Lincoln County had hoped that some day a railroad would have built north of Fayetteville as the DC&NO had originally been proposed.[131] With the NC's purchase, any hopes of extending the line north toward Nashville were dashed. Also dashed was any chance that a railroad would rise to compete against the NC&St.L to lower freight rates.

---

130   Ibid, page 261.
131   Professor Elmer G. Sulzer in his book *Ghost Railroads of Tennessee* says that the DC&NO did have trackage north of Fayetteville to the town of Booneville, Tennessee, but that this line was never capable of operating on a regular basis and was abandoned between 1893 and 1897.

For almost thirty years, from the turn of the century forward, the NC&St.L attempted to sustain a profitable operation on the former Middle Tennessee & Alabama. It simply was never able to do so and the ICC granted the NC's petition for abandonment in 1928.[132]

The Fayetteville to Capshaw branch or the Jeff, as it was called, operated a local roundtrip between the two towns six days a week. The line held the distinction of being the next to last branch to be purchased by the NC (the Orme Branch in southeast Tennessee being the last) and it was the first branch on the system to be closed and abandoned by them.

On January 12, 1912, construction started on the Lewisburg & Northern Railroad, a subsidiary of the L&N. The Lewisburg & Northern was to connect Brentwood, Tennessee to Athens, Alabama and pass through Lewisburg. Two-and-one-half years later, the line was completed. It opened on July 15, 1914. On that date the citizens of Lewisburg celebrated Railroad Days to welcome the passenger trains. With the arrival of a second railroad in Marshall County, the citizens of the county voted to float a $20,000 bond for the construction of a new depot. This station became a union station at the crossing of the NC&St.L and the new Lewisburg & Northern. The depot was built between April and August 1914.

---

132   Richard E. Prince, *Nashville, Chattanooga & St. Louis Railway: History and Steam Locomotives.* 1967, page 62.

Map of the Huntsville Division

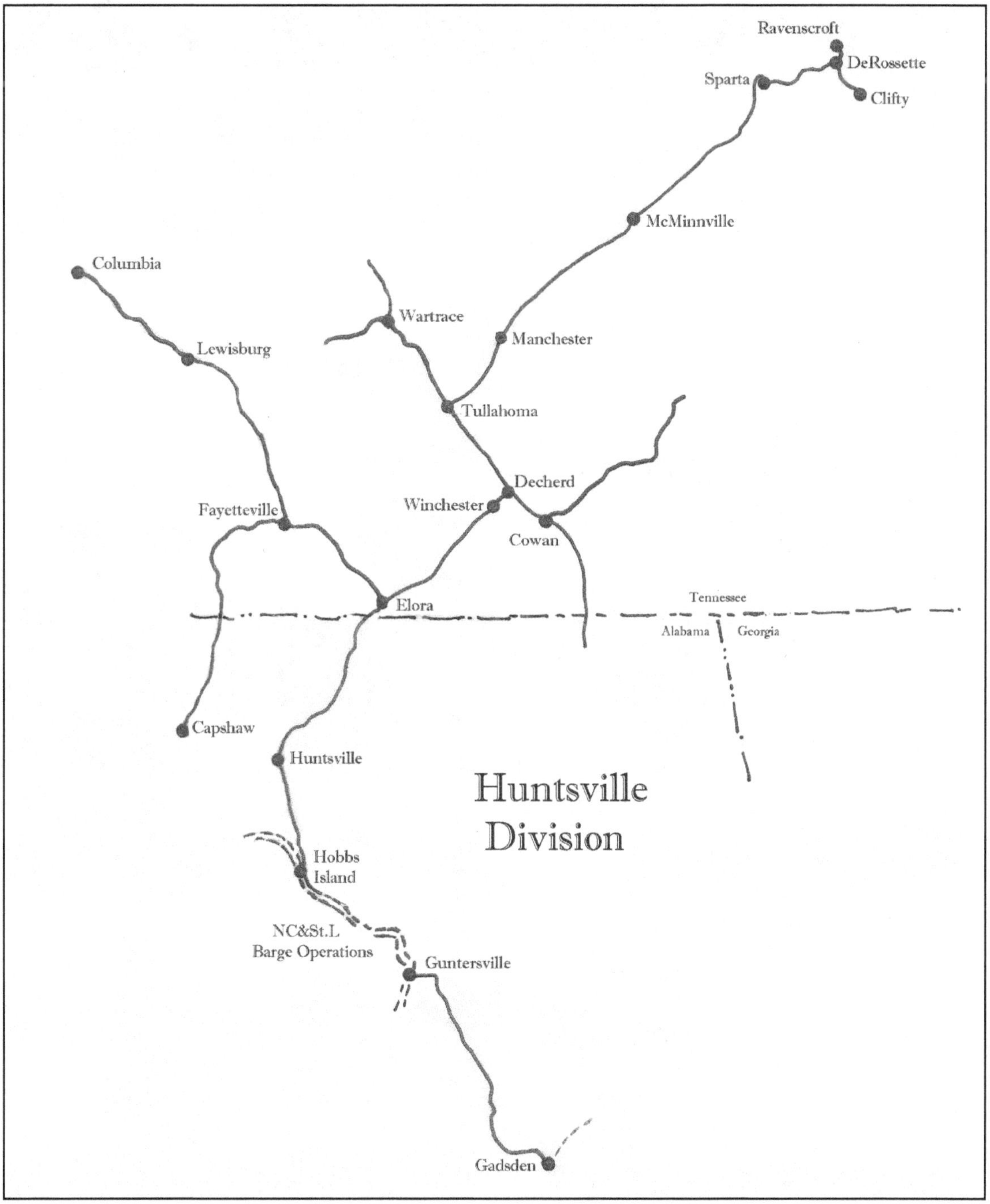

Huntsville Division Main Line

Bell Factory, Alabama Mile Marker 119.0.
-*Bob Baudendistel Collection*

Chase, Alabama Mile Marker 124.0. The Chase station is unique in that it may be the smallest union station in the US. Built in 1937 on the site of an earlier station, this depot was privately owned by the Chase family, who chose this location on which to start their nursery business in the 1880. Today the depot is still located aside two railroads. The Norfolk Southern tracks to Huntsville and the Chase & Mercury tourist railroad tracks are located to each side of the depot. This structure contains the ticket office of the tourist railroad as well as the North Alabama Railroad Museum.
-*National Archives*

Gadsden, Alabama Mile Marker 203.0, built 1896. This station was used jointly by the NC&St.L and the L&N and was a L&N design. Standing until the early 1970s, there was a hotel that served the depot across the tracks. -*Terry L. Coats Collection*

Guntersville, Alabama Mile Marker 167.0, built 1909. This refurbished station now serves as a railroad museum and contains railroad artifacts and has a small auditorium. -*Terry L. Coats photographer*

Hobbs Island, Alabama Mile Marker 144.0, built 1893. Depicted in this photo at its original site. Note that the agent's office in this structure and the one at New Market, Alabama did not have a window. -*Bob Baudendistel Collection*

Huntsville, Alabama Freighthouse. -*L&N Collection, University of Louisville*

Huntsville, Alabama. Old and new freight depots. The new prefabricated building would soon replace the older one in the background. This photo was made in the interim between the building of the new one and the destruction of the older one. -*Bernie Wooler Collection*

New Market, Alabama Mile Marker 112.0. Note the structure did not have windows. -*Bernie Wooler Collection*

Normal, Alabama Mile Marker 125.0. This small 11 x 12½ foot station included an 80 foot by 5 foot platform trackside. -*Bob Baudendistel Collection*

Plevna, Alabama Mile Marker 108.0. -*National Archives*

COLUMBIA BRANCH OF THE HUNTSVILLE DIVISION

Fayetteville, Tennessee Mile Marker 122.0, ca. 1939, built 1899. -*Terry L. Coats Collection*

Belfast, Tennessee Mile Marker 144.0. By the time this photograph was made in the early 1950s, the old passenger station was being used exclusively as a freight depot and there was a small passenger shelter next to the depot. -*Bob Bell, Jr. Collection*

Belvidere, Tennessee Mile Marker 90.0. This station is now in private hands as is a section house from this area. The owner of these structures is living in the section house and is using the depot as a crafts workshop. -*Tennessee State Library and Archives*

Columbia, Tennessee Mile Marker 170.0. Union station for the NC&St.L and the L&N Railroads. This structure still stands and is privately owned and is being remodeled for commercial use. -*Terry L. Coats Collection*

Elora, Tennessee Mile Marker 103.0. -*National Archives*

Fayetteville, Tennessee. Freighthouse built in the 1850s by the Winchester & Alabama Railroad. Even after the newer passenger depot (shown on the next page) was abandoned this antebellum structure continued to serve the people of Fayetteville. -*Bob Bell, Jr. Collection*

Fayetteville, Tennessee Mile Marker 122.0 Passenger Depot, built 1899. -*Nashville, Chattanooga & St. Louis Railway*

Flintville, Tennessee Mile Marker 108.0. -*Louis Winsett Collection*

Howell, Tennessee Mile Marker 129.0. -*Margaret Harris Shutt.*

Huntland, Tennessee Mile Marker 98.0. -*Tennessee State Library and Archives*

Kelso, Tennessee Mile Marker 114.0. Still standing, this station is currently used as a storage facility. -*Terry L. Coats photographer*

Lewisburg, Tennessee Mile Marker 150.0. This brick union station served both the NC&St.L and the L&N Railroads and was razed in 1995. -*L&N Collection, University of Louisville*

Lewisburg, Tennessee Freight Depot. -*Tennessee State Library and Archives*

Maxwell, Tennessee Mile Marker 94.0. Still standing, the station is now used as a private residence. -*Terry L. Coats photographer*

Petersburg, Tennessee Mile Marker 135.0. This station was razed about 1961. -*Gail G. Sanders Collection*

Talley, Tennessee Mile Marker 139.0. -*Terry L. Coats photographer*

Jeff Branch of the Huntsville Division

Coldwater, Tennessee Mile Marker 135.0, built 1904 and enlarged in 1911. -*Tennessee State Library and Archives*

Toney, Alabama Mile Marker 144.0. This depot still stands and is the only remaining depot on what was the Fayetteville, Tennessee to Jeff, Alabama branch and is currently used for storage. -*David Ellenburg photographer*

Sparta Branch of the Huntsville Division

Campaign, Tennessee Mile Marker 114.0, built 1908. -*Nashville, Chattanooga & St. Louis Railway*

Bon Air, Tennessee Mile Marker 137.0, built 1904. Enlarged in 1912, this depot was purchased by a local family and was dismantled board by board. In the 1930s, the materials were loaded on a boxcar leased from the NC&St.L and transported to the Price's Switch area where the they were used to construct a private residence. This house still stands. -*Tennessee State Library and Archives*

Price's Switch Mile Marker 133.0. Telephone booth moved from its original location currently used as a storage house. -*Terry L. Coats photographer*

Eastland, Tennessee Mile Marker 148.0, ca.1909, built 1905. -*Bondecroft History Center*

Hickerson, Tennessee Mile Marker 73.0. -*National Archives*

Quebeck, Tennessee Mile Marker 119.0. This photograph is of the depot as it sat in its original location. The structure was moved approximately fifteen miles from its original location on the Sparta Branch. Today the depot is used as a storage unit at the home of its owner. -*Kenton Dickerson photographer*

Rock House, Tennessee Mile Marker 135.0. Rock House was built between1835 and 1839 and served as a tollhouse on a private road. The road served as a primary link between Middle Tennessee and the east coast. President Andrew Jackson was known to stop here often on trips from Nashville to Washington. With the extension of the NC&St.L Railway from Sparta to the mining area of DeRossett and beyond, the old house was used as a passenger depot for the trains. Note the railroad to the right of the photograph and US Highway 70 to the left. Today the railroad is removed and the highway has been raised some 40 to 50 feet in elevation, leaving the little structure completely invisible from the roadway. -*Rock House Museum*

Rock Island, Tennessee Mile Marker 115.0, built 1893. This station was originally located in Farley (Rocket), Alabama, moved to Rock Island and is currently used as rental property. The freight room portion of this depot was removed years ago and incorporated into another building that is also used as rental property. -*Terry L. Coats photographer*

Sparta, Tennessee Mile Marker 131.0. Passenger depot, built 1917. The original 1896 depot burned in 1915 and was replaced with this one. Still standing on its original site, this depot is currently used as a business. The Carpenter Gothic freight depot that once stood a short distance away has been razed. -*Bob Bell, Jr. Collection*

Walling, Tennessee Mile Marker 117.0, built 1910. -*Lee Yoder Collection*

Summitville, Tennessee Mile Marker 89.0. -*Tennessee State Library and Archives*

DeRossett, Tennessee Mile Marker 141.0, built 1904. enlarged in 1911, built 1904. Enlarged in 1911, this photograph depicts the station as it stood in its original location. -*Bob Bell, Jr. Collection*

McMinnville, Tennessee Mile Marker 104.0, built 1917. This photo from the early 1900s shows the Sparta Branch local at the depot. This Carpenter Gothic station was replaced with a brick Queen Anne station by the early 1920s and this station would be used as the freighthouse. -*McMinn County, Tennessee Library*

Doyle, Tennessee Mile Marker 123.0, built 1910. This depot was razed and a simpler shelter was built in its place. -*Nashville, Chattanooga & St. Louis Railway*

DeRossett, Tennessee Roundhouse, ca. 1916. -*National Archives*

Manchester, Tennessee Mile Marker 81.0. -*Bob Bell, Jr. Collection*

Morrison, Tennessee Mile Marker 94.0, built 1910. -*Bob Bell, Jr., photographer*

Paducah & Memphis Division
Tennessee Midland Railway Company

As early as 1836, rail service between Memphis and Knoxville had been discussed at a railroad convention in Knoxville. It would take an additional fifty years for any rail to be laid. The Tennessee Midland Railway Company was chartered December 29, 1886. Parties interested in the company subscribed $1,250,000 to start the enterprise. The principal backers were from Memphis and Richmond, Virginia.

Paducah, Kentucky Combination Station This station was used as the passenger station in Paducah until the NC&St.L and the IC built a new combination station in 1900. After 1900, this station was used as a freight depot. -*National Archives*

Construction began in 1887, and by 1888, eighty-six miles of track had been laid from Memphis to Jackson, Tennessee. The first train to enter Jackson from Memphis occurred on June 1, 1888. The train called the Illinois Central freight house at Jackson its depot.

The following year, the track was extended through Midland City (Lexington) to the west banks of the Tennessee River at Perryville. The first through train ran between Memphis and Perryville on February 4, 1889. The original charter allowed the Tennessee Midland Railway to build eastward from Memphis through the state capitol, through Knoxville and eventually to the Virginia state line. In reality, the plan fell considerably short of its goal. The Tennessee River landing at Perryville some 135 miles from Memphis would be the culminating point of this railroad; the river was never bridged for rail traffic, and no rail was ever laid east of the river. The Tennessee Midland maintained a small 70 foot turntable in Perryville for turning their engines for the return trips to the west.

The Tennessee Midland was to be part of a much grander scheme to build a railroad from Tennessee across the country to the Pacific Ocean. The Tennessee Midland was to have been a portion of an elaborate railroad that would build east from Tennessee to the Atlantic Ocean and west from the state to the opposite shore. The Tennessee & Pacific Railroad Company had chartered in Tennessee in 1865 and was to have been a part of this same transcontinental railroad. The T&P was to build from Knoxville to Nashville, then from Nashville to Jackson, and then on to Memphis. Only this Memphis to Perryville and a portion of this line between Nashville and Lebanon, Tennessee were ever completed. The middle Tennessee section of the T&P would be purchased on October 1, 1877 by the NC&St.L and would become its Lebanon branch.

Paducah, Tennessee & Alabama Railroad

Wreck along the P&M Division, Hazel, Kentucky. -*Cabin Antiques, Sharon Ray Collection*

In 1889, the city of Paducah, Kentucky issued $100,000 in bonds to build in a southeasterly direction the Paducah, Tennessee & Alabama Railroad toward Tennessee. By 1891, the PT&A Railroad had completed building tracks from Paducah southward through Murray, Kentucky to Paris, Tennessee where it intersected with the tracks of the Louisville & Nashville Railroad. By October 1892, the tracks had been extended to Hollow Rock (later Bruceton, Tennessee), where it met the Nashville, Chattanooga & St. Louis on its Nashville to Hickman line. Continuing south, the following year the PT&A connected to the Tennessee Midland Railway at Lexington. The linking of these two lines completed a through passage from the Mississippi River at Memphis to the Ohio River at Paducah, a distance of 254 miles.

Not long after the Paducah, Tennessee & Alabama and the Tennessee Midland connected in 1892, the Paducah, Tennessee & Alabama acquired the latter road under a thirty year lease agreement. This business contract was short lived, by 1893 both the Paducah, Tennessee & Alabama and the Tennessee Midland were in receivership. The receivership lasted three years until December 1895 when the companies were sold in foreclosure to the Louisville & Nashville Railroad. In 1896, the Louisville & Nashville, in what may have been a forced deal, leased this newly acquired prize to the Nashville, Chattanooga & St. Louis. Up until this time, the NC&St.L had gained entrance to Memphis over the L&N through its connection with the L&N at McKenzie. By leasing this trackage, the NC&St.L now had its own egress to the Bluff City. With this acquisition, the line between Hollow Rock and Memphis became part of the Nashville, Chattanooga & St. Louis' main line, while the section from Hollow Rock to Paducah and the line between Lexington and Perryville were reduced to branch line status. The acquisition of the line to Paducah also allowed the NC an additional river port on the Ohio River at Paducah.

World's Longest Single Truss Bridge

After establishing itself in Paducah, the NC&St.L entered into a business agreement with the Chicago, Burlington & Quincy Railway to bridge the Ohio River between Metropolis, Illinois and Paducah and to build, maintain, and operate a short railroad linking the two railroads. In February 1910, The NC and the CB&Q railroads formed a new company and incorporated the Paducah & Illinois Railroad Company. At the time of the incorporation, three

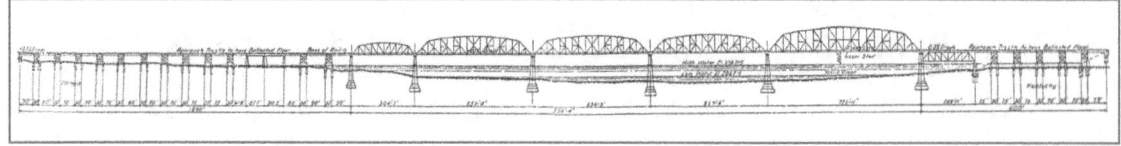

Metropolitan Bridge, built 1914-7. -*Railway Age Magazine*

additional companies, the Illinois Central, Chicago & Eastern Illinois, and the Cleveland, Cincinnati, Chicago & St. Louis expressed interest in financing the construction of the bridge; all would have a change of heart and none participated in the initial construction.

Started in 1914, the double track bridge, the world's longest single truss bridge opened to rail traffic in December 1917. Three years later the Illinois Central Railroad had a change of mind about investing in the P&I railroad Company. The IC became a partner in the railroad when the NC and the CB&Q sold to that company one-third interest in the bridge and the 13 miles of railroad operated by the P&I.

1875 Nashville Chattanooga & St. Louis Railway Pass. -*Terry L. Coats Collection*

After the demise of the NC, the L&N diverted traffic from this route, choosing to route traffic over its St. Louis Division instead. Likewise, the consolidation of the CB&Q into the giant Burlington (BNSF) system took traffic off this route. Eventually the IC became the sole owner of the bridge. The Illinois Central sold all rights to the bridge in 1986. Today the bridge is owned by Four Rivers Transportation, Inc. and is used in short line operations.

HOLLOW ROCK AND THE BRUCETON YARDS

Originally, there had been a small yard in Hollow Rock, Tennessee, the junction point of the P&M Division and the Nashville Division. The P&M also maintained an intermediate terminal at Lexington. As business increased, it became necessary to improve and expand the facilities at Hollow Rock. In 1920, plans were completed to construct a larger more modern yard and new mechanical facilities at the junction. New engine house and car repair shops were erected as well as an expansion of the yard capacity to nearly four-fold of that which it had previously. With the building of these new facilities, the old terminal at Lexington was closed and employees were reassigned.[133] With the opening of new shop facilities, those who had worked at Paducah were transferred as well.

---

133   NC&St.L Railway Bulletin. September 1946, page 6.

Bruceton, Tennessee Scales. -*Nashville, Chattanooga & St. Louis Railway*

Because Hollow Rock was only an interchange point of the rails, it became necessary for the NC to purchase adjacent property to accommodate the construction of businesses, a depot, and other railroad related structures. By 1922 this new area named, Junction City was populated by a passenger depot replete with covered train sheds, a yard office, dispatcher's office, a hotel, and a myriad of train servicing amenities. The name Junction City was short lived, it was soon discovered that the state of Tennessee already had a Junction City and so the name was changed to Bruceton in honor of the then General Manager of the NC&St.L Railway, W. P. Bruce.[134]

Over time, Bruceton would become one of the busiest places on the entire NC&St.L system. Aside from the engine maintenance facilities, Bruceton was a major passenger depot as well. Because of its strategic location, passenger trains from north, south, east, and west would interchange daily in Bruceton. Trains from Memphis, Chattanooga, Tennessee, and Hickman and Paducah, Kentucky were scheduled to arrive at approximately 11:25 AM each morning. If you were lucky enough to have been in Bruceton during the first quarter of the twentieth century, you would have been able to see four trains enter the station and grind to a halt on parallel tracks next to the covered train platform. On the northern most tracks, one would have been able to see the Nashville to Memphis train. On the next track over would be a small accommodation train about to depart north taking her passengers up the Hickman line to the Mississippi River city. The third track would hold the train that would lumber its way up the north leg of the P&M to Paducah and on the fourth track would stand the crack train the *Lookout,* which was the Memphis to Chattanooga train.

Bruceton, Tennessee Roundhouse -*Terry L. Coats photographer*

Bruceton, Tennessee City of Memphis train crew. -*Nashville, Chattanooga & St. Louis Railway*

---

134   Ibid, page 17.

For about five minutes, these four trains sat side by side. Passengers alighting from one train hurrying to pass to one of the three sister accommodations made the Bruceton platforms a beehive of activity. Baggage carts filled with mail and express would weave in and out between the passengers as their drivers hurried to transfer their cargo to the correct RPO. At 11:30 AM, one would hear the conductors on the Nashville to Memphis train and the train to Hickman call, *"All Aboard,"* and soon the two were off to their appointed destinations. Within a few minutes more, the other two trains were also off to their respective destinations and all was quiet until the same time the following day.

The mainline of the P&M Division from Memphis to Paducah operated through the 1957 merger though the last passenger service on the upper part of the division ceased operating on March 31, 1951. At its demise, the NC&St.L was still using a wooden passenger car on this run. This was probably the last regular long-run railroad in America to still be using a wooden car.[135]

The Perryville to Lexington branch affectionately known as the *Pea Vine* was abandoned and the tracks removed in 1936. The main line of the P&M tracks from Burkitt (just west of Jackson) to Cordova were abandoned in 1967, leaving this section of country without a railroad for the first time since the 1880s.

In the early 1980s the line between Bruceton to Beech Bluff and Hardin to Paducah was abandoned. The latter section of this line was given a short reprieve when in 1994 it was rebuilt and for about 10 years the Hardin Southern Railroad operated a tourist railroad between Hardin and Murray. In 2009 the ties and rails were finally removed.

A 45 mile long portion of the P&M from Bruceton, Tennessee to Murray, Kentucky is still operated by the Kentucky & West Tennessee Railroad, (K&WT). They transport chemicals, clay, agriculture products, automobile parts, and building materials.

Cancelled Letter from the City of Memphis

---

135   Karl R. Koenig, *The Story of the Hardin Southern Railroad.*

Map of the Paducah & Memphis Division

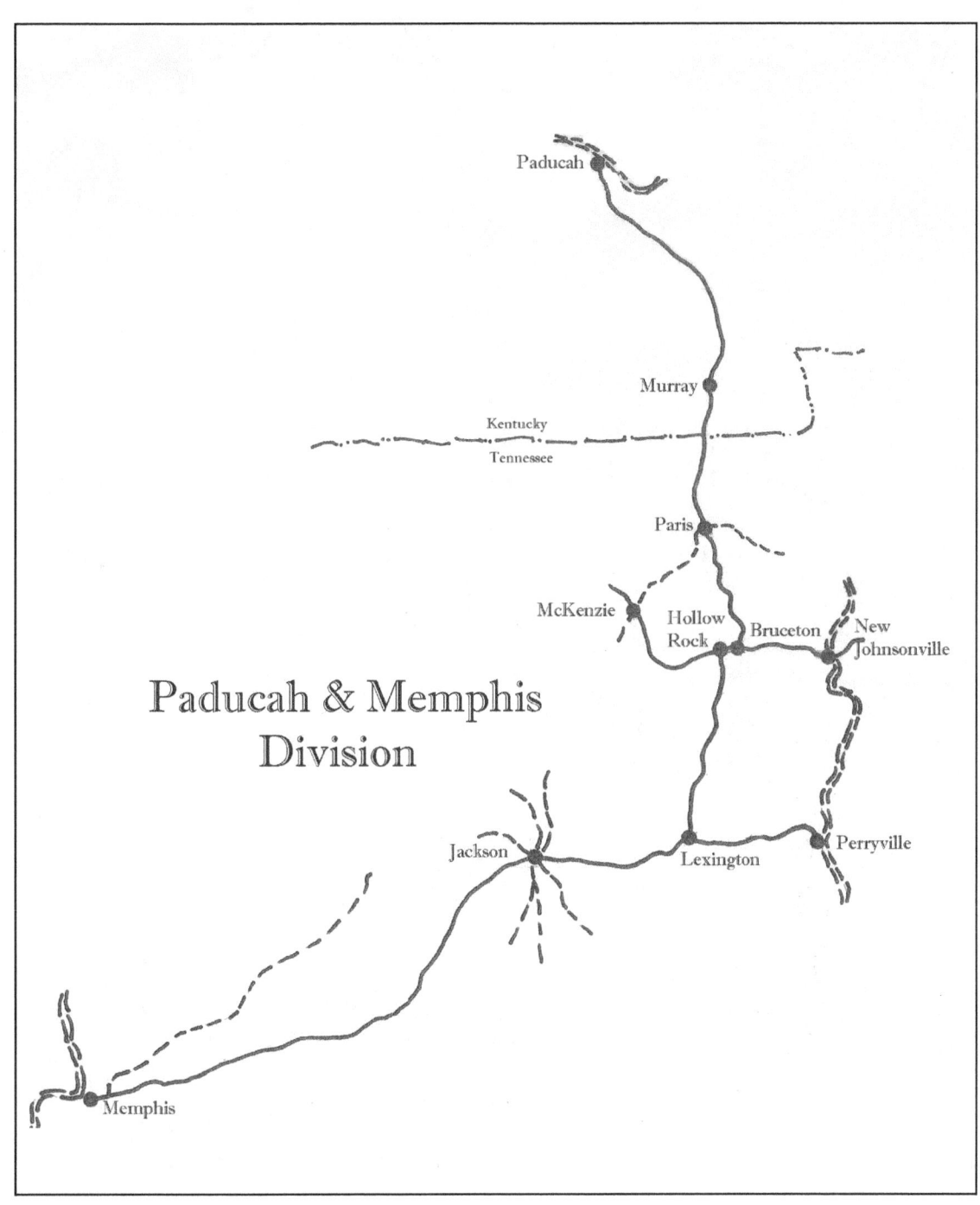

Paducah & Memphis Division Main Line

Almo, Kentucky Mile Marker 145.0, built 1911. -*Allen Hicks Collection*

Almo, Kentucky. It is thought that at least for a short while train tickets were sold from this business house. -*Terry L. Coats Collection*

Beech Bluff, Tennessee Mile Marker 142.0. -*Allen Hicks Collection*

Benton, Kentucky Mile Marker 160.0. -*Terry L. Coats Collection*

Buena Vista, Tennessee Mile Marker 101.0. -*National Archives*

Cordova, Tennessee Mile Marker 217.0, built 1885. In recent years the station was used as the county library. The station has been purchased privately and is being used as retail space. -*Tom R. Knowles photographer*

Memphis, Tennessee Mile Marker 235.0 Aulon Tower. -*National Archives*

Benton, Kentucky Freight Station. -*National Archives*

Benton, Kentucky Mile Marker 160.0 Passenger Station. -*National Archives*

Denmark, Tennessee Mile Marker 165.0. -*National Archives*

Dexter, Tennessee Mile Marker 147.0. -*National Archives*

Elva, Kentucky Mile Marker 168.0 Combination Station, built 1912. -*National Archives*

Hardin, Kentucky Freight Station. -*National Archives*

Hardin, Kentucky Mile Marker 152.0 Passenger Station. This small depot was part of a three building compound that included the station, a separate freighthouse, and a baggage house. -*National Archives*

Hatchie, Tennessee Mile Marker 172.0. -*National Archives*

Hazel, Kentucky Mile Marker 133.0 Passenger Depot, built 1911. -*National Archives*

Hazel, Kentucky Freight Platform. -*National Archives*

Huron, Tennessee Mile Marker 136.0. The Huron Station is shown here in original standardized Tennessee Midland Railway architecture. -*National Archives*

Jackson, Tennessee Freight Station. -*National Archives*

Jackson, Tennessee Passenger Station Mile Marker 152.0, built 1907. Prior to the opening of this station in 1907 the NC&St.L used the Tennessee Midland Railway depot built in 1888 as its Jackson station. With the construction of this station, the Tennessee Midland depot was moved approximately 200 yards east of its original location and was used as a general freight office. -*National Archives*

Laconia, Tennessee Mile Marker 188.0. -*National Archives*

Lenox, Tennessee Mile Marker 236.0. -*Tennessee State Library and Archives*

Luray, Tennessee Mile Marker 139.0. The station in Luray was originally built in 1891. The small double shed must have been the replacement for the original structure. -*Allen Hicks Collection*

Lexington, Tennessee Mile Marker 127.0, 1953 Depot. -*James Ozment photographer; -Western Rail Images Collection*

Mansfield, Tennessee Mile Marker 106.0. *-Michael Keipp Collection*

Murray, Kentucky Mile Marker 142.0. *-Terry L. Coats photographer*

Murray, Kentucky. This station was replaced by the Queen Anne depot shown in the upper right photo. *-National Archives*

Murray, Kentucky Freight Station. *-Terry L. Coats photographer*

Paducah Kentucky Freighthouse, ca. 1925. In 1917, the NC&St.L and the CB&Q jointly built a bridge between Metropolis, Illinois and Paducah, Kentucky. In anticipation of expanding the amount of traffic coming into Paducah over this bridge, the NC constructed this freighthouse. Included in the plans was space on the second floor for the division superintendent's office in addition to the local freight office and warehouse on the main floor. From the 1930s to the 1970s this freighthouse was the center for distribution of fruits and vegetables from all over the country. By 1974 the way the railroads handled produce changed radically and the warehouse closed. By late 1975 the warehouse was in private ownership and continued handling produce through the 1980s. By the early 1990s the railroad removed all tracks to the building and it was used as an antique mall. In 1996 the local chapter of the National Railway Historical Society was invited to use the second floor for their meeting and to open a museum. The building was sold and the museum moved to a nearby location.
-Paducah Railroad Museum

Paducah, Kentucky Freight Station. -*L&N Collection, University of Louisville*

Paducah, Kentucky Interior. -*Paducah Museum*

Paris, Tennessee Mile Marker 117.0, built 1903. This station still stands about 2 blocks from the courthouse square in Paris. At this writing, it is not in use. The last known application for the building was as an antique store. The track serving this station ran down the middle of one of the city's streets. -*Kenton Dickerson Collection*

Puryear, Tennessee Mile Marker 129.0. -*Terry L. Coats Collection*

Puryear, Tennessee Shelter. -*Tennessee State Library and Archives*

Paducah, Kentucky Mile Marker 182.0. Built in 1900, the Illinois Central and the NC&St.L Railway built this depot as a combination passenger station. It was razed in 1964. *-Terry L. Coats Collection*

Paducah, Kentucky Eight-stall Roundhouse. *-National Archives*

Somerville, Tennessee Mile Marker 195.0. *-L&N Collection, University of Louisville*

Somerville, Tennessee Freighthouse. *-National Archives*

Whiteville, Tennessee Mile Marker 181.0. The car to ther right served as a Railroad Post Office. *-Eric Fleet Collection*

Wildersville, Tennessee, ca.1950s. Shown here is the small passenger shed that replaced the older full size Tennessee Midland Station. *-Terry L. Coats Collection*

Wildersville, Tennessee Mile Marker 116.0, built 1923. *-Terry L. Coats Collection*

Yuma, Tennessee Mile Marker 111.0. This station survives today though severely altered from its original appearance in this photograph made in 1916. It is now privately owned and has been turned 90 degrees and moved back from the old right-of-way. As originally built, the structure was 77 feet, 10 inches in length. Today, after the baggage end of the station was removed it now measures a mere 32 feet, 6 inches. *-National Archives*

Early American Homestead in the South

Oakland, Tennessee Open Air Shed. *-National Archives*

Mercer, Tennessee Mile Marker 169.0. *-National Archives*

Oakland, Tennessee Mile Marker 205.0. *-National Archives*

Vildo, Tennessee Mile Marker 175.0. -*National Archives*

Timberlake, Tennessee Mile Marker 121.0.
-*National Archives*

Warren, Tennessee Mile Marker 201.0. -*National Archives*

Warren, Tennessee. -*Allen Hicks Collection*

Westport, Tennessee Mile Marker 107.0. Westport has been moved a short distance for its original location. Today it is still in the community and has several additions and serves as private residence. -*National Archives*

Wilderville, Tennessee Mile Marker 116.0. -*National Archives*

Van Dyke, Tennessee Mile Marker 110.0. -*Allen Hicks Collection*

Perryville Branch of the Paducah & Memphis Division

Chesterfield, Tennessee Mile Marker 135.0, built 1889-90. -*National Archives*

Beacon, Tennessee Mile Marker 140.0, built 1913. -*National Archives*

Bluff, Tennessee Mile Marker 131.0, built 1909. -*National Archives*

Parsons, Tennessee Mile Marker 144.0, ca. 1918. The original depot in Parsons was moved on a flatcar from Thompson Station on the mainline. It was a small structure, but large enough to sell tickets and to carry on rudimentary business. That station burned and this Tennessee Midland Station was built to replace it. -*Terry L. Coats Collection*

Perryville, Tennessee Mile Marker 151.0. -*National Archives*

Darden, Tennessee Mile Marker 138.0. -*National Archives*

Warrens Bluff, Tennessee (aka Bluff), built 1918. -*Terry L. Coats Collection*

Western & Atlantic Division

In the 1830s, before the coming of the railroad, Charleston, South Carolina was in direct competition with Mobile, Savannah and New Orleans as an export and import seaport. Charleston, however, was at a distinct disadvantage to the other three ports in that it was the only city not located at the mouth of a river. New Orleans, Mobile and Savannah received goods from inland via a waterway. Charleston, on the other hand, was forced to receive what it would ship by overland wagon. Charlestonians turned to the newly emerging railroad as an alternative to their lacking river traffic.

Atlanta car shed, 1864. -*National Archives*

Opening an additional seaport to Charleston would not only be a boom to the city but it would also be a boom to the farmers and industrialist who were shipping their products to market. Up to this time, New Orleans had a monopoly on most of the raw materials flowing in from the Mississippi Valley. Farmers from Tennessee, Mississippi, Kentucky, and Alabama used the connecting Cumberland, Tennessee and Ohio Rivers to ship down the Mississippi River to the Crescent City. Without the competition from any other shipping center, the brokers in New Orleans were free to hold down the prices paid for these raw materials and then to charge exorbitant prices for the same materials when they were shipped to the Northeast United States or abroad. The establishment of a competing route of trade from the mid south to the east coast would place the new port in direct competition with New Orleans, and in doing so, inflate the market in favor of the supplier and producer.

Seeking an inlet for commerce, Charleston was instrumental in helping charter the South Carolina, Canal & Railroad Company. By October 1833, the SCC&RC had constructed 135 miles of track west from Charleston to Hamburg, South Carolina. At that time it was the longest railroad in the world. Hamburg is located directly across the Savannah River from Augusta, Georgia. Augusta had long been a marketplace for north Georgia cotton commerce. The SCC&RC was eager to tap into the cotton shipping trade by giving the Georgia farmers a quick and economical outlet, first to the sea, and then to international markets. Up until that time, cotton had been loaded on packet boats and transported to Savannah down the Savannah River. With the building of the railroad across South Carolina, the cost per mile to ship the cotton to an ocean port was considerably reduced.

With a railroad built in South Carolina, it was now Georgia's turn to develop a railroad to push inward. Begun in Savannah in 1833, by 1836 the Georgia Railroad built west from a connection to the SCC&RC in Augusta to the city of Madison, Georgia. After a short hiatus, it was decided that they needed to connect to other railroads currently under construction toward the center of the state.

The building of a railroad to connect middle and northern Georgia to the sea had actually been an afterthought to the movers and shakers of antebellum Georgia. In 1826, Hamilton Fulton, Georgia State Engineer, and Wilson Lumpkin, a member of the Georgia Board of Public Works and later Governor of Georgia, set out from Savannah by horseback to map the best route for a *systematic plan of internal improvements*. At the time of their undertaking, the two envisioned a network of canals carrying goods from the Tennessee River in north Georgia to the seaport. The coming to the region of the railroad quashed the idea of building an expansive waterway and the state turned its attention to building a railroad from Savannah instead.

As American commerce grew, it became apparent to the states in the South that a coordinated effort was needed to develop a transportation system to link different parts of the country. A convention was held in Knoxville on July 4, 1836. The subject of this convention was the construction of a railroad that would connect ports in the Deep South to the river port in Cincinnati via Tennessee and Louisville. A battle ensued on the floor of the convention when different factions lobbied for the route of the proposed line to go though their part of the country. Both South Carolina and Georgia had told the attendees that they were willing to build a rail system across their respective state at the taxpayers' expense, but for Georgia delegates it was to no avail. Knoxville delegates held the convention in upper East Tennessee because they wanted the rail lines to come through Knoxville and along with Louisville and Charleston came away as winners when the final vote was taken. It was decided that the road would be built from Charleston up the French Broad River to Asheville, North Carolina and through Knoxville to Louisville and Cincinnati.

The delegates from Chattanooga, Savannah, and Georgia were furious over the vote at the convention. Not to be out done, in November of that same year, the state of Georgia held its own railroad convention in Macon. At that convention the Georgia legislature was asked to approve funds to build a railroad that would be owned and operated entirely by the state. In a report to the legislators, a committee recommended that a railroad should be built to connect central Georgia to a place called, "Ross' Landing, Tennessee or some neighboring point on the Tennessee River." This location was chosen because Ross' Landing was the first available point at which the Tennessee River cleared the southern range of the Cumberland Mountains and would facilitate a landing point of railroad and river.

On December 21, 1836, Georgia Governor Schley signed an act authorizing the building of the railroad, funds were approved and soon the newly chartered Western & Atlantic Railroad was building north toward Tennessee. The Western & Atlantic was so named by the legislature of the state of Georgia with aspirations of connecting the Atlantic Ocean to railheads upon rivers that lead to the great expanses of the Western United States.

About the same time, the Central Georgia Railroad, later the Georgia Railroad and Banking Company, was taking shape as the route of some very prime railroad property. The Georgia Railroad began to push westward from Madison, Georgia. Likewise, the Monroe Railroad, later to be called the Macon & Western, located in Forsyth, Georgia began building north toward the terminus of the W&A.

The W&A began construction on July 4, 1837, but to a slow start. All railroad building, as was almost all commerce in the state, was affected greatly by a national business setback known as the *Panic of 1837*. Between 1837 and 1840, construction on all Georgia railroads crawled to an almost complete stop. The W&A only managed to complete some surveying and grading north of Marietta during that four year period. Not to put to waste, in Marietta, the efforts made in grading the right-of-way in an unused section of roadbed became a horse racetrack until construction could be resumed. It was not until 1841 that construction began again in earnest on all the lines.

Corporate offices for the W&A were located in Marietta with the railroad running between a northern terminus at Ross' Landing, Tennessee, later to be renamed Chattanooga, and a southern terminus approximately twenty miles south of Marietta. This southern end of the line was given the non-descript name of *Terminus*.

By the fall of 1842, the rail lines between Marietta and Terminus (now known as Atlanta) had been completed and arrangements were made to have a locomotive delivered to the railroad from Madison, Georgia. The locomotive *Florida* was brought as far as Madison, which was at that time the terminus of the Georgia Railroad. A sixteen mule team then transported the locomotive and a boxcar overland in time to make its inaugural run from Terminus to Marietta on December 24, 1842.

As the W&A prospered and the community around Terminus grew, a proper name was needed to replace the outmoded moniker. With the linking of the Georgia Railroad and the Monroe Railroad to the W&A, the location was no longer a terminus, but had now become a junction point and, thus, the name Terminus was no longer appropriate. In the 1840s, the former governor of Georgia, the honorable Wilson Lumpkin, was now the Disbursing Agent for the W&A. Lumpkin had a daughter by the name of Martha. On December 23, 1843, to honor the Lumpkin family the name of Terminus was officially changed to Marthasville. The ten to twelve families that inhabited the area around Marthasville approved of the name and Marthasville incorporated. It was now a city proper consisting of two stores, a saw mill, and a railroad office. So small was the town and so poor were the residents, no one there would be able to justify the building of a church. Yet, there was a need for religious services for those who lived in the area so, when not in use by the railroad, the Western & Atlantic office building was used for church services.[136]

---

136   *History of Atlanta, Georgia*. Edited by Wallace Putman Reed. 1889.

The name of Marthasville would be short lived. John Edgar Thomson was the chief civil engineer for the Georgia Railroad. He was instrumental in laying out the routes of the Western & Atlantic to Chattanooga and later the initial route of the Nashville & Chattanooga. Thomson envisioned a great city one day emerging from the hamlet where the Georgia, the Monroe (Macon & Western), and the Western & Atlantic Railroads converged. In his opinion, the name Marthasville was simply too countrified and provincial to be the name of a great city. Thomson considered the name Atlanta; the feminized version of the word Atlantic from the Western & Atlantic, sounded like a much more proper name and suggested that the name be changed. The name caught on and the name was officially changed from Marthasville to Atlanta by the Georgia legislature in December 1847.

On December 22, 1843, the state legislature approved work to north of the Etowah River. Within a short time, the W&A built a depot near the Cooper Furnace Works and the town of Etowah was established. As the W&A worked its way northward, small towns began to spring up along the right-of-way. In many cases, the railroad was such a vital connection for these small towns that *instead of the railroad coming to the town, the town would come to the railroad.* When the Adairsville depot was built a half-mile from the city center, the city fathers elected to move the town to the depot. When the W&A passed close to, but not through the town of Rome, it was not possible to move the town. Seeking the next best solution they built an 18 mile short line to Kingston and there created a rail yard connection to the W&A. In 1847, the W&A had reached Cross Keys, Georgia. Shortly after building a depot, Cross Keys changed its name to Dalton and the town limits were defined as a one-mile circumference from that depot.

The first train moved across Georgia into Chattanooga on December 1, 1849. To make the run, the W&A had to shuttle train passengers and freight around the yet to be completed tunnel at Tunnel Hill, Georgia. The arriving train from Atlanta brought passengers to the southern side of Chetoogetta Mountain … the last obstacle to completing the line between the cities. The engine and cars were portaged around the mountain and the passengers and freight taken by carriage and wagon to the tracks on the other side. At that point, the passengers re-boarded the train to continue the trip to their destination. Over the coming months two construction crews pecked their way toward each other from the two sides of the mountains. A breakthrough was finally accomplished and a train finally traversed the entire line from Terminal to Ross' Landing on May 9, 1850.[137]

The Western & Atlantic was the link between two cities that would become synonymous with the term *railroad town*. It can be said that neither Chattanooga nor Atlanta would have existed had they not been rail centers. The Western & Atlantic was the anchor rail line in both cities to which other lines would connect. By 1845, the Georgia Railroad had linked with the W&A in Terminus, Georgia. At 173 miles in length, it was the longest railroad

---

137   Gilbert E. Govan, *The Chattanooga Union Station*. Tennessee Historical Quarterly, Volume 29. 1970.

in the world at the time, and in February 1854, the Nashville & Chattanooga steamed into Chattanooga. That same year, the fourth rail line, the Atlanta & LaGrange Railroad (later the Atlanta & West Point Railroad), entered Atlanta from the southwest. There was now a completed rail system from Nashville to the sea with Atlanta as a major hub.

Western & Atlantic during the Civil War

The W&A had a very vivid history in the War years between 1861 and 1865. With the fall of the city of Nashville in 1862 and the withdrawal of the Confederate Army from Murfreesboro to Tullahoma, and eventually to Chattanooga, Confederate General Braxton Bragg was following the path of the Nashville & Chattanooga Railroad on his withdrawal into the Bluff City. After the battles of Lookout Mountain and Missionary Ridge, Chattanooga fell in November 1863. Again, the Army of Tennessee, now under the command of General Joseph E. Johnston, was forced to retreat, this time toward Atlanta. This retreat followed directly down the Western & Atlantic. After leaving Chattanooga, General Johnston fell back through north Georgia to Ringgold, Adairsville, Dalton, and eventually Kennesaw Mountain overlooking the tracks. At Kennesaw Mountain, Johnston would turn and make a stand of resistance. Even while in retreat, General Johnston understood the importance of this railroad and he never ventured from this vital line of communication and supply.

As the Army of Tennessee was about to enter Atlanta on July 18, 1864, General Johnston was called back to Richmond to join President Davis' staff as an advisor. In his stead, Davis assigned Lieutenant General John Bell Hood. By the time General Hood established his army in Atlanta, the railroad behind him all the way to the north lay in control of the Federals. General William T. Sherman used the railroads abandoned by the Confederates as his primary supply line. Sherman used the L&N, N&C, and the W&A back to Nashville and beyond to build up the materiel he needed to track down Hood's besieged army in defense of Atlanta.

Hood realized the tenuous situation Sherman was in by having his supply line relying on a 250 mile long single main back to Nashville. He knew that his only hope of counteracting Sherman's stranglehold on Atlanta was to cut the Federal railroad supply line. In early August Hood dispatched *Fighting* General Joe Wheeler and his cavalry north to cut the lines of the W&A and the N&C. Wheeler and his horsemen were able to burn the bridge over the Etowah River as well as destroying about 35 miles of Yankee iron. For a short while, the Confederate flag flew again over northern Georgia rail.

The repair of 35 miles of track was made in short order by the United States Military Railroad. The repair, maintenance, and improvement of the rapidly deteriorating T-rail became a problem. The South had not produced a single piece of rail and had imported only a minute amount of rail from overseas since 1861. By 1864, the lines of the N&C and the W&A

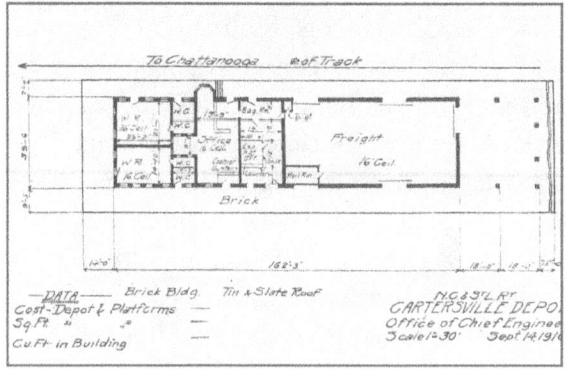

Cartersville Depot (top) & Floor Plan (bottom)

were in very poor shape. Many of the smaller branch lines feeding these two roads had been closed and the rail used on mainlines. With heavy traffic south of Nashville, the Federals were punishing the rails at an alarming rate. To accommodate the extra load, they replaced the old U-rail the N&C and the W&A had used to build their lines with T-rail; extended many sidings, and enlarged water stations. Additionally, Confederate raids against the Tennessee and Georgia railroads were a constant thorn in the side of the Federals. From 1864 to 1865 alone, the cost of repair was over four million dollars. The Yankees had to rebuild some of the bridges as many as five times as a result of raids and washouts.

In the early part of the Atlanta campaign the supply of materiel over the Nashville to Chattanooga to Atlanta route was so heavy that General Burnside and General Sherman were forced to divert return traffic north over a different route. Instead of sending the trains over the N&C from Chattanooga, they were sent to Stevenson, then 80 miles east over the Memphis and Charleston Railroad to Decatur, Alabama, then north 120 miles over the Nashville and Decatur Railroad to Nashville. This route was almost 90 miles farther than the conventional route, but it was necessary.

During the height of the campaign the W&A moved 100,000 men and 35,000 horses over a period of 196 days. The W&A received shipments from the L&N and N&C from Nashville, the East Tennessee & Georgia out of Knoxville, and over the Memphis & Charleston from Mississippi and Alabama. These movements by train replaced tens of thousands of mules and wagons that would have been needed to transport men, supplies, and livestock. General Sherman would write in his memoirs after the War that, "The Atlanta Campaign would simply have been impossible without the railroads…"[138]

The standoff in Atlanta between General Sherman and General Hood lasted from July to September 1864. During the siege, as the Federals increased their stranglehold on the Confederates, the W&A, the Georgia Railroad, and the Macon & Western Railroads all fell to Yankee occupation. Only the Atlanta & West Point Railroad to the southwest of Atlanta

---

138   Thomas Weber, *The Northern Railroads in the Civil War 1861-1865*. Page 199.

stayed in Confederate hands. It was over this line that the citizenry and the Army evacuated south from the city after its fall. With the evacuation of Hood toward Tennessee, all railroads in Georgia were now in Federal hands.

GEORGIA POLITICS AND THE RAILROADS

Rufus Bullock, a transplanted New Yorker, was in 1860 working as the manager of the Augusta, Southern Express Company. After the War he became president of the Macon and Augusta Railroad. Seeking higher aspirations, Bullock resigned his railroad positions to run against Confederate General John B. Gordon, a Democrat, for the office of Georgia Governor. Bullock was elected and took office in 1868.

It has often been said that power corrupts and the administration of Governor Bullock was truly no exception to this adage. Bullock made a point of surrounding himself with political cronies. One of those cronies was Foster Blodgett, a radical member of the Republican Party. To keep Blodgett close at hand, Bullock appointed him as Superintendent of the Western & Atlantic Railroad. Unfortunately, Blodgett, Bullock's political *yes man*, knew little or nothing about the operation of a railroad. Within a short time after taking control of the railroad, Blodgett went about dismissing hundreds of long time W&A employees. One of those included in the mass dismissal was William A. Fuller, hero of the *Great Locomotive Chase*.

Blodgett's radical manner of operating the state owned W&A raised the ire of Georgia legislators. In 1870, the legislators took control of the railroad and then dictated to Governor Bullock that he was to find a *qualified operator* to take control of the W&A and he was to lease the line to that operator.[139] On December 27, 1870 after some political wrangling, Governor Bullock accepted a twenty year lease from a group of operators that included former Georgia Governor Joseph Brown and Confederate Vice President Alexander H. Stevens.

Twenty years later, as the lease entered into by Governor Brown and his associates was drawing to an end. It had cost the Brown compendium $25,000 per year to lease the W&A. Thinking this amount to be entirely too small, the Georgia legislators would up the ante for the new lease. The new minimum requirement the state would accept for the new lease would be $35,000 per year for a period of 20 years, $40,000 for a period of 30 years, and $50,000 per year for a 50 year term. The higher dollar amounts required by the state effectively eliminated smaller investors like Governor Brown's group and opened the bidding to only larger investors.

After the bidding closed only two companies, the Richmond & Danville, and the Nashville, Chattanooga & St. Louis had presented an offer for the lease. When the bids were

---

139   Les R. Winn, *Ghost Trains and Depots of Georgia*. Page 88.

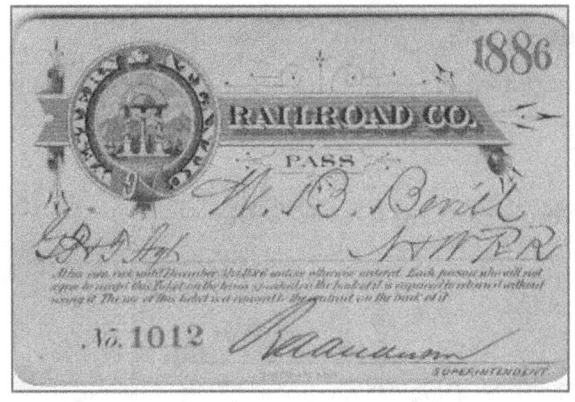

1886 Western & Atlantic Railroad Pass. -*Dain L. Schult Collection*

opened, the Richmond & Danville had offered $35,000 for a lease of 29 years. The offer from the NC&St.L was $35,001 for the same 29 year.

Was the $35,000 plus $1.00 bid an almost miraculous guess ... probably not? Some years before, the NC&St.L had helped the Southern Railroad gain entrance into Chattanooga. It had long been assumed that the Southern had prior knowledge concerning the Richmond & Danville bid and had given inside information to the NC&St.L for their help with the Chattanooga dealings. Whatever the case, the NC&St.L had fulfilled a dream of NC&St.L president Cole and had procured passage into Atlanta. Unfortunately, by the time the NC gained control of the Western & Atlantic, Cole had long since been deposed as president and the L&N owned the NC&St.L.

Locomotive #582 at Atlanta, Georgia. -*Marietta Museum of History*

Vinning, Georgia Locomotive #569, ca. 1948. -*Nashville, Chattanooga & St. Louis Railway*

The Atlanta Division of the NC would serve the railroad well. In the 1920s and 1930s, it would be over these tracks that some of America's most pristine trains, the Dixie Trains would run. First-class, Pullman service between Chicago and Florida upon the Dixie Flyer or the Dixie Limited was without a peer. Even the coach service on the Dixie Express was certainly the talk of the town.

In the 1940s this section of rail would become one of the heaviest traveled and most important in the United States. As America entered WWII, massive amounts of troops, materiel, and fuel oil traveled over these rails from the Midwest to the east coast to embark to Europe. So heavy was the traffic that the NC&St.L purchased twenty of the 4-8-4, J3 steam engines in 1942-3. Additionally, in order to relieve wartime congestion south of Chattanooga, the company installed CTC (Centralized Traffic Control) signaling systems from Cartersville to Atlanta, Georgia. In 1943, a portion of the Atlanta Division was used by both the L&N and the NC&St.L for egress into Atlanta and was the most heavily used portion of the entire line. On an average day, there would be some 50 to 65 trains, including six passenger trains and three fast freights, scheduled over the line between

Junta just outside Cartersville and the Hills Park Yard in Atlanta. The NC was bringing traffic south from Nashville and the L&N had two divisions spilling trains onto NC tracks at this gateway as well. The NC installed signals on 41 miles of single and 2 miles of double track to reduce congestion and to speed the movement of the trains. Today this line still remains one of the heaviest prowled lines in the country.

Rome Railroad

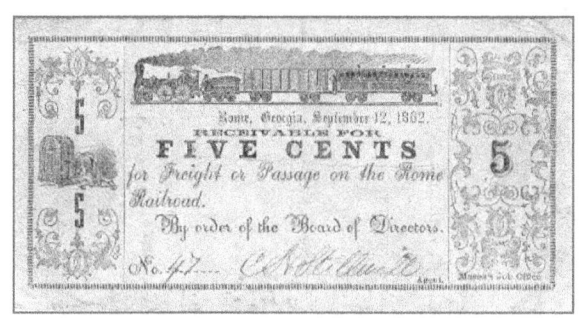

Rome Railroad 5¢ Voucher. Good for transportation on the Rome Railroad between Rome and Kingston, Georgia.
-Terry L. Coats Collection

When the state legislature announced that they would construct the state owned W&A Railroad between Atlanta and the Tennessee River, the businessmen of Rome recognized the economic impact connecting to the line. The new line had bypassed Rome by a few miles. To make the connection to the Western & Atlantic, the Memphis Branch Railroad & Steamship Company of Georgia built a branch railroad 18 miles long between Rome and Kingston, Georgia, which was completed in December 1849. In Kingston the MBRR&SSCO terminated in a yard and there connected with the W&A. It seems that the Memphis Branch Railroad & Steamship Company was just too much of a mouthful for most people to say so in 1850 the name of the railroad was changed to the Rome Railroad. Kingston became a focal point along the W&A with its connection and yard interchanging with the Rome Railroad.

During the War Between the States, the Rome Railroad played an essential role for both armies. There were extensive factories and a machine shop located in Rome that was used by the Confederates. During the 1862 Great Locomotive Chase, James Andrews and his men were almost captured when they were forced to delay at Kingston for well over an hour waiting for traffic to clear. The Andrews raiders only pulled out on the stolen *General* five minutes before the arrival of William Fuller and the pursuers. Fuller was forced to abandon his pursuit engine in Kingston and it was on the Rome Railroad's engine *William R. Smith* that he continued the chase north of Kingston. In July 1864, the line was taken over by the USMRR. The road was used by the Federals to ferry soldiers to the Battle of Allatoona Pass.

During the 1880s and 1890s the Rome Railroad had a fairly significant operation. They ran two passenger trains each day to and from their eastern terminus at Kingston as well as having a substantial freight business servicing the industries in Rome.

In 1896 the NC&St.L purchased the Rome Railroad. The purchase was made despite the fact the state of Georgia lessee of the W&A would more than likely never sell that line to the NC.

The NC&St.L operated the Rome Railroad as one of its branches. At the request of the U. S. Government, this line was closed as a conservation matter during WWII. The last train ran on this branch in October 1943; shortly afterward the line was closed.

Map of the Western & Atlantic Division

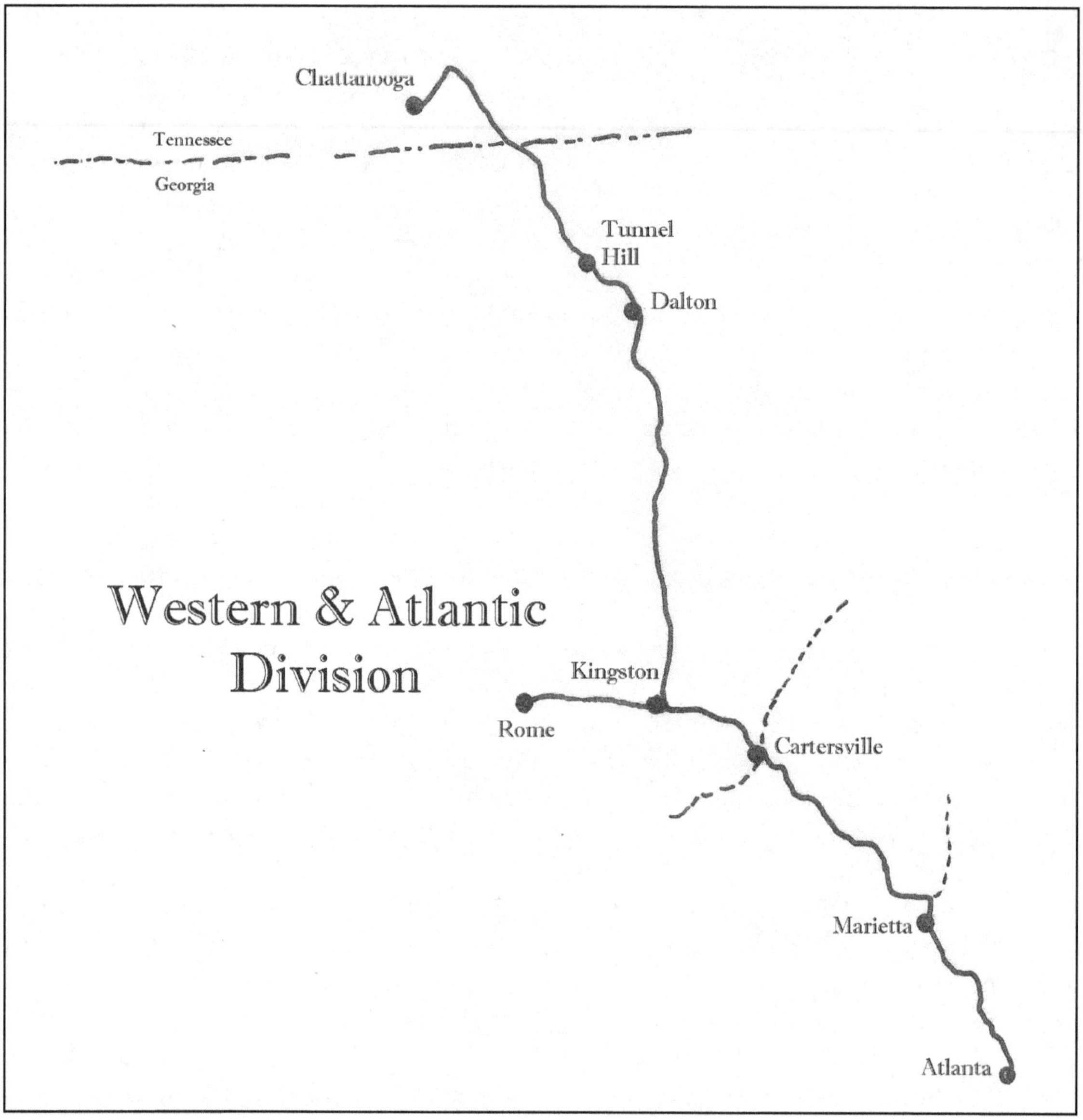

WESTERN & ATLANTIC MAIN LINE

Acworth, Georgia Mile Marker 254.0. The Acworth station still stands, though today it is in two pieces. As was common after the closing of these depots, the passenger and the freight ends of the depot were separated from one another. -*National Archives*

Adairsville, Georgia Mile Marker 220.0. The Western & Atlantic Railroad built this beautiful old station in 1891. Adairsville was a major repair center for the W&A Railroad. It was from this station that the locomotive Texas joined in the Great Locomotive Chase. Today this station serves as a Welcome Center for the city of Adairsville. -*Adairsville History Center Collection*

Boyce, Tennessee Mile Marker 155.0. -*Tennessee State Library and Archives*

Brookmont, Georgia Mile Marker 276.0. -*National Archives*

Calhoun, Georgia Mile Marker 211.0, built 1854. Restored a few years ago to its former grandeur, the station is used today for community events and meetings. -*National Archives*

Cartersville, Georgia Mile Marker 241.0. The Cartersville Depot is currently serving the city as its Downtown Development Authority offices and as the Cartersville and Barton County Visitors Bureau. -*National Archives*

Cass, Georgia Mile Marker 236.0, ca. 1854. Cass was originally a water and wood station on the W&A Railroad. Though no longer standing, note the standardization the W&A created between this station and the ones at Cass, Ringgold, and Tunnel Hill. The latter two are still with us. This photo of Cass was made around 1916. -*National Archives*

Cave, Georgia Mile Marker 233.0. This small wood structure is shown in a 1916 photograph. -*National Archives*

Chickamauga, Tennessee Mile Marker 162.0. -*Tennessee State Library and Archives*

Dalton, Georgia Freight Station. The W&A RR built the Dalton station in 1852. Today it is used as an upscale restaurant. Of interest is a plaque in the floor of the station indicating at its location is the exact center of the town. -*National Archives*

Dalton, Georgia Mile Marker 189.0 Passenger and Baggage Station (aka Crossplains). -*National Archives*

Emerson, Georgia Mile Marker 246.0. This station was originally called Stegall. Shown in this photo is the station agent's house and general store at Stegall. -*Joe Bozeman Collection*

Gilmore, Georgia Mile Marker 279.0, ca. 1916. Shown are a small passenger shed and a water tower. -*National Archives*

Gilmore, Georgia Freight Station. -*National Archives*

Junta, Georgia. -*National Archives*

Kennesaw, Georgia Mile Marker 260.0 1917 Depot, built 1893. In 1862, Kennesaw was known as Big Shanty. It was from this location that on April 12, 1862 a group of Yankee saboteurs stole a train of the Western & Atlantic Railroad with the intent of burning bridges and disrupting rail traffic between Atlanta and Chattanooga. Today the restored station is a museum and is used for city activities. -*Joe Bozeman Collection*

Kennesaw, Georgia Depot with Water Tank. Shown are the depot, water tower and the original W&A depots. -*Joe Bozeman Collection*

Kennesaw, Georgia Depot, ca. 1900. This photograph depicts the nineteenth century Kennesaw depot that may have been the first depot in town. This structure can be seen as the white building in the center of photo at left. -*Joe Bozeman Collection*

Kingston, Georgia Mile Marker 230.0, built 1911. This station was built to replace the previous station that burned. Kingston was the intersection of the W&A and the Rome Railroads. On the date of the Great Locomotive Chase, it was in Kingston that W&A conductor William Fuller almost caught his stolen train arriving just minutes after the General and its train steamed away. *-Adairsville History Depot Collection*

Marietta, Georgia Mile Marker 269.0 Passenger Depot, built 1898. This station today serves as the Marietta Visitors Welcome Center. It stands beside the Kennesaw House Hotel. It was in the Kennesaw House that saboteurs of the Great Locomotive Chase spent the night before boarding the train the following morning. *-Terry L. Coats Collection*

Marietta, Georgia Noonday Tower. This tower was identical to the one at Bass, Alabama. *-Allen Hicks Collection*

Marietta, Georgia Queen Anne Style Freighthouse. *-L&N Collecation, University of Louisville*

Resaca, Georgia Mile Marker 205.0. *-National Archives*

Ringgold, Georgia Mile Marker 174.0, built 1849. Ringgold is the oldest station still remaining of those built by the Western & Atlantic Railroad. This stone building still shows the battle scars from the Civil War. It was in Ringgold that James Andrews and the raiders of the locomotive General abandoned the stolen train in 1862. Today the station has been restored and serves the city for civic meetings. *-Terry L. Coats photographer*

Rogers, Georgia Mile Marker 239.0. -*National Archives*

Smyrna, Georgia Mile Marker 274.0, built 1906. -*Joe Bozeman Collection*

Tilton Georgia Mile Marker 198.0, built 1900. -*National Archives*

Tunnel Hill, Georgia Mile Marker 182.0. The Tunnel Hill station still stands just north of the famous W&A and the NC&St.L tunnels though Chetoogetta Mountain. Until recently, this station was used as part of a milling operation. -*Terry L. Coats Collection*

Vinning, Georgia Mile Marker 278.0, built 1896. -*National Archives*

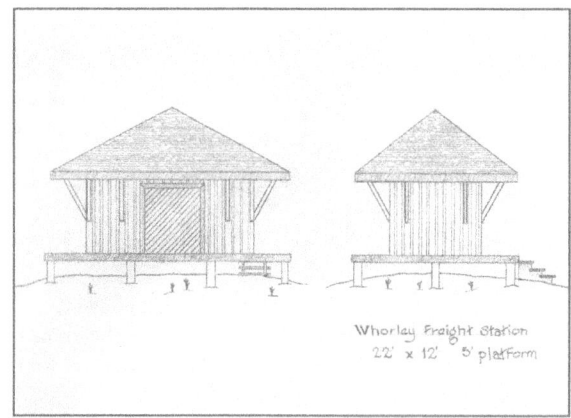
Whorley, Tennessee Mile Marker 153.0. This small station sat at the area near the current intersection of I-75 and East Brainerd Road in Chattanooga. -*Drawing by Terry L. Coats*

Rome Branch of the Western & Atlantic Division

Bass, Alabama Mile Marker 106.0, ca. 1916. This tower is identical to the one found at Marietta, Georgia and referred to as the Noonday Tower. -*National Archives*

Rome, Georgia Mile Marker 248.0. This station replaced an earlier one built in 1897. Rome was the home base of the Rome Railroad, a short line bought and operated by the NC&St.L. The Rome Railroad intersected the W&A at Kingston, Georgia.
-*National Archives*

Adaptive Uses

Though the Nashville, Chattanooga & St. Louis Railway ceased operations over fifty years ago, today there are over sixty railroad depots, a round house, a countless amount of section houses as well as other railway structures still in existence. These structures can be found spread entirely across what was the original railroad system. These structures can be found in every condition from abandoned and sorely in need of rescue, to fully restored and fully functional.

Almost without exception, all the remaining structures have lived on to find a rejuvenated use. The Bruceton roundhouse is but a shell of its former self and today sits empty and gutted, but all other known structures are in use serving some secondary purpose.

In 2009, there were several old NC&St.L depots still in the ownership of the CSX Railroad. The depots at Tullahoma, Dickson, Murfreesboro and McKenzie are still owned by the CSX and continue in service to that railroad as storage, maintenance of way, or as crew facilities. The remaining structures are in private, corporate, or municipal ownership.

Elva, Kentucky Section House. -*Terry L Coats photographer*

The depot in Lyle, Tennessee is part of a rehabilitation center. The depots at Victoria, Westport, DeRossett, Rock Island, and Centerville, Tennessee are private residences. The latter two are unique in that one is rental property, the other as a bed and breakfast guesthouse.

Most of the privately owned buildings are currently used for storage. The depots at Kelso, Belfast, Belvidere, Quebeck, Orme, Yuma, Greeley, and Leeville, Tennessee are being used for that purpose.

A gentleman in Sparta is using an old telephone booth that once served the Price's Station area as a very small storage shed. His parents bought the Bon Air depot from the railroad after that line was abandoned. They disassembled the structure and loaded it board by board into a boxcar they leased from the NC. After transporting the material down the mountain, they parked the boxcar on a siding, unloaded it, and built a house using the parts of the old station. This house still stands.

Centerville, Tennessee Today the Centerville depot has been moved to Duck River, Tennessee. It is now used as bed and breakfast lodging. -*Terry L. Coats photographer*

Other depots have been purchased by the cities in which they were located and are being used for municipal or civic purposes. There are chambers of commerce in the depots at Hohenwald and Jasper; Shelbyville is an adult education center. The station in Sparta, Tennessee was converted and is now being used as offices and storage for a gasoline distribution business. The Winchester station is the Franklin County Roads Commission office. The Lebanon depot is also part of a business.

DeRossett, Tennessee Mile Marker 141.0 built 1904, enlarged 1911. This photograph depicts the station as it stood in its original location. -*Bob Bell Collection*

Tucker's Gap on the abandoned Nashville to Lebanon branch was purchased at auction in the summer of 2005 and was relocated to the Wilson County fairgrounds in Lebanon. Over the next year, the depot was restored to the way it looked at the time it was constructed in 1870s. In August 2006, this beautiful little building, the smallest NC&St.L station in Middle Tennessee, was dedicated to the people of Wilson County and has taken its place along with other historic buildings from Wilson County in the reconstructed village of *Fiddlers Grove*. The station now houses a collection of NC&St.L memorabilia and a model train layout. In 2008, the county purchased a caboose and moved it next to the Tucker's Gap station. Though not a NC&St.L caboose, it is painted in NC&St.L lettering.

DeRossett, Tennessee, ca. late 1990s. This station was moved to Fairfield Glade Resort from its original location and for a number of years the old depot was used as the clubhouse on the resort's golf course. -*Terry L. Coats Collection*

The depots at Jackson and Cowan, Tennessee, Marietta and Kennesaw, Georgia, Chase and Guntersville, Alabama, and the old freight depot in Paducah, Kentucky are now railway museums.

Nashville's Union Station traveled a very arduous road toward destruction before finally being saved from the wrecking ball. The station went into a steep decline after World War II that continued to the eventual condemning of the building in 1975. After suffering through several

DeRossett, Tennessee Station extensively reworked, ca. 2007. The DeRossett station in its third reincarnation as a private residence in Crossville, Tennessee. -*Terry L. Coats photographer*

Quebeck, Tennessee. *-Terry L. Coats photographer*

Tuckers Gap at Wilson Co. Fairgrounds *-Terry L. Coats photographer*

Hobbs Island, Alabama. Shown in this photograph is the station as it appears today. It was moved from Hobbs Island to New Market, Alabama where it currently serves as a beautifully refurbished guesthouse to a private residence. *-Terry L. Coats photographer*

changes of ownership and continuing years of neglect, 1985 saw a turn of fortune and new life when developers revitalized the building for use as a hotel.

It is unfortunate that we have lost the majority of our old depots and terminals. On the other hand, it is comforting to know that even though the NC&St.L closed for business over fifty years ago, there are so many of these old buildings that have been saved and are in use in such diverse ways.

One of the most numerous structures to survive into the twenty-first century would be the NC&St.L section houses. These section houses built as company housing for the track repair and construction gangs have long since passed into the private sector. Many of these stoic buildings are still used for residential purposes and were constructed before 1900, making them some of the oldest structures to survive.

Some of the oldest stations to serve the NC&St.L are among those that have survived. The Western & Atlantic Railroad built these stations dating back to 1849. The stations in northern Georgia were participates in the famous 1962 silver screen movie *Great Locomotive Chase*. The surviving stations are the Acworth – now abandoned and cut into two pieces, Adairsville – used as a welcome center, Calhoun – used for community meetings, Dalton freight house – now a restaurant, Tunnel Hill – previously used as part of a business, Cartersville – now a welcome center, Kennesaw – a museum, Marietta – now a visitor center, and Ringgold - used as a community center. The communities along this section of the NC&St.L can be proud of their preservation efforts that saved their depots.

ELEVATION DRAWINGS

Atlanta Watch Shanty and Drawing.
-*Nashville, Chattanooga & St. Louis Railway*

Atlanta Watch Shanty Drawing Front and Side Elevations. -*Drawing by Terry L. Coats*

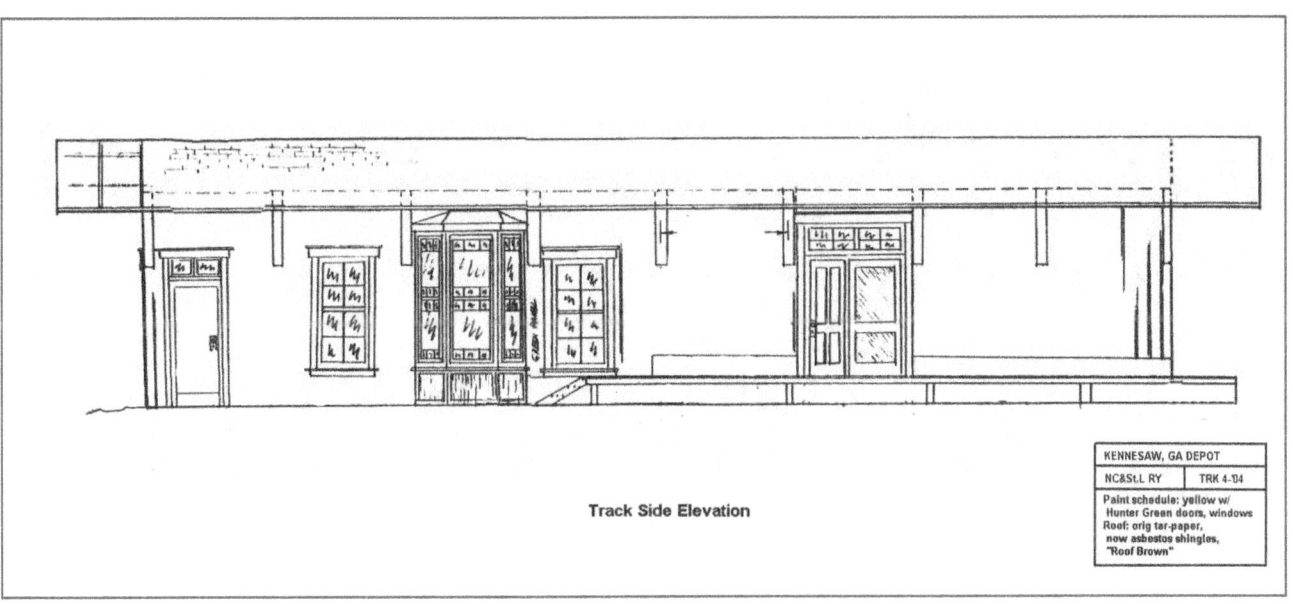

NC&St.L Station, Kennesaw, Georgia. Front Elevation. -*Drawing by Tom R. Knowles*

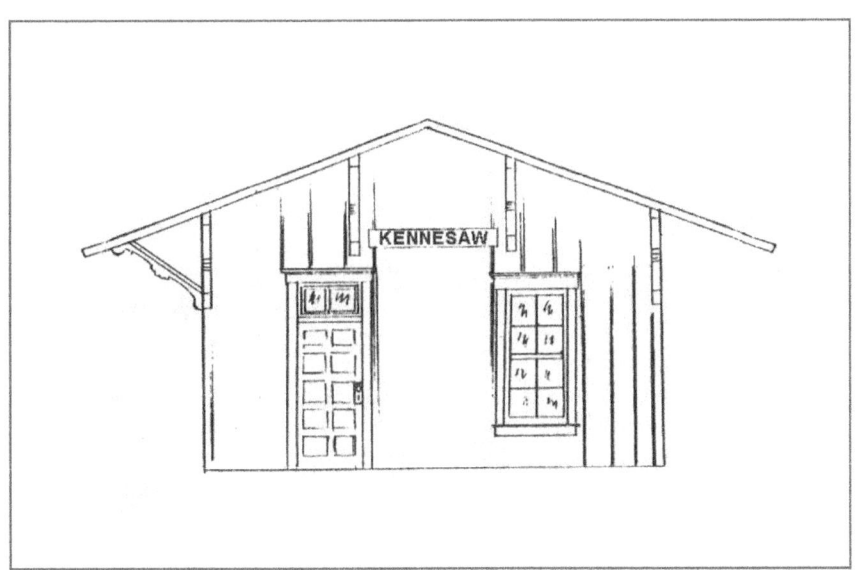

NC&St.L Station, Kennesaw, Georgia. End Elevation. -*Drawing by Tom R. Knowles*

NC&St.L Station, Craggie Hope, Tennessee. Front Elevation. -*Drawing by Terry L. Coats*

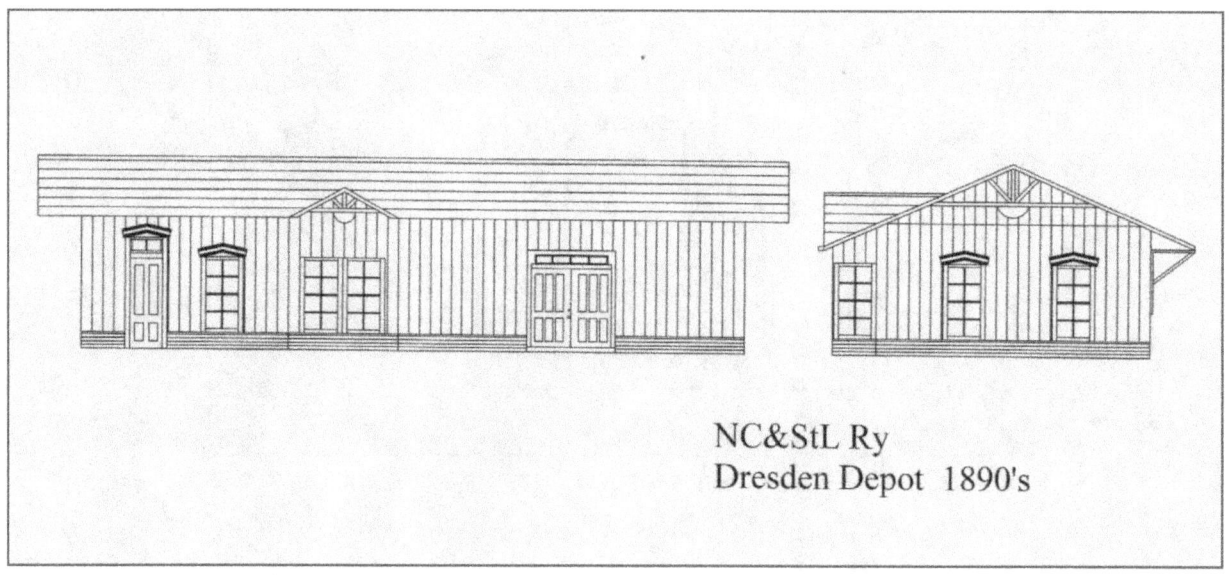

N&NW Station, Dresden, Tennessee. Front and Side Elevations. -*Drawing by Mark Perry*

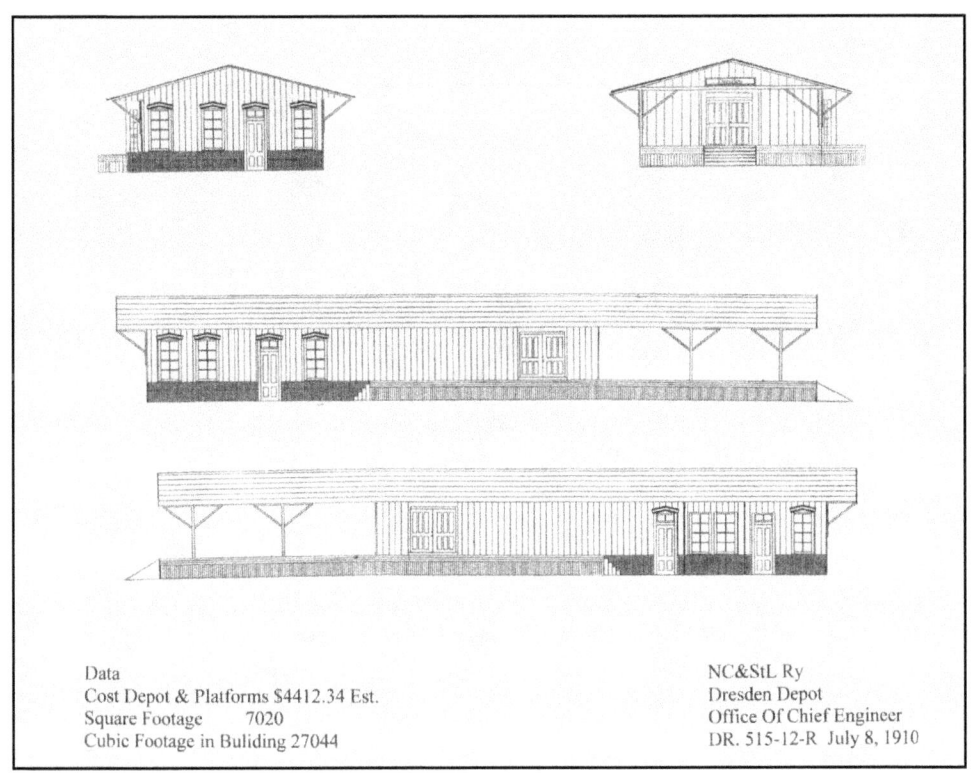

NC&St.L Station, Dresden, Tennessee. Front, Rear and Side Elevations. *-Drawing by Mark Perry*

NC&St.L Station, Hardin, Kentucky. Front, Rear and Side Elevations. *-Drawing by Terry L. Coats*

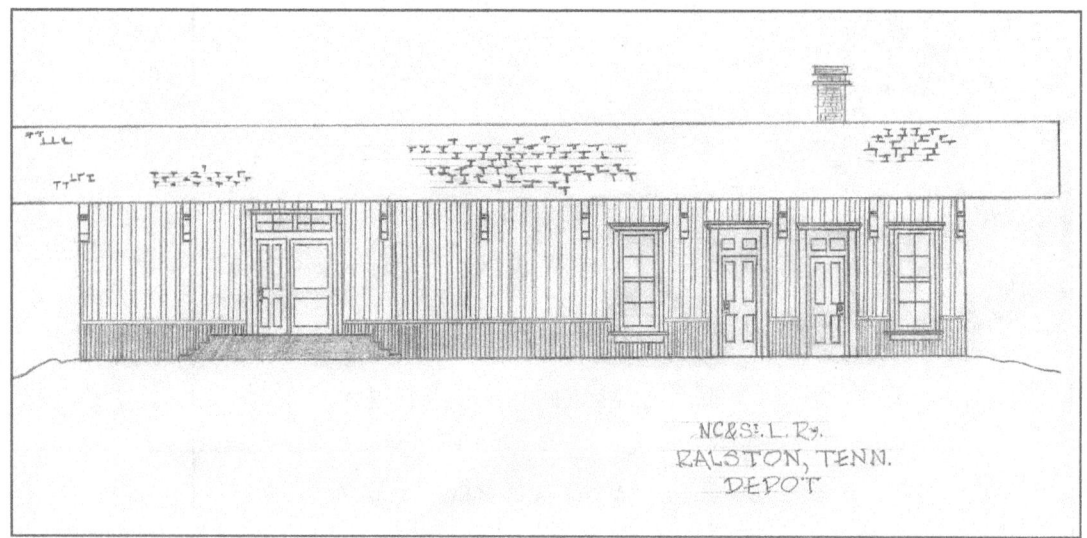

NC&St.L Station, Ralston, Tennessee. Front and Side Elevations. -*Drawing by Terry L. Coats*

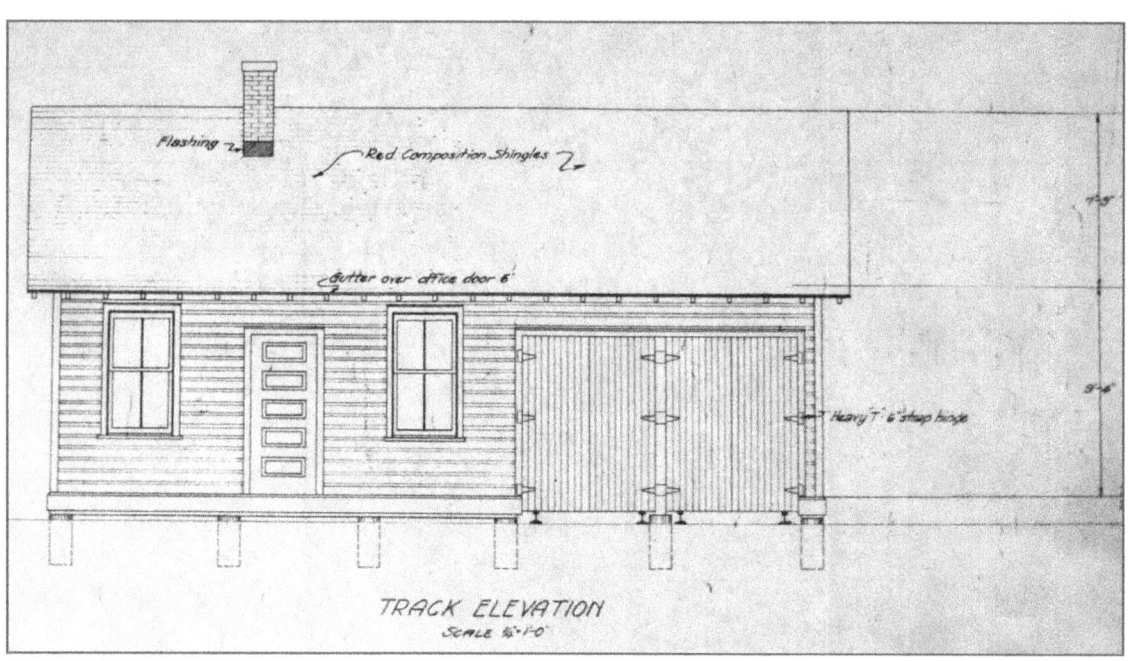

NC&St.L Tool House — W&A Division Front Elevations. -*NC&St.L Railway*

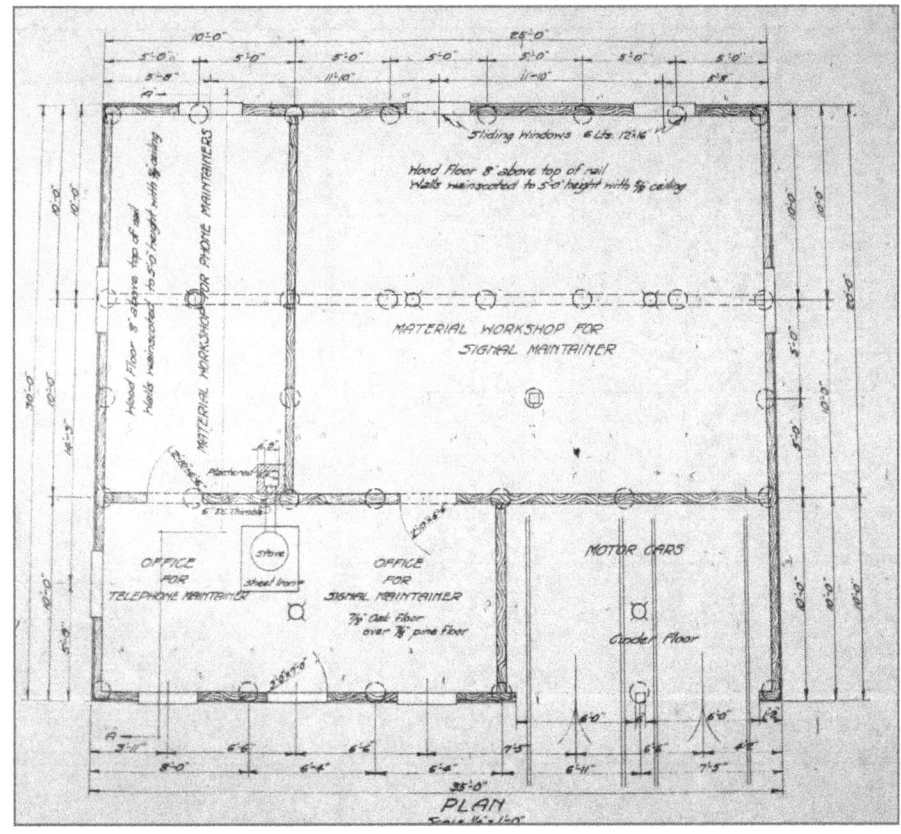

NC&St.L Tool House — W&A Division Floor Plan. *-NC&St.L Railway*

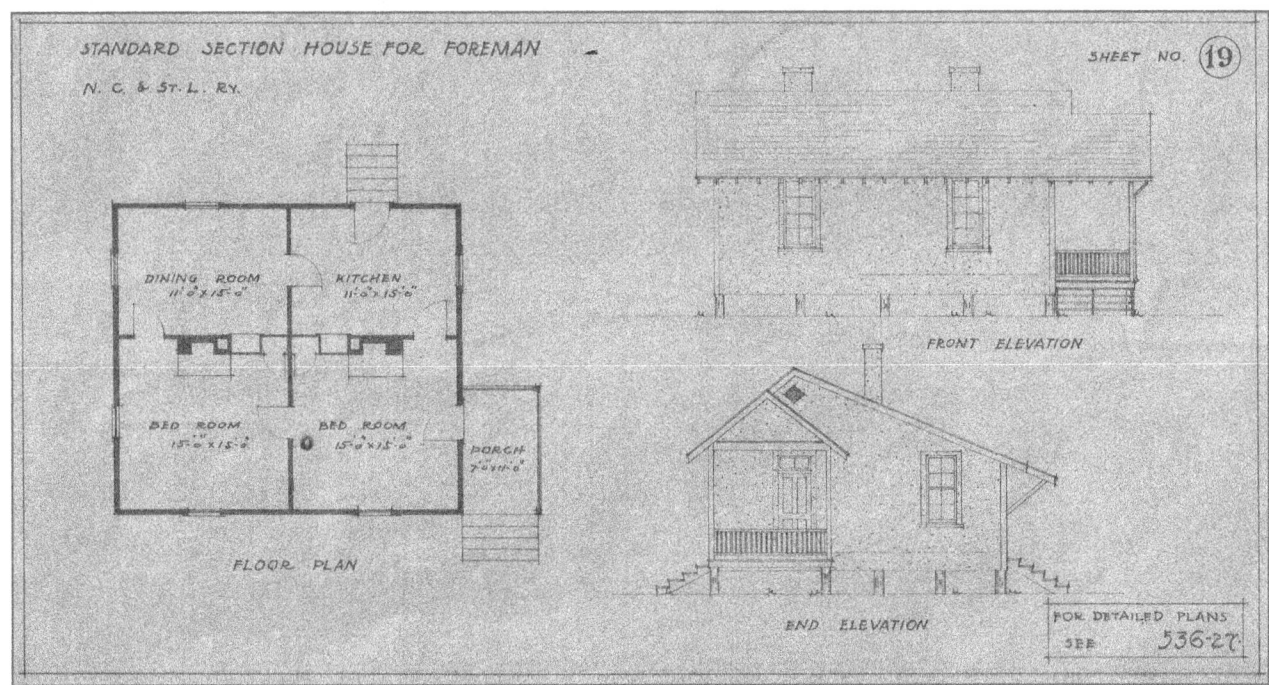

Typical NC&St.L Foreman and Laborers Section House with Floor Plans. These houses were the standard construction for a foreman or laborer of a maintenance of way crew. Both houses were the same size. Because he was the supervisor the foreman would receive the entire four rooms. The laborers house would have been divided for the use of two families. *-NC&St.L Railway*

Elevation drawing of the Cowan, Tennessee Railway Station. -*Drawing by Tom R. Knowles*

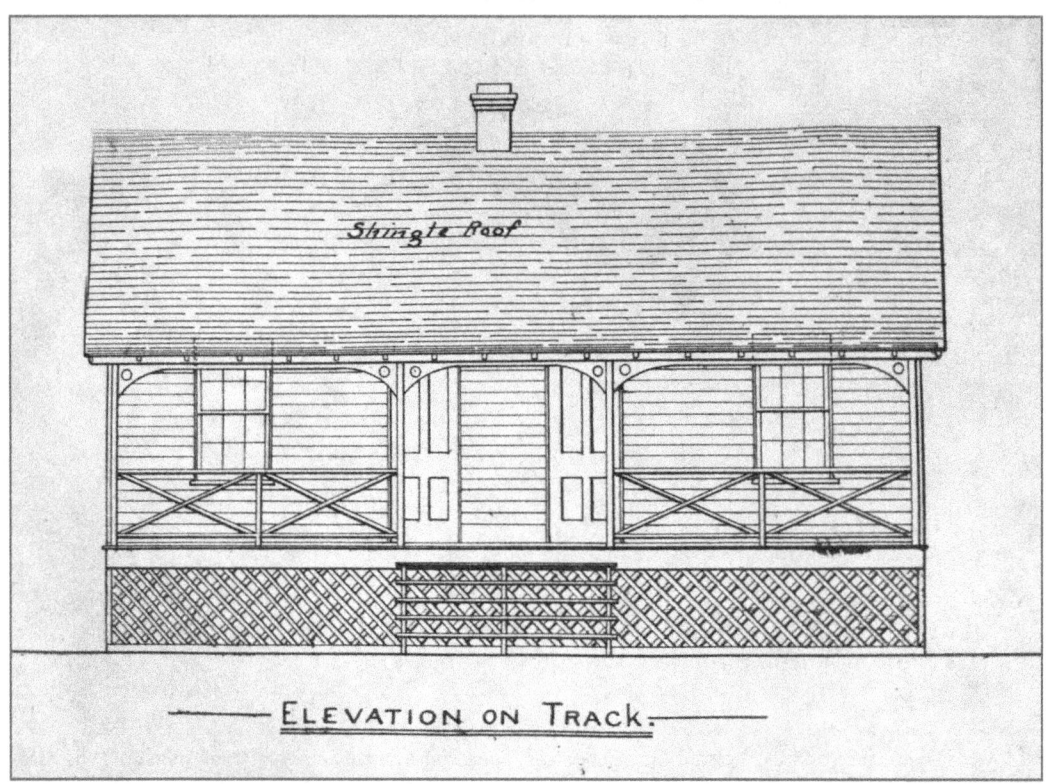

Maintenance of Way Foreman's House front elevation. -*Nashville Chattanooga & St. Louis Railway*

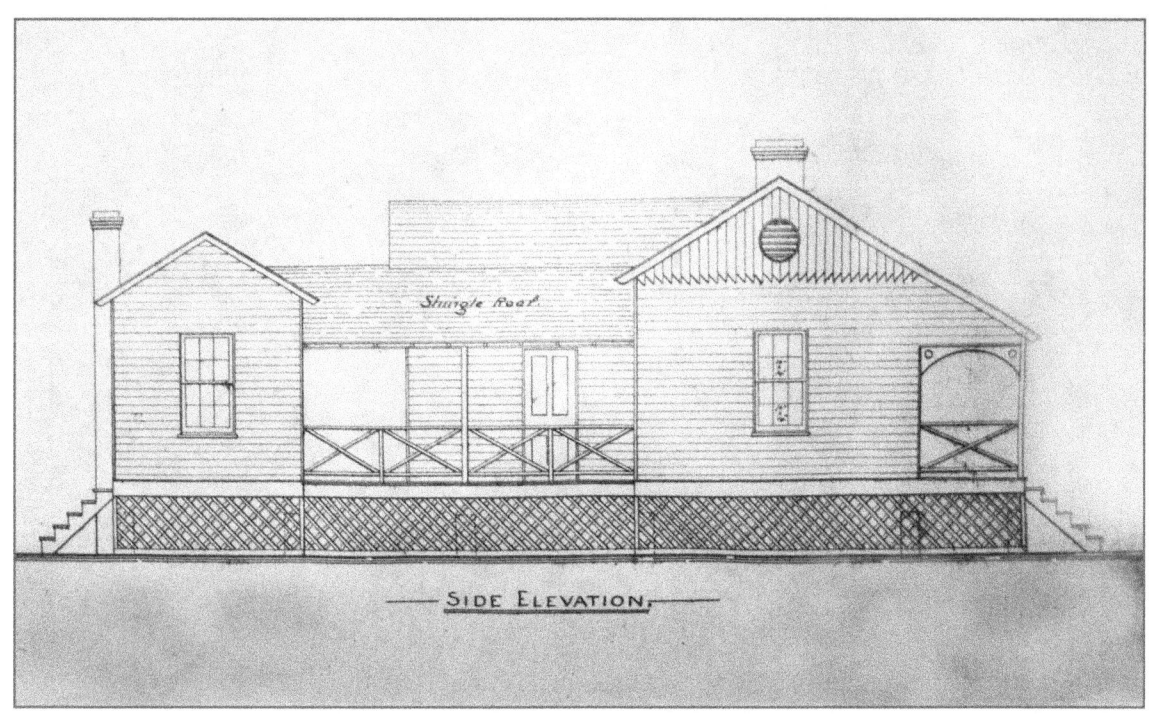

Maintenance of Way Foreman's house side elevation. -*Nashville, Chattanooga & St. Louis Railway*

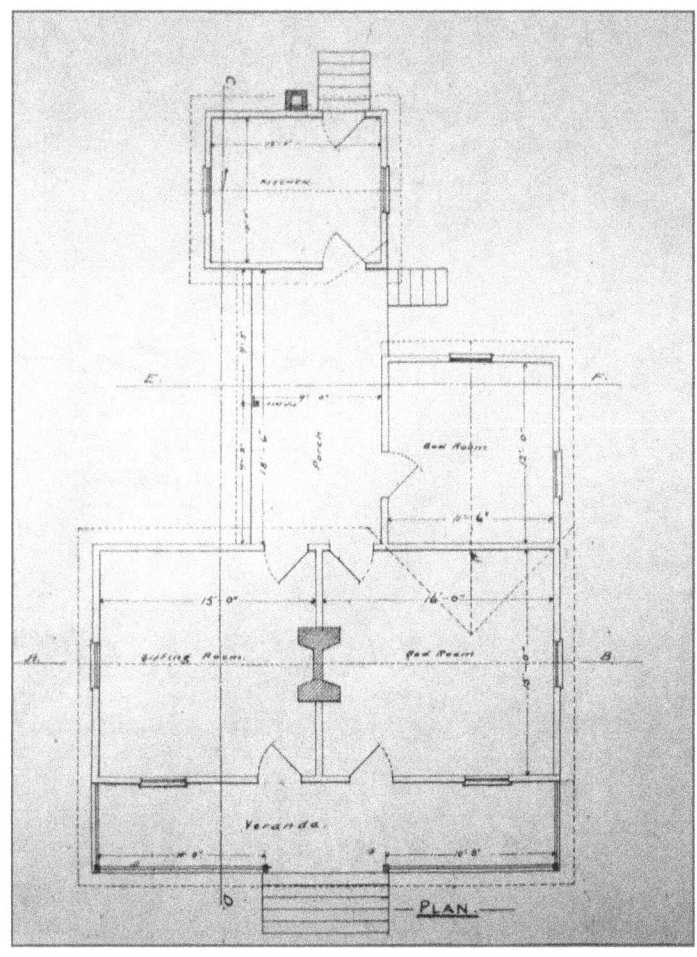

Maintenance of Way Foreman's house. -*Nashville, Chattanooga & St. Louis Railway*

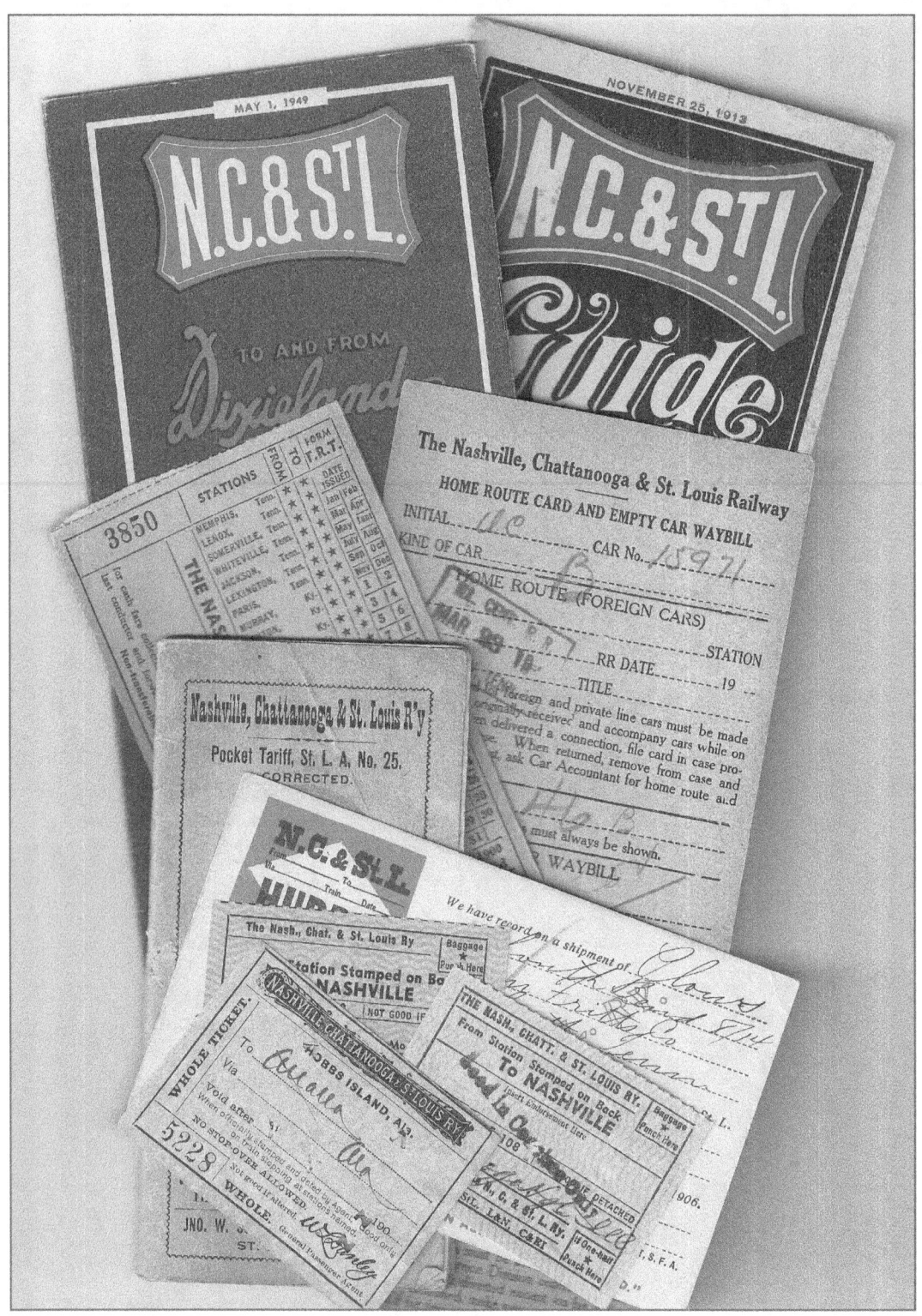

To Our Patrons and Friends

The employees of this station extend to you a cordial welcome.

Some of us may not see you or know you, but all of us want you to be our guest and feel at home.

Whatever rules we have are made for your protection and comfort, not to annoy you.

You may be starting or ending a journey.

Maybe you are greeting or saying good-bye to a loved-one or friend. Whatever your purpose here we want you to find courtesy and friendliness and pleasing service.

If we fail to serve you properly, please let us know.

We are grateful for you visit with us and we hope you will come again.

Employees of the Nashville Chattanooga & St. Louis Railway at this station.

To Our Patrons and Friends Station Sign. This sign could be found in the depots of the NC&St.L. Its message illustrates the genuine esteem the company and its employees held for the most important people in the world, its patrons.

Appendix A
Railroad Abbreviations and Names

Abbreviation	Railroad Name
AB&C RR	Atlanta, Birmingham & Coast Railroad
A&LaG RR	Atlanta & LaGrange Railroad (Atlanta & West Point Railroad)
A&WP RR	Atlanta & West Point Railroad
ACL RR	Atlantic Coast Line Railroad
AGS RY	Alabama Great Southern Railway Company
AMTRAK	National Railroad Passenger Corporation
CE&I RR	Chicago and Eastern Illinois Railroad
C&B RR	Cincinnati & Birmingham Railroad
C&BCG	Central Railroad & Banking Company of Georgia
CA&A RR	Cincinnati, Alabama & Atlantic Railroad
CB&Q RR	Chicago, Burlington & Quincy Railroad
CF&W RR	Caney Fork & Western Railroad
CM&G RR	Chicago, Memphis & Gulf Railroad
CNO&TP RY	Cincinnati, New Orleans & Texas Pacific Railway Company
CofG RR	Central of Georgia Railroad
CSX RR	CSX Railroad
DC&NO RR	Decatur, Chesapeake & New Orleans Railroad
DR NG RR	Duck River Valley Narrow Gauge Railroad

Abbreviation	Railroad Name
E&K RR	Edgefield & Kentucky Railroad
ET&G RR	East Tennessee & Georgia Railroad
ET&V RR	East Tennessee & Virginia Railroad
ETV&G RR	East Tennessee, Virginia & Georgia Railroad
Franklin RR	Franklin Railroad
Georgia RR	Georgia Railroad
H&E RR	Huntsville & Elora Railroad
H&O RR	Hickman & Obion Railroad
Hiwassee RR	Hiwassee Railroad
HS RR	Hardin Southern Railroad
IC RR	Illinois Central Railroad
KCFS&M RR	Kansas City, Ft. Scott & Memphis Railroads (Rock Island)
K&WT RR	Kentucky & West Tennessee Railroad
L&N RR	Louisville & Nashville Railroad
L&N RR	Lewisburg & Northern Railroad
L&NTC	Louisville & Nashville Terminal Company
LaG&M RR	LaGrange and Memphis Railroad
LCC RR	Louisville, Cincinnati & Charleston Railroad
M&A RR	Macon & Augusta Railroad
M&B RR	Memphis & Birmingham Railroad (Frisco)
M&C RR	Memphis & Charleston Railroad

Abbreviation	Railroad Name
M&M RR	McMinnville & Manchester Railroad
M&O RR	Memphis & Ohio Railroad
MT&A RY	Middle Tennessee & Alabama Railway
M&T RR	Mississippi & Tennessee Railroad
M&W RR	Macon & Western Railroad (Monroe Railroad)
MBR&SCG RR	Memphis Branch Railroad & Steamship Company of Georgia (Rome Railroad)
MC RR	Mississippi Central Railroad
MC&L RR	Memphis, Clarksville & Louisville Railroad
MH RR	Mineral Homes Railroad
MRTC	Memphis Railroad Terminal Company
N&C RR	Nashville & Clarksville Railroad
N&C RR	Nashville & Chattanooga Railroad
N&D RR	Nashville & Decatur Railroad
N&E RR	Nashville & Eastern Railroad
N&K RR	Nashville & Knoxville Railroad
N&NW RR	Nashville & Northwestern Railroad
N&TR RR	Nashville & Tuscaloosa Railroad Company
NC	Collectively any reference to the Nashville, Chattanooga & St.Louis Railroad systems
NC&St.L RY	Nashville Chattanooga & St. Louis Railway
NCMTC	NC&St.L Motor Transit Company

Abbreviation	Railroad Name
New Orleans RR	New Orleans Railroad
NO&O RR	New Orleans & Ohio Railroad
NY&H RR	New York & Harlem Railroad
NY&HN RR	New York & New Haven Railroad
NYC&H RR	New York City & Hudson River Railroad
O&N RR	Owensboro & Nashville Railroad
P&I RR	Paducah & Illinois Railroad
PT&A RR	Paducah, Tennessee & Alabama Railroad
R&D RR	Richmond & Danville Railroad
Reading RR	Reading Railroad
Rome RR	Rome Railroad
SAL RR	Seaboard Airlines Railroad
SCC&RC	South Carolina, Canal & Railroad Company
SCT RR	South Central Tennessee Railroad
SMC RR	Sewanee Mining Company Railroad
Southern RR	Southern Railroad
St.L&SE RR	St. Louis & South Eastern Railroad
SV RR	Sequatchie Valley Railroad
SW RR	Southwestern Railroad
T&A RR	Tennessee & Alabama Railroad
T&C RR	Tennessee & Coosa Railroad

Abbreviation	Railroad Name
T&P RR	Tennessee & Pacific Railroad
TA&G RR	Tennessee, Alabama & Georgia Railroad
TC RR	Tennessee Central Railroad
TC&R RR	Tennessee Coal & Railroad Company
TCI&R RR	Tennessee Coal, Iron & Railroad Company
TM Ry	Tennessee Midland Railway
USMRR	United States Military Railroad
USRA	United States Railroad Administration
W&A RR	Western & Atlantic Railroad
W&A RR	Winchester & Alabama Railroad
WH&E RR	Walking Horse & Eastern Railroad

Appendix B
Railroad Terms and Definitions

Definitions selected from compilation by Tom R. Knowles

Amtrak	Quasi-governmental agency/corporation that began passenger trains nationwide in May 1971. Railroad companies were eager to divest themselves of passenger train operation at that time. Amtrak owns locomotives, cars, some facilities and repair and maintenance equipment, but leases use of track and facilities from the railroads where it runs.
Association of American Railroads	Abbreviation AAR. A railroad organization for setting practices, standards and general operating rules adaptable to use by most railroads.
Ballast	Gravel applied to the right of way as anchor and drainage for track.
Block	Section of track governed by one set of signals.
Board-and-Batten	Methods of constructing the outside wall of a building where broad boards are installed vertically next to each other in succession. The joint between boards are covered by thin wooden strips, called battens. Common construction practice by railroads.
Brakeman	Person(s) on a train that before the advent of air brakes was responsible to the engineer for manual setting of brakes and coupling/uncoupling of cars as needed.
Branch Line	Trackage connected to a main line serving smaller communities - usually "dead ended."
Brass	Slang for non-unionized upper railroad management.
Combination Station	A station providing shelter and service for both passengers and freight.
Commodities	Goods having value to be shipped.

Conductor	Person on a train who conducts the train's business and serves as each train's mobile boss. Responsible to the trainmaster.
Consist	Term used to describe the make-up of a train.
Craft	Special and individual descriptions of certain skilled jobs on the railroad. Usually unionized.
Depot	See station, usually staffed twenty-four hours a day and seven days per week.
Diesel-Electric Locomotive	Locomotive engine using an oil-fired internal combustion reciprocating engine to turn an electric generator or alternator that in turn by control means is routed to electric motors geared to the driving wheels. Requiring much less maintenance then steam engines and eliminating smoke issues with municipalities. Diesel replaced steam completely in all United States mainline service by about 1960.
Division	A defined operating district of a larger railroad. Usually between two larger cities or terminals.
Engine	See also locomotive power for a train.
Engine House or Round House	Facility usually located in conjunction with a railroad yard used for maintenance and repair of locomotives.
Engineer	Person who operates an engine in train service.
Facilities	Any improvement along the lines that helps serve the railroad's needs.
Federal Railway Administration	Abbreviation FRA. A government agency setting and enforcing universal regulations of United States railroads.
Fireman	In steam engine days, the person responsible for keeping the steam up, locomotive care, engine "housekeeping" and signal spotting. Occasionally acts as the engineer to gain operating experience. In diesel days, mainly relieved engineer on long runs and watched his side of the train.

Freight Station, Freight House, or Freight Depot	A station serving a town's freight traffic, shipping, receiving, and billing. This structure used as a storage facility for goods or cargo carried by trains
Gauge	Distance measured in increments. United States and other nation's railroads are standard gauge: 4 feet, 8.5 inches between rails.
Highball	Slang for clear track, proceed according to rules. Before semaphore and lighted signals, travel was often governed by the position of a large moveable ball, high position being proceed.
Junction	Place where two or more track routes meet, connect, or cross each other.
Local	Short for local train. A train the plies between almost all stations along its route and stops to call at each.
Main Line	Trackage on right of way mainly used for through traffic from one major geographic point to another, for example, the track from Nashville to Chattanooga.
Order Hoop	Loop or wye shaped device used to pass orders to train crews given from trackside without stopping the train.
Passenger Station	A station serving a town's passenger traffic.
Platforms	Improved piece of land next to railroad track made of gravel, wood, concrete or steel for use by railroad personnel and customers. Could also be used as a loading dock.
Right of Way	A more or less continuous strip of land where a road may proceed.
ROW	Abbreviation for Right of Way.
Rules Book	A set of standards issued to all employees governing the operations of trains as well as the rules of safety and economy the employees are to follow for the protection of themselves and their customers.
Section	For maintenance purposes, lengths of track kept in good repair by one set of workers (section gang) usually about 10 miles, but sometimes much more.

Semaphore	Type of visual trackside signal for benefit of trainmen using a moving arm to indicate its message.
Side Track (Siding)	Section of track deviating from the main used for storage of railroad cars not in transit, to serve an industry or shipper, or for the use of a second train to clear the main when two trains meet.
Signals	Devices and procedures to allow communication between train crew (each other) and operation personnel.
Spur Track	Track, like a branch line, usually quite short serving basic purposes of connection to industry storage.
Station Agent	Person responsible for the day-to-day business of a station or depot; usually assigned to one particular place long term; may also be called station master.
Station or Station House	A structure next to trackage used as a shelter for operations personnel and passengers or freight.
Steam Locomotive	Locomotive Engine - a machine that can propel itself by boiling water into its gaseous phase and pressuring it. Steam under pressure is used in cylinders or turbines to expand and do work. Steam engine categories are defined in America by the Whyte System, whereby support and guiding wheels are differentiated from driving wheels by counting them and putting them in hyphenated standard form. A locomotive with four front support and guiding wheels followed by eight (usually larger diameter) driving wheels, then four more support wheels behind that gives USA 4-8-4. Different wheel arrangements were for differing needs. Certain names were also applied to various wheel arrangements.
Stock Pen	Facility used for holding livestock until they can be transported or after they were delivered by rail.
Streamliner	Aerodynamic style of locomotives and passenger cars (usually as a matched set) became especially popular in the late 1930s.

Switch	Device built into tracks to allow the merging and diverging of trains.
Terminal	A facility where trains stop to load or unload, change engines, get service, etc.
Tie	Support for railroad rails, set at right angles to the rails, mostly wooden. Rails for track are nailed (spiked) to them.
Traffic	Progression of commerce from one place to another for hire.
Train	Any mobile railroad equipment authorized to travel on tracks, usually refers to rolling stock behind an engine. An engine alone can also be a train if authorized and fulfilling other rules.
Train order	Paper authorization for the make-up and intended operation of a train if not provided for by timetable.
Turntable	A rotating platform for turning railroad locomotive, so that it is facing another direction or for the alignment of locomotives into the respective bays of an engine house.
Union	Labor organizations, workers joined forces to have a unified voce when negotiating with management.
Union station	Station cooperatively operated by at least two separate railroads.
Varnish	Shiny, clear, wood coating, also applied to passenger cars interiors. Slang referring to any fancy passenger train.
Yard	Collection of tracks usually at large businesses, terminals and junctions. These tracks provide room for shuffling of cars into new trains, train meets and storage of rolling stock.

Appendix C
Constructions, Acquisitions, and Leases of the N&C and NC&St.L Railway 1850-1957[140]

Chattanooga Division: Main line was chartered as the Nashville & Chattanooga Railroad Company in 1845. The corporate name was changed in 1873 to the Nashville, Chattanooga & St. Louis Railway. Construction was completed from Nashville to Murfreesboro in 1851; from Murfreesboro to Bridgeport in 1853; and to a connection in Chattanooga with the Western & Atlantic Railroad in 1854.

Nashville Division: Main line was chartered in Tennessee as the Nashville & Northwestern Railroad Company in 1852 and in Kentucky in 1856. Construction was completed from Nashville to Kingston Springs in 1861 and from Kingston Springs to Johnsonville on the Tennessee River in 1864. Construction from Johnsonville to Union City was completed in 1867, though most of the construction had occurred before the War Between the States. The line from Hickman to Union City was chartered as the Hickman & Ohio Railroad in 1853-4. It was purchased by the Nashville & Northwestern in 1855-6. The entire line was sold to the NC&St.L in 1872.

Atlanta Division: Main line was built by the State of Georgia as the Western & Atlantic Railroad in an Act approved in 1836. This line was leased to the NC&St.L Railway in 1890 and again in 1919. Construction was completed from Atlanta to Marietta in 1843; to Kingston in 1845; to Dalton in 1847; and to the Tennessee River in Chattanooga in 1849.

Paducah and Memphis Division: Main line was leased from the Louisville & Nashville Railroad Company in 1896 by the NC&St.L for a period of ninety-nine years. The line from Memphis to Lexington was chartered in 1875 as the Tennessee Midland Railway Company, but it was not until 1887-8 that construction was completed through Lexington to the Tennessee River at Perryville. The line from Paducah to the Tennessee-Kentucky line was chartered in 1854, 1873, and 1888 and from the state line to Lexington in 1875 and 1888. A consolidation of these charters took place in 1889 into the Paducah, Tennessee & Alabama Railroad Company. Construction was completed from Paducah to the Tennessee line in 1890; from there to Paris in 1891, and 1892 a connection was made with the Tennessee Midland.

Centerville Branch: Main line was chartered in 1877 as the Nashville & Tuscaloosa Railroad Company and under that name built to Kimmins. The line from Dickson to the Duck River was deeded to the NC&St.L in 1883 and to Kimmins in 1884. From Kimmins to Allens

---

140   The Nashville, Chattanooga & St. Louis Railway 1866-1942. The Nashville, Chattanooga & St. Louis Railway Employees Education Service, Lesson Number 4. Nashville, Tennessee. 1942, page 28.

Creek the line was built for the Southern Iron Company and was deeded to the NC&St.L in 1892. Construction was completed from Dickson to Graham in 1879 and to Duck River in 1882; from the Duck River (at Centerville) to Kimmins in 1883; and from Kimmins to Allens Creek in 1883. This line was originally built as a narrow gauge and was changed to standard gauge in 1894.

Shelbyville Branch: Line was built by the Nashville & Chattanooga Railroad in 1852-3.

Sparta Branch: Line was chartered as the McMinnville & Manchester Railroad Company in 1850, was built in 1855, and was sold to the NC&St.L in 1877. The Southwestern Railroad Company chartered the line from McMinnville to Sparta in 1852; this portion of the line was sold to the Nashville, Chattanooga & St. Louis Railway in 1877 as an unfinished right of way. The NC&St.L completed the line from McMinnville to Rock Island in 1883; from Rock Island to Doyle in May 1884; and from Doyle to Sparta in October 1884. In 1883 the NC&St.L also purchased the Bon Air Railway from the coalmines in DeRossett south to Sparta. This branch of the railroad operated out of the Huntsville Division.

Tracy City Branch: Line was chartered in 1851-2 as the Sewanee Mining Company and construction began in 1853. The completed line from Cowan was acquired by the NC&St.L in 1887. The branch was extended by the NC&St.L to Coalmont in 1904 and to Palmer in 1917.

Columbia Branch: Line was chartered in 1850 as the Winchester & Alabama Railroad Company to build from Decherd, through Winchester, to Fayetteville. The Fayetteville to Columbia line was chartered in 1872, as the Duck River Narrow Gauge Railroad Company and was constructed in 1854 from Decherd to Winchester, from Winchester to Fayetteville in 1859, from Columbia to Petersburg in 1879, and Petersburg to Fayetteville in 1882. The NC&St.L purchased the lines from Decherd to Fayetteville in 1877 and from Columbia to Fayetteville in 1887. The narrow gauge was broadened to standard gauge in 1889.

Huntsville Division: Line was chartered and constructed in 1887 as the Huntsville & Elora Railroad Company from Elora south to Huntsville. In 1893, under a different charter it was extended to the Tennessee River at Hobbs Island. The NC&St.L acquired the line in 1887. The line from Guntersville to Gadsden was chartered in 1884 as the Tennessee & Coosa Railroad Company, and was sold to the NC&St.L in 1891. Construction started in Gadsden and at the time of the sale extended about thirty-nine miles. The NC&St.L completed the construction to Guntersville in 1891. Under the same charter the NC&St.L built from Hobbs Island to Huntsville. Chartered in 1887 to build from Gallatin to Decatur, the Decatur, Chesapeake & New Orleans Railroad only constructed tracks from the Alabama/Tennessee state line to Fayetteville. By 1893 the DC&NO had failed to fulfill its charter and reorganized as the Middle Tennessee & Alabama Railway. The MT&A was unable to complete the railroad and in 1897 was sold to the NC&St.L to extend the line from Jeff to Capshaw.

Orme Branch: Construction began in 1902 and was completed in 1904. It was built by the Needmore Coal Company and The Nashville, Chattanooga & St. Louis Railway. The Needmore Coal Company sold its interest to the Campbell Coal & Coke Company and that concern sold the line to the NC&St.L in 1904.

Sequatchie Valley Branch: The line from Bridgeport to Jasper was built by The Nashville & Chattanooga Railroad Company in 1867 under Acts passed in 1858-60. A charter was granted in 1868 from Jasper to Pikeville in the name of the Sequatchie Valley Railroad Company. Construction on the line from Jasper to Victoria was completed in 1878, following which, the trackage and franchise was conveyed to the NC&St.L. The NC&St.L completed the line to Whitwell in 1887, to Dunlap in 1888, and to Pikeville in 1891.

Rome Branch: Line was chartered in 1839 under the name Memphis Branch Railroad & Steamboat Company of Georgia. In 1849, the line was completed and opened from Kingston to Rome. The name of the corporation changed in 1850 to the Rome Railroad Company and was sold to the NC&St.L in 1896.

Lebanon Branch: Line was chartered in 1866 as the Tennessee & Pacific Railroad Company to build between Memphis and Knoxville. The portion between Nashville and Lebanon was sold to the NC&St.L in 1877. This branch of the railroad operated out of the Chattanooga Division.

Appendix D
Historical Timeline

1831	First railroad charters issued by the Tennessee legislature - six were issued, none were built.
1831	Forced removal began for five civilized Native American tribes from the southern United States.
1836	Western & Atlantic Railroad chartered.
1837	Western & Atlantic Railroad began building toward Ross' Landing on the Tennessee River.
1837	The Panic of 1837 stopped railroad construction across South.
1838	Hiwassee Railroad became the first chartered railroad to lay track in Tennessee.
1842	The first depot, a log structure, was built in Atlanta by the Western & Atlantic Railroad.
1845	Nashville & Chattanooga Railroad chartered by an Act of the State of Tennessee.
1845	Southern and Western Convention held in July and November in Memphis with much future railroad construction planned at these two conventions.
1846	Memphis & Charleston Railroad chartered by State of Tennessee.
1848	Nashville & Chattanooga began construction of a tunnel on Cumberland Mountain.
1848	In March, the Nashville & Chattanooga began construction from Nashville toward Chattanooga.
1848	January 24, The first Nashville & Chattanooga stockholders meeting was held in Nashville with Vernon K. Stevenson elected as the railroad's first president.
1848	9.7 miles of track completed toward Chattanooga by April 13th and train ran to end of the line.
1848	61 miles of track were in place and the Nashville & Chattanooga were operating two trains daily to tracks end by December.
1850	Western & Atlantic reached Chattanooga, Tennessee.

1851	The Western & Atlantic Railroad built the first depot in Chattanooga, Tennessee.
1852	Tennessee legislature passed General Internal Improvement Law spurring a boom in building of railroads in the state.
1853	The 1842 log cabin depot in Atlanta was replaced with a more substantial structure, which was burned during the Civil War.
1854	Nashville & Chattanooga reached Chattanooga, Tennessee.
1854	Nashville & Chattanooga completed building terminals in Chattanooga and Nashville as well as a multitude of stations between.
1859	The Western & Atlantic, Nashville & Chattanooga, and Memphis & Charleston Railroads built a Union Station in Chattanooga, replacing the 1851 structure built by the Western & Atlantic.
1859	Louisville & Nashville Railroad extended its line from Louisville to Nashville.
1861	Nashville & Northwestern Railroad completed from Hickman, Kentucky to McKenzie, Tennessee.
1864	Nashville & Northwestern Railroad is completed from Nashville to the Tennessee River at Johnsonville.
1864	U.S. Army turns over repair and operation of the Nashville & Chattanooga and Nashville & Northwestern to the United States Military Railroad.
1865	Nashville & Chattanooga and Nashville & Northwestern Railroads returned to company ownership by the Federal government.
1866	A log structure was built in Atlanta to replace the depot burned in 1864.
1867	Nashville & Northwestern Railroad is completed from Tennessee River at Johnsonville to McKenzie, Tennessee completing the line to Hickman, Kentucky.
1871	Union Station in Atlanta completed to replace the temporary log cabin built in 1866. The temporary station replaced the station burned during the War Between the States.
1873	Nashville & Chattanooga Railroad petitioned for a name change and becomes the Nashville, Chattanooga & St. Louis Railway.

1873	Nashville, Chattanooga & St. Louis Railway adopts a new slogan, "From St. Louis to the Sea."
1877	Line from Jasper to Pikeville, Tennessee purchased.
1877	Line from Decherd to Fayetteville, Tennessee purchased.
1877	Line from Tullahoma to McMinnville, Tennessee purchased.
1879	Louisville & Nashville and Nashville, Chattanooga & St. Louis Railway began purchasing controlling interests in railroads in Kentucky with each railroad trying to out pace the other in an attempt to gain trackage between Nashville and St. Louis.
1879	Nashville & Chattanooga president Edmund Cole approached the Louisville & Nashville with a proposition that the two railroads merge. The Louisville & Nashville would have nothing to do with the idea.
1879	In a move to head off Nashville & Chattanooga president Cole from gaining the upper hand in his attempt to become the largest railroad in the South, Louisville & Nashville president H. V. Newcomb does an end run and purchases controlling interest in the Nashville, Chattanooga & St. Louis from founder and principal stockholder Vernon K. Stevenson.
1880	Vernon K. Stevenson relinquishes his stock in the Nashville, Chattanooga & St. Louis Railway to the Louisville & Nashville.
1880	NC&St.L Railway became subsidiary of L&N Railroad.
1881	A three story office building erected at 930 Broadway in Nashville. Later the former residence next door was also purchased and used as an annex.
1882	Nashville & Chattanooga completed construction of a new Union Station in Chattanooga.
1883	Line from Colesburg to Duck River, Tennessee purchased.
1883	Line from McMinnville to Sparta, Tennessee built.
1884	Line from the Duck River to Kimmins, Tennessee purchased.
1887	Line from Cowan to Tracy City, Tennessee purchased.
1887	Line from Fayetteville to Columbia, Tennessee purchased.
1887	Line from Elora, Tennessee to Hobbs Island, Alabama purchased.

1890	Line from Chattanooga, Tennessee to Atlanta, Georgia leased.
1890	The shops in the "Gulch" downtown Nashville are replace with new facilities on Charlotte Pike, which remain the primary shops for the railroad through 1957.
1892	Line from Kimmins to Allen Creek, Tennessee purchased.
1893	Nashville, Chattanooga & St. Louis and Louisville & Nashville jointly operate the terminal and yards in the "Gulch" in Nashville.
1893	Barge and paddle wheel service began on the Tennessee River in Alabama to ferry train cars between Hobbs Island and Guntersville.
1895	Line from Memphis, Tennessee to Paducah, Kentucky leased from L&N Railroad.
1896	Line from Kingston to Rome, Georgia purchased.
1896	Nashville, Chattanooga & St. Louis leases Paducah, Tennessee & Alabama Railroad giving it its own through line to Memphis, which later became the Paducah & Memphis Division of the Nashville, Chattanooga & St. Louis Railway.
1896	Nashville's Union Station remodeled to receive visitors to the Tennessee Centennial and Exposition.
1897	Nashville & Chattanooga instrumental in bringing the Tennessee Centennial and Exposition to Nashville and Tennessee.
1898	Line from Guntersville to Gadsden, Alabama purchased.
1899	The Nashville, Chattanooga & St. Louis leased trackage between Fulton, Kentucky and Martin, Tennessee over which the Nashville, Chattanooga & St. Louis routed the famous Dixie Flyer.
1900	Nashville, Chattanooga & St. Louis and Louisville & Nashville completed a new terminal at Nashville.
1900	Chattanooga's 1882 Union Station received a major renovation.
1902	Atlantic Coast Line Railroad purchased controlling interest in the Louisville & Nashville (including the Nashville, Chattanooga & St. Louis).
1904	Line from Bridgeport, Alabama to Orme, Tennessee purchased.
1904	Line from Tracy City to Coalmont, Tennessee built.

1907	Cravens Yards at the base of Lookout Mountain replaced the downtown yards in Chattanooga.
1912	New Union Station built in Memphis.
1917	Line from Coalmont extended to Palmer, Tennessee.
1917	Chicago, Burlington & Quincy Railroad and the Nashville, Chattanooga & St. Louis enter into an agreement to build a bridge 5,400 feet long across the Ohio River between Paducah, Kentucky and Metropolis, Illinois. Up until that time the railroads had used a ferry to transport rail cars in the interchange.
1917	The United States government consolidates all railroads to form the United States Railroad Authority.
1918	On July 9th two passenger trains on the Nashville, Chattanooga & St. Louis collide approximately 5 miles west of Nashville, Tennessee the death toll including passengers and Nashville, Chattanooga & St. Louis Railway employees climbed to 130. The high death toll is the deadliest train accident on American soil.
1918	The Nashville, Chattanooga & St. Louis constructs a branch line to the Dupont plant in Old Hickory, Tennessee.
1923	The 1881 Nashville, Chattanooga & St. Louis office building at 930 Broadway is replaced with an eight-story building at 1000 Broadway.
1926	Gulf Mobile & Northern Railroad leased trackage between Jackson, Tennessee and Paducah, Kentucky over the Paducah & Memphis Division.
1928	The 1850s tunnel at Tunnel Hill, Georgia closed and a new larger bore was dug adjacent to the old one.
1929	Between 1929 and 1937 the Nashville, Chattanooga & St. Louis was hit had by the depression. Branches are closed (Lebanon), other operations are curtailed, and personnel are either let go or had hours cut back.
1930	Nashville, Chattanooga & St. Louis completed building a new terminal at Atlanta.
1930	The 1871 Union Station in Atlanta replaced by a new terminal.
1941	In anticipation of impending World War II, Nashville, Chattanooga & St. Louis president Hall ordered a large number of freight cars. His hunch paid off when the railroad used the cars to carry materiel during WWII.

1941	The first diesel locomotives on the Nashville, Chattanooga & St. Louis were placed in switcher service.
1943	A total of twenty, 4-8-4, J-3, steam locomotives were ordered. These locomotives became the workhorses during the WWII. The Nashville, Chattanooga & St. Louis handled as many as 6-8 tank car trains daily carrying fuel from Texas to the east coast.
1943	The NC begins installing Central Traffic Control. The railroad would have most of its line from Atlanta to Memphis under the control of CTC by 1953.
1946	The Nashville, Chattanooga & St. Louis built in its Nashville Shops the streamline passenger train the "City of Memphis." The train ran from Memphis to Nashville and returned to the Bluff City daily.
1948	The first of fifty-two F-3 and F-7, A and B unit diesel road locomotives are placed in service. The "B" units are equipped with steam generators for use with passenger cars.
1950	Thirty-Seven GP-7 diesel locomotives arrived for service. All were painted maroon and yellow with the exception of five units, which were equipped with steam generators and were painted blue and Confederate gray similar to the F-3s.
1951	Louisville & Nashville president Tilford announced the joint building of new facilities at Radnor Yards in Nashville. He went on to say that as soon as that project was completed it was the company's goal to merge the Nashville, Chattanooga & St. Louis into the Louisville & Nashville.
1953	On January 4th the railroad made its last run of trains using steam engine as motive power.
1954	Radnor Yards in Nashville replaced the old yards next to Nashville's Union Station.
1957	August 31st marked the last day of operations for the Nashville, Chattanooga & St. Louis Railway. The Nashville, Chattanooga & St. Louis had operated for 112 years as one of the finest railroads in the country.

Appendix E
Stations, Locations, Mile Markers, and Facilities

Note: Some Stations Changed Names as the Years Passed

Station	Mile Marker	County	State	Facilities	Still Standing
Nashville Division					
Mississippi River					
Hickman	171	Fulton	Kentucky	Depot, Water Tank	
Ryan	168	Fulton	Kentucky	Depot	
Curran	166	Fulton	Kentucky		
Dodds	165	Fulton	Kentucky	Depot, Stock Pens	
Shucks Switch	163	Fulton	Kentucky		
Dresden Crossing	162	Fulton	Kentucky		
Matson Switch	161	Fulton	Kentucky	Depot	Station
State Line	161	Fulton	Kentucky & Tennessee		
Woodland Mills	160	Obion	Tennessee	Depot	
Brevards	157	Obion	Tennessee		
Union City	154	Obion	Tennessee	Depot, Interchange with GM&O RR	Station
Gibbs	151	Obion	Tennessee	Depot, Interchange with IC RR	
Shoffner	150	Obion	Tennessee	Depot	
Terrell	147	Weakley	Tennessee	Depot, Stock Pens	

Station	Mile Marker	County	State	Facilities	Still Standing
Gardner	144	Weakley	Tennessee	Depot	
Martin	141	Weakley	Tennessee	Depot, Section House, Stock Pens, Water Tank, Interchange with IC RR	
Ralston	138	Weakley	Tennessee	Passenger and Freight Shelter	
Rhoadsdale	134	Weakley	Tennessee	Cinder Plant	
Dresden	132	Weakley	Tennessee	Depot, Stock Pens, Sidings	
Gleason	125	Weakley	Tennessee	Depot, Section House	
McKenzie	117	Carroll	Tennessee	Depot, Freight Depot, Water Tank, Stock Pens, Interchange with L&N RR	Station
Trabue	114	Carroll	Tennessee		
Hico	113	Carroll	Tennessee	Depot, Section House, Siding	
Huntington	105	Carroll	Tennessee	Depot, Freight House	
Rosser	100	Carroll	Tennessee	Section House	
Bruceton	96	Carroll	Tennessee	Depot, Hotel, Roundhouse, Yard	
Bruceton	96	Carroll	Tennessee	Roundhouse, Yard	Roundhouse
Hollow Rock	96	Carroll	Tennessee	Depot, Interchange with P&M Division	
Bruceton	94	Carroll	Tennessee	Depot, Freight House, Roundhouse, Yards	
Big Sandy	93	Carroll	Tennessee		
Hamrick	93	Carroll	Tennessee		

Station	Mile Marker	County	State	Facilities	Still Standing
Sawyers Mills	91	Benton	Tennessee		
Lipe	90	Benton	Tennessee		
Camden	86	Benton	Tennessee	Depot, Stock Pens, Section House	
Troy	84	Benton	Tennessee		
Eva	80	Benton	Tennessee	Depot	
Tennessee River	78	Benton	Tennessee		
New Johnsonville	78	Humphreys	Tennessee	Depot	Station
Johnsonville	77	Humphreys	Tennessee	Depot, Water Tank, Yard	
Denver (Box)	75	Humphreys	Tennessee	Shelter, Depot at one time	
Franks	73	Humphreys	Tennessee		
Pursley	72	Humphreys	Tennessee	Siding	
Short Switch	70	Humphreys	Tennessee	Section House	
Waverly	67	Humphreys	Tennessee	Depot, Water Tank	
Gorman	62	Humphreys	Tennessee	Section House	
McEwen	57	Humphreys	Tennessee	Depot	
Donnegan	54	Humphreys	Tennessee	4 Section Houses	
Tennessee City	50	Dickson	Tennessee	Depot, Section House	

Station	Mile Marker	County	State	Facilities	Still Standing
Pond	44	Dickson	Tennessee	Depot, Siding	
Dickson	42	Dickson	Tennessee	Depot, Freight House, Turntable, Stockpens, Yard	Station
Colesburg	39	Dickson	Tennessee	Depot, Yard, Water Tank	
Burns	37	Dickson	Tennessee	Depot, Section House	
Franklin Crossing	35	Dickson	Tennessee		
Crow	34	Dickson	Tennessee		
Bakers Crossing	34	Dickson	Tennessee		
White Bluff	30	Dickson	Tennessee	Depot, Passenger and Freight Shelter	
Glendale	27	Cheatham	Tennessee		
Craggie Hope	25	Cheatham	Tennessee	Depot	
Kingston Springs	24	Cheatham	Tennessee	Depot	Station
Pegram	20	Cheatham	Tennessee	Depot (built 1906)	Station
Newsom	16	Davidson	Tennessee	Depot	
Bellevue	12	Davidson	Tennessee	Depot	
Hicks	11	Davidson	Tennessee		
Vaughn's Gap	9	Davidson	Tennessee	Depot, Section House	
Harding	7	Davidson	Tennessee	Shelter	

Station	Mile Marker	County	State	Facilities	Still Standing
WhiteBridge	5	Davidson	Tennessee		
Belle Meade Plantation	4	Davidson	Tennessee	Flag Stop	
New Shops	2	Davidson	Tennessee	Main Shops for the Railroad, Coal Tower, Yard, Interchange with TC RR	
Stock Yards	1	Davidson	Tennessee		
Nashville	0	Davidson	Tennessee	Terminal, Interchange with Chattanooga Division L&N RR	Station

Cumberland River

West Nashville Branch

Station	Mile Marker	County	State	Facilities	Still Standing
West Nashville	3	Davidson	Tennessee	Depot, Freight Depot	

Paducah & Memphis Division

Ohio River

Station	Mile Marker	County	State	Facilities	Still Standing
Paducah	182	McCracken	Kentucky	Union Depot, Roundhouse, Interchange with IC RR	Freight House
Oaks	173	McCracken	Kentucky		
Overby	170	McCracken	Kentucky		
Elva	168	Marshall	Kentucky	Depot, Section House	Section House
Millikens	165	Marshall	Kentucky		

Station	Mile Marker	County	State	Facilities	Still Standing
Iola	164	Marshall	Kentucky		
Benton	160	Marshall	Kentucky	Depot, Stock Pens, Water Tank	
Glade	156	Marshall	Kentucky		
Hardin	152	Marshall	Kentucky	Freight and Passenger Depot	
Dexter	147	Calloway	Kentucky	Depot, Passenger Shelter, Stock Pens	Shelter
Almo	145	Calloway	Kentucky	Depot	Store
Murray	142	Calloway	Kentucky	Depot, Stock Pens	Station, Freight House
Tobacco	141	Calloway	Kentucky	Depot	
Hazel	133	Calloway	Kentucky	Depot, Freight House, Section House	
State Line	133	Calloway	Kentucky & Tennessee		
Puryear	129	Henry	Tennessee	Depot, Passenger Shelter, Section House, Stock Pens	
Whitlock	123	Henry	Tennessee	Depot	
Hilltop	121	Henry	Tennessee		
Paris	117	Henry	Tennessee	Depot, Turntable, Water Tank, Stock Pens, Section Cabins	Station
Van Dyke	110	Henry	Tennessee	Depot	
Mansfield	106	Henry	Tennessee	Depot, Section House, Shelter	
Vale	100	Carroll	Tennessee	Depot, Section Houses	

Station	Mile Marker	County	State	Facilities	Still Standing
Snyder	97	Carroll	Tennessee		
Bruceton	94	Carroll	Tennessee	Depot, Freight House, Roundhouse, Hotel, Yards	Roundhouse
Hollow Rock	96	Carroll	Tennessee	Interchange with Nashville Division	
Buena Vista	101	Carroll	Tennessee	Depot, Section House	
Westport	107	Carroll	Tennessee	Depot, Section House (shelter at some time)	Station as Home
Yuma	111	Carroll	Tennessee	Depot, Section House	Station
Wildersville	116	Henderson	Tennessee	Depot, Passenger Shelter, Section House	
Timberlake	121	Henderson	Tennessee	Shelter	
Wards	125	Henderson	Tennessee		
Lexington	127	Henderson	Tennessee	Depot, Coal Tower, Stock Pens	
Hinson Springs	130	Henderson	Tennessee		
Life	133	Henderson	Tennessee	Shelter	
Huron	136	Henderson	Tennessee	Depot Shelter, Section House	
Luray	139	Henderson	Tennessee	Depot, Shelter, Stock Pens	
Beech Bluff	142	Madison	Tennessee	Depot, Shelter, Section House	
Ranger	144	Madison	Tennessee		
Alexander	148	Madison	Tennessee		

Station	Mile Marker	County	State	Facilities	Still Standing
Rose Hill	151	Madison	Tennessee	Siding	
East Union	151	Madison	Tennessee		
Jackson	152	Madison	Tennessee	Depot, Interchange GM&O	Station as Museum
Burkitt	156	Madison	Tennessee	Siding	
Grover	159	Madison	Tennessee	Platform	
Neely	161	Madison	Tennessee	Shelter, Section House	
Denmark	165	Madison	Tennessee	Depot, Stock Pens, Siding	
Mercer	169	Madison	Tennessee	Depot	
Hatchie	172	Madison	Tennessee	Depot, Shelter, Water Tank	
Big Hatchie River	173	Madison	Tennessee		
Vildo	175	Hardeman	Tennessee	Depot, Shelter, Section House	
Augustus	177	Hardeman	Tennessee	Platform	
Whiteville	181	Hardeman	Tennessee	Depot, Section House, Stock Pens	
Ina	186	Fayette	Tennessee		
Laconia	188	Fayette	Tennessee	Depot, Section House, Stock Pens	
Somerville	195	Fayette	Tennessee	Depot, Section House, Freight House	Station
Warren	201	Fayette	Tennessee	Depot, Shelter, Stock Pens	
Oakland	205	Fayette	Tennessee	Depot, Stock Pens, Open Air Shed, Section Houses, Hotel	

Station	Mile Marker	County	State	Facilities	Still Standing
Hickory Withe	209	Fayette	Tennessee	Water Tank	
Eads	209	Shelby	Tennessee	Depot, Section Houses, Stock Pens	
Knox	213	Shelby	Tennessee		
Cordova	217	Shelby	Tennessee	Depot, Stock Pens	Station
Clay	221	Shelby	Tennessee	Siding	
Mullins	222	Shelby	Tennessee	Depot	
Berclair	226	Shelby	Tennessee		
Alta	228	Shelby	Tennessee		
Montgomery Park	231	Shelby	Tennessee		
K.C. Junction	233	Shelby	Tennessee		
Aulon	235	Shelby	Tennessee	Interlocking Tower	Tower
Lenox	236	Shelby	Tennessee	Depot	
Memphis	237	Shelby	Tennessee	Union Station Terminal	
Mississippi River					

Perryville Branch

Station	Mile Marker	County	State	Facilities	Still Standing
Lexington	127	Henderson	Tennessee	Depot, Coal Tower, Stock Pens	
Warren's Bluff	131	Henderson	Tennessee	Depot	
Chesterfield	135	Henderson	Tennessee	Depot	

Station	Mile Marker	County	State	Facilities	Still Standing
Darden	138	Henderson	Tennessee	Depot	
Beacon	140	Decatur	Tennessee	Depot	
Parsons	144	Decatur	Tennessee	Depot, Water Tower	
Perryville	151	Decatur	Tennessee	River Connection, Turntable	
Tennessee River					
Atlanta Division					
Atlanta	289	Fulton	Georgia	Southern, Georgia, CofGeorgia, Interchange with SAL Ry	
Howell	288	Fulton	Georgia	SAL Ry, L&N RR	
Hills Park	285	Fulton	Georgia	Yards	
Cleburne	284	Fulton	Georgia		
Bolton	282	Fulton	Georgia	Depot	
Chattahoochee River	281	Fulton	Georgia		
Iceville	280	Cobb	Georgia		
Gilmore	279	Cobb	Georgia	Flag Station	
Vinning	278	Cobb	Georgia	Depot, Siding	
McIvors	277	Cobb	Georgia		
Smyrna	274	Cobb	Georgia	Depot	

Station	Mile Marker	County	State	Facilities	Still Standing
Lockair	272	Cobb	Georgia		
Rosewood	270	Cobb	Georgia		
Marietta	269	Cobb	Georgia	Passenger and Freight Depot, Yards	Station
Elizabeth	267	Cobb	Georgia	Interchange w/ L&N RR	
Kennesaw	260	Cobb	Georgia	Depot, Siding	Station
Moon	258	Cobb	Georgia		
Acworth	254	Cobb	Georgia	Depot	Station
Ruby	251	Bartow	Georgia		
Allatoona	249	Bartow	Georgia	Depot	
Bartow	247	Bartow	Georgia		
Emerson	246	Bartow	Georgia	Depot	
Etowah	244	Bartow	Georgia	Section Houses	
Etowah River	243	Bartow	Georgia		
Cartersville	241	Bartow	Georgia	Depot, Yard, SAL Ry	Station
Junta	240	Bartow	Georgia		
Rogers	240	Barton	Georgia	Small Depot	
Atco	239	Bartow	Georgia		

Station	Mile Marker	County	State	Facilities	Still Standing
Cass	236	Bartow	Georgia	Depot	
Bests	235	Bartow	Georgia		
Cave	234	Bartow	Georgia	Small Freight Depot	
Gains Mill	233	Bartow	Georgia		
Kingston	230	Bartow	Georgia	Depot, Yard, Wye	
Halls	225	Bartow	Georgia	Depot, Siding	
Adairsville	220	Bartow	Georgia	Depot, Yard	Station
McDaniels	214	Gordon	Georgia	Siding	
Calhoun	211	Gordon	Georgia	Depot, Siding	Station
Oostanaula River	209	Gordon	Georgia		
Resaca	205	Gordon	Georgia	Depot, Siding	
Tilton	198	Gordon	Georgia	Depot	
Dalton	189	Gordon	Georgia	Passenger and Freight Depot, Yards, Section House	Freighthouse
Rocky Face	185	Gordon	Georgia	One-room Freight Depot	
Tunnel Hill Tunnel	183	Gordon	Georgia		
Tunnel Hill	182	Gordon	Georgia	Depot	Station
Catoosa	176	Gordon	Georgia		
Ringgold	174	Gordon	Georgia	Depot	Station

Station	Mile Marker	County	State	Facilities	Still Standing
Graysville	168	Gordon	Georgia	Depot	
State Line	167	Gordon	Georgia & Tennessee		
Chickamauga	162	Hamilton	Tennessee	Depot, Section Houses	
Whorley	160	Hamilton	Tennessee	Freight Station	
King's Bridge/Tyner	157	Hamilton	Tennessee	Siding	
Boyce	155	Hamilton	Tennessee	Depot, CNO&TP Ry	
Chattanooga	151	Hamilton	Tennessee	Union Depot	
Rome Branch of Atlanta Division					
Kingston	230	Bartow	Georgia	Station	
Wooleys	233	Bartow	Georgia		
Murchison	234	Bartow	Georgia		
Eves	237	Floyd	Georgia	Flag Station	
Bass Ferry	239	Floyd	Georgia	Flag Station	
Dykes	241	Floyd	Georgia		
Freeman	242	Floyd	Georgia	Flag Station	
Rome	248	Floyd	Georgia	Passenger and Freight Station	
Chattanooga Division					
Chattanooga	151	Hamilton	Tennessee	Union Depot	

Station	Mile Marker	County	State	Facilities	Still Standing
Cravens	149	Hamilton	Tennessee	Yards	
N.Y. Tower	148	Hamilton	Tennessee		
Lookout	147	Hamilton	Tennessee	Shelter	
Wauhatchie	145	Hamilton	Tennessee	Small Depot, Yard	
State Line	143	Hamilton	Tennessee & Georgia &Tennessee	Short section goes in and out of Georgia then in and out of Tennessee	
Hooker	141	Dale	Georgia	Yards	
State Line	140	Dale	Georgia & Tennessee		
Summit	139	Marion	Tennessee		
Etna Mines	138	Marion	Tennessee	Water Tank	
Whiteside	137	Marion	Tennessee	Depot	
Vulcan	134	Marion	Tennessee	One-room Depot	
Ladds	130	Marion	Tennessee	Depot	
Shellmound	129	Marion	Tennessee	Depot, Water Tower	
Moore's Crossing	127	Marion	Tennessee		
State Line	126	Marion	Tennessee & Alabama		
Long Island	125	Jackson	Alabama	Depot	
Draw Bridge	123	Jackson	Alabama	Depot	

Station	Mile Marker	County	State	Facilities	Still Standing
Tennessee River	122	Jackson	Alabama		
Bridgeport	122	Jackson	Alabama	Depot, Freight House, Yard	Station as Museum
Bolivar	117	Jackson	Alabama		
Stevenson	112	Jackson	Alabama	Passenger and Freight Depot, Hotel, Section House	Station
Cards	111	Jackson	Alabama		
Bass	106	Jackson	Alabama	Depot	
State Line	102	Jackson	Alabama & Tennessee		
Anderson	101	Franklin	Tennessee	Depot	
Sherwood	96	Franklin	Tennessee	Depot, Yard	
Tantallon	94	Franklin	Tennessee	Siding	
Rockridge	90	Franklin	Tennessee		
Cumberland Tunnel	89	Franklin	Tennessee		
Cowan	87	Franklin	Tennessee	Depot, Hotel, Yards	Station as Museum
Decherd	82	Franklin	Tennessee	Depot, Yard	
Estill Springs	77	Franklin	Tennessee	Depot, Yard	
Elsie	71	Coffee	Tennessee		
Tullahoma	69	Coffee	Tennessee	Passenger and Freight Depot, Stock Pens, Yards	Station

Station	Mile Marker	County	State	Facilities	Still Standing
Camp Forrest	67	Coffee	Tennessee		
Normandy	62	Bedford	Tennessee	Depot, Siding	
Cortner	61	Bedford	Tennessee	Depot	
Haley	58	Bedford	Tennessee	Depot, Section House	
Wartrace	55	Bedford	Tennessee	Passenger and Freight Depot, Stock Pens, Toolhouse	
Bell Buckle	51	Bedford	Tennessee	Passenger and Freight Depot, Yard	
Fosterville	45	Rutherford	Tennessee	Depot, Siding	
Christiana	42	Rutherford	Tennessee	Depot, Siding	
Rucker	38	Rutherford	Tennessee	Depot, Siding	
Winsted	36	Rutherford	Tennessee		
Murfreesboro	32	Rutherford	Tennessee	Depot, Section House, Yard	Station
Stones River	30	Rutherford	Tennessee		
National Cemetery	29	Rutherford	Tennessee	Shelter	
Russell	28	Rutherford	Tennessee		
Florence	26	Rutherford	Tennessee	Siding Depot	
Wade	22	Rutherford	Tennessee	Shelter	
Smyrna	20	Rutherford	Tennessee	Depot, Coal Shed	Station

Station	Mile Marker	County	State	Facilities	Still Standing
Jefferson Pike	18	Rutherford	Tennessee		
Lavergne	16	Rutherford	Tennessee	Depot, Yard	
Kimbro	14	Davidson	Tennessee		
Mt.View	12	Davidson	Tennessee		
Antioch	10	Davidson	Tennessee	Depot, Section House, Yard	
Asylum	8	Davidson	Tennessee		
Danley	7	Davidson	Tennessee	One-room Depot	
Curry	6	Davidson	Tennessee		
Glencliff	5	Davidson	Tennessee	One-room Depot, Yard	
Lebanon Junction	2	Davidson	Tennessee		
Nashville	0	Davidson	Tennessee		Terminal as Hotel

Cumberland River

Columbia Branch of Huntsville Division

Station	Mile Marker	County	State	Facilities	Still Standing
Decherd	82	Franklin	Tennessee	Depot, Yard	
Winchester	85	Franklin	Tennessee	Depot, Yard	Station
Kasserman	87	Franklin	Tennessee		
Belvidere	90	Franklin	Tennessee	Depot, Siding	Station

Station	Mile Marker	County	State	Facilities	Still Standing
Maxwell	94	Franklin	Tennessee	Depot	Station
Beans Creek	96	Franklin	Tennessee	Depot, Siding	
Huntland	98	Franklin	Tennessee	Depot, Stock Pens	
Elora	103	Lincoln	Tennessee	Depot, Section House, Start of the Huntsville Division	
Milner	105	Lincoln	Tennessee		
Flintville	108	Lincoln	Tennessee	Depot	
Brighton	110	Lincoln	Tennessee	Shelter	
Kelso	114	Lincoln	Tennessee	Depot, Stock Pens, Double Sidings	Station
Douglass	116	Lincoln	Tennessee		
Buchanan	117	Lincoln	Tennessee		
Fayetteville	122	Lincoln	Tennessee	Depot, Branch south to Capshaw Alabama, Wye, Section House	
Harris	125	Lincoln	Tennessee		
Howell	129	Lincoln	Tennessee	Depot	
Bidwell	131	Lincoln	Tennessee		
Petersburg	135	Lincoln	Tennessee	Depot	
Dahney	137	Marshall	Tennessee		
Talley	139	Marshall	Tennessee	Depot	Station as Barn

Station	Mile Marker	County	State	Facilities	Still Standing
Blackwell	142	Marshall	Tennessee		
Belfast	144	Marshall	Tennessee	Depot	Station
Orr	146	Marshall	Tennessee		
Lewisburg	150	Marshall	Tennessee	Depot, Connection with NW RR	
Ewing	151	Marshall	Tennessee	Boxcar Depot	
South Berlin	155	Marshall	Tennessee		
Silver Creek	157	Marshall	Tennessee	Section House	
Bryant	158	Maury	Tennessee	Depot	
Park	160	Maury	Tennessee		
Hill	162	Maury	Tennessee	Line between Columbia and Lewisburg removed in 1946	
Fountain Creek	163	Maury	Tennessee		
Blue Cut	165	Maury	Tennessee		
Rankin	166	Maury	Tennessee		
Columbia	170	Maury	Tennessee	Depot, Stock Pens, Coal Platform, Turntable and Small Yard Interchange at Columbia with L&N RR	Station
Fayetteville to Capshaw Branch of Huntsville Division					
Fayetteville	122	Lincoln	Tennessee	Depot	

Station	Mile Marker	County	State	Facilities	Still Standing
Harms	127	Lincoln	Tennessee		
Tillman	128	Lincoln	Tennessee		
Wilson	129	Lincoln	Tennessee		
Deford	131	Lincoln	Tennessee		
Pearl City	131	Lincoln	Tennessee		
Sumner	132	Lincoln	Tennessee		
Hobbs	133	Lincoln	Tennessee		
Coldwater	135	Lincoln	Tennessee	Depot	
Blanche	137	Lincoln	Tennessee		
Patterson	138	Lincoln	Tennessee	Depot	
Taft	141	Lincoln	Tennessee	Depot	
State Line	143	Lincoln	Tennessee & Alabama		
Norwood	144	Madison	Alabama		
Elkwood	147	Madison	Alabama		
Madison Cross Roads (Toney)	149	Madison	Alabama	Depot	Station
Jeff (Harvest)	152	Madison	Alabama		
Coalton	154	Madison	Alabama		

Station	Mile Marker	County	State	Facilities	Still Standing
Clark	155	Madison	Alabama		
Capshaw	158	Madison	Alabama		
Huntsville Branch of Huntsville Division					
Elora	103	Lincoln	Tennessee	Depot	
State Line	105	Lincoln	Tennessee & Alabama		
Roseboro	106	Madison	Alabama		
Plevna	108	Madison	Alabama	Depot	
Toliver	110	Madison	Alabama		
New Market	112	Madison	Alabama	Depot, Stock Pens	
Fanning	114	Madison	Alabama		
Deposit	116	Madison	Alabama	Depot	
Bell Factory	119	Madison	Alabama	Depot	
Mercury	123	Madison	Alabama	Depot	
Chase	124	Madison	Alabama	Depot	Station as Museum
Normal	125	Madison	Alabama	One-room Depot	
Huntsville	130	Madison	Alabama	Depot, Freight House, Yard, Interchange with Southern RR	
Redstone	134	Madison	Alabama		

Station	Mile Marker	County	State	Facilities	Still Standing
Lily Flagg	136	Madison	Alabama	Shelter	
Mathews	137	Madison	Alabama		
Rocket/Farley	140	Madison	Alabama	Original building moved to Rock Island Tennessee	
Burrows	142	Madison	Alabama	Cinder Platform	
Norton	143	Madison	Alabama		
Hobbs Island	144	Madison	Alabama	Depot	Station as House
Incline	144	Madison	Alabama	Ramp to Barges	

Tennessee River

Gadsden Branch of Huntsville Division

Tennessee River

Station	Mile Marker	County	State	Facilities	Still Standing
Gunther's Landing	165	Marshall	Alabama	Ramp to Barges	
Guntherville	167	Marshall	Alabama	Depot, Wye	Station as Museum
Wyeh City	168	Marshall	Alabama		
Rayburn	169	Marshall	Alabama		
Lane Switch	173	Marshall	Alabama		
McNarrows	174	Marshall	Alabama		
Albertville	177	Marshall	Alabama	Depot, Stock Pens, Section House	Station

Station	Mile Marker	County	State	Facilities	Still Standing
Sara	179	Marshall	Alabama	Carbody Depot	
Boaz	182	Etowah	Alabama	Depot, Water Tower	
Upton	185	Etowah	Alabama		
Mountainboro	186	Etowah	Alabama	Depot	
Carlisle	188	Etowah	Alabama	Section House	
Sligo	191	Etowah	Alabama	Carbody Depot	
Littleton	192	Etowah	Alabama		
Attalla	197	Etowah	Alabama	Depot	
Alabama City	201	Etowah	Alabama	L&N RR Yards	
Gadsden	203	Etowah	Alabama	Depot, Freight Depot, Interchange with L&N RR	

Sequatchie Valley Branch of Chattanooga Division

Station	Mile Marker	County	State	Facilities	Still Standing
Bridge port	123	Jackson	Alabama	Depot	
Orme Junction	125	Jackson	Alabama	Branch back to Orme	
State Line	125	Jackson	Alabama & Tennessee		
Richard City/ Copenhagen	126	Marion	Tennessee	Depot, Passenger Shelter, Section House	
South Pittsburg	129	Marion	Tennessee	Freight Depot	
Kimball	131	Marion	Tennessee		

Station	Mile Marker	County	State	Facilities	Still Standing
Browder	133	Marion	Tennessee		
Jasper	135	Marion	Tennessee	Depot, Section House	Station
Sequatchie	138	Marion	Tennessee	Shelter	
Victoria	142	Marion	Tennessee	Depot, Turntable for run to mine	Station as Home
Whitwell	146	Marion	Tennessee	Depot, Wye	
Sweetwater	147	Marion	Tennessee		
Shirleyton	149	Marion	Tennessee		
Harris	150	Marion	Tennessee		
Morganville	151	Marion	Tennessee		
Condra	152	Marion	Tennessee		
Cartwright	153	Sequatchie	Tennessee	Shelter, Water Tank	
Daus	156	Sequatchie	Tennessee	Depot, Passenger Shelter	
Dunlap	161	Sequatchie	Tennessee	Depot, Section House	
Brush Creek	163	Sequatchie	Tennessee		
Mt. Airy	166	Sequatchie	Tennessee	Shelter	
Pailo	168	Bledsoe	Tennessee		
Atpontley Junction	170	Bledsoe	Tennessee		

Station	Mile Marker	County	State	Facilities	Still Standing
College	172	Bledsoe	Tennessee	Depot	
Lees	175	Bledsoe	Tennessee	Depot	
Pikeville	180	Bledsoe	Tennessee	Depot	
Inman Branch					
Abandoned between 1900-1915					
Victoria	142	Marion	Tennessee	Depot	Station as Home
Hutton	146	Marion	Tennessee		
Inman	147	Marion	Tennessee		
Orme Branch of Chattanooga Division					
Orme Junction	125	Jackson	Alabama		
Johnson Crossing	127	Jackson	Alabama		
Cumberland	130	Jackson	Alabama	Depot	
Mt. Carmel	132	Jackson	Alabama		
Montague	133	Jackson	Alabama	Depot	
State Line	135	Jackson	Alabama & Tennessee		
Orme	136	Marion	Tennessee	Depot, Yards, Small Turntable	Station

Station	Mile Marker	County	State	Facilities	Still Standing
Tracy City Branch of Chattanooga Division					
Cowan	87	Franklin	Tennessee		Station as Museum
St. Marys	93	Franklin	Tennessee		
Sewanee	95	Franklin	Tennessee	Depot, Freight Depot	
St. Andrews	96	Franklin	Tennessee		
Sand Switch	97	Franklin	Tennessee		
Monteagle	101	Grundy	Tennessee		
Fairmont	102	Grundy	Tennessee		
Summerfield	103	Grundy	Tennessee	Shelter	
Clouse Hill	103	Grundy	Tennessee		
Hayes Crossing	105	Grundy	Tennessee		
Werner Spur	106	Grundy	Tennessee		
Tracy City	107	Grundy	Tennessee	Depot, Roundhouse, Section Houses	
Saunders	110	Grundy	Tennessee	Prior Ridge Branch - TC RR to Prior Ridge abandoned 1930	
Lockhart	115	Grundy	Tennessee	Several other mine spurs from TC abandoned in 1930s	
Coalmont	115	Grundy	Tennessee	Section House, Spur	
S.F.& I. Coal Company	117	Grundy	Tennessee		

Station	Mile Marker	County	State	Facilities	Still Standing
Swiss	118	Grundy	Tennessee		
Gruetli	119	Grundy	Tennessee	Depot, Passing Siding	
Luchsinger	120	Grundy	Tennessee		
Henleys Spur track	122	Grundy	Tennessee		
Collins	124	Grundy	Tennessee	Passenger and Freight Shelter, Passing Track, Siding	
Lick Branch Spur	125	Grundy	Tennessee		
Palmer	127	Grundy	Tennessee	Depot, Shelter House, Sawmill, Tipple, Water Tower, Wye, Yard	

Sparta Branch of Huntsville Division

Station	Mile Marker	County	State	Facilities	Still Standing
Tullahoma	69	Coffee	Tennessee	Station	Station
New Antwerp	72	Coffee	Tennessee	Spur	
Hickerson	73	Coffee	Tennessee		
Belmont	75	Coffee	Tennessee	Shelter	
Black Jack	76	Coffee	Tennessee	Siding	
Manchester	81	Coffee	Tennessee	Depot	
Forrest Mills	84	Coffee	Tennessee		
Summitville	89	Coffee	Tennessee	Depot, Section House	

Station	Mile Marker	County	State	Facilities	Still Standing
Albright	91	Coffee	Tennessee		
Morrison	94	Warren	Tennessee	Depot, Section House, Siding	Section House
Old Well	96	Warren	Tennessee	Carbody Depot	
Smarts (Smartt)	99	Warren	Tennessee	Depot, Siding	
Hickory Creek	102	Warren	Tennessee	Spur	
McMinnville	104	Warren	Tennessee	Depot, Section House	
Jones Crossing	107	Warren	Tennessee		
Rowland	110	Warren	Tennessee	Depot, Siding	
Campaign	114	Warren	Tennessee	Depot	
Rock Island	115	Warren	Tennessee	Depot	Station
Walling (Teeter)	117	Warren	Tennessee	Boxcar Depot	
Quebeck (Holders)	119	White	Tennessee	Depot	Station
Onward (Ward)	121	White	Tennessee	Stock Pens	
Doyle	123	White	Tennessee	Depot, Section House	
Moores	127	White	Tennessee		
East Sparta	130	White	Tennessee	Shelter	
Sparta	131	White	Tennessee	Brick Station, Siding, abandoned to Clifty mid 1930s	Station

Station	Mile Marker	County	State	Facilities	Still Standing
Price	133	White	Tennessee	Siding	
Mine #1	134	White	Tennessee	Spur	
Mine #4	134	White	Tennessee	Siding	
Rock House	135	White	Tennessee	Depot, 3 Section Houses, Boxcar Depot, Water Tank, Spur	Station as Museum
Bon Air	137	White	Tennessee	Depot, Spur, Mechanical Hoist to pull cars up the grade	
Tip Top	139	White	Tennessee	Siding	
DeRossett	141	White	Tennessee	Depot, Section Houses, Yard, Water Tank, Coal Chute, Wye	Station as House, 3 Section Houses
Ravenscroft	143	Putnam	Tennessee	Depot, Yard, Small 2 mile branch from DeRossett	
Sourwood	145	White	Tennessee	Platform	
Owens	146	White	Tennessee	Platform	
Eastland	148	White	Tennessee	Section House, Yard, Wye, Spur to mines	
Clifty	149	White	Tennessee	Depot, Spur to mines, Hotel	

Shelbyville Branch of Chattanooga Division

Station	Mile Marker	County	State	Facilities	Still Standing
Wartrace	55	Bedford	Tennessee	Passenger and Freight Depots	
Haliburton	56	Bedford	Tennessee		

Station	Mile Marker	County	State	Facilities	Still Standing
Greeley	56	Bedford	Tennessee	Passenger Shelter	Shelter
Bomarhill	57	Bedford	Tennessee		
Caldwell	58	Bedford	Tennessee		
Gray	59	Bedford	Tennessee		
Ebo	60	Bedford	Tennessee		
Sanders	60	Bedford	Tennessee		
Shelbyville	63	Bedford	Tennessee	Passenger and Freight Depots, Stock Pen	Station
Lebanon Branch of Chattanoooga Division					
Nashville	0	Davidson	Tennessee	Union Station	
Lebanon Junction	2	Davidson	Tennessee		
Woodycrest	2	Davidson	Tennessee	Shelter	
Easton	3	Davidson	Tennessee	Depot	
Mill Creek	5	Davidson	Tennessee		
Mud Tavern	6	Davidson	Tennessee	Enclosed Shelter	
Donelson	8	Davidson	Tennessee	Depot	
Hermitage	11	Davidson	Tennessee	Depot	
Tulip Grove	14	Davidson	Tennessee		

Station	Mile Marker	County	State	Facilities	Still Standing
Green Hill	15	Wilson	Tennessee	Depot	
Mount Juliet	17	Wilson	Tennessee	Depot, Passenger Shelter	
Silver Springs	21	Wilson	Tennessee	Water Tank	
Leeville	23	Wilson	Tennessee	Depot	Station
Tuckers Gap	25	Wilson	Tennessee	Depot	Station as Museum
Lillard	28	Wilson	Tennessee		
Lebanon	31	Wilson	Tennessee	Depot, Freight House	Station
Centerville Branch of Nashville Divison					
Dickson	42	Dickson	Tennessee	Depot, Freight House, Turntable, Stock Pens, Yard	Station
Colesburg	44	Dickson	Tennessee	Depot, Coal Chute, Water Tower	
Pomona	47	Dickson	Tennessee	Section House	
Tidwell	49	Dickson	Tennessee		
Ambrose	49	Dickson	Tennessee		
Iron Hill	50	Dickson	Tennessee		
Abiff	51	Hickman	Tennessee		
Bon Aqua	53	Hickman	Tennessee	Depot	
Lyle	59	Hickman	Tennessee	Depot, Section House	Station

Station	Mile Marker	County	State	Facilities	Still Standing
Bates	61	Hickman	Tennessee		
Rodemer	63	Hickman	Tennessee	Depot	
Brown	64	Hickman	Tennessee		
Graham	67	Hickman	Tennessee	Depot, 4 Section Houses	Section Houses
Nunnelly	69	Hickman	Tennessee	Depot, Stock Pens	
Goodrich	70	Hickman	Tennessee	Depot, Track Scales	
Elkins	71	Hickman	Tennessee		
Moore's	72	Hickman	Tennessee		
Grinders	73	Hickman	Tennessee	Depot	
Duck River	75	Hickman	Tennessee		
Centerville	76	Hickman	Tennessee	Depot, Stock Pens	Station
Twomey	77	Hickman	Tennessee	Depot, Scales, Coal Chute, Branch to mines	Section House
Wiss	78	Hickman	Tennessee		
Deans	78	Hickman	Tennessee	Section House	Section House
Watson	80	Hickman	Tennessee	Siding	
Buffalo	82	Hickman	Tennessee	Spur	
Aetna	85	Hickman	Tennessee	Depot, Section House	

Station	Mile Marker	County	State	Facilities	Still Standing
Kimmins	88	Lewis	Tennessee	Depot, Stock Pens	
Blondy	93	Lewis	Tennessee	Siding	
Theodore	94	Lewis	Tennessee	Wye, Siding	
Hohenwald	95	Lewis	Tennessee	Depot, Stock Pens	Station
Shubert	97	Lewis	Tennessee	Abandoned to Allen's Creek 1920s	
Lovel	98	Lewis	Tennessee		
Kitchens	100	Lewis	Tennessee		
McLean	101	Lewis	Tennessee		
Nancy	102	Lewis	Tennessee		
Howard	103	Lewis	Tennessee		
N. Riverside	103	Lewis	Tennessee		
Riverside	104	Lewis	Tennessee	Depot	
Allen's Creek	106	Lewis	Tennessee	Depot, Stock Pens	

Index

Note: cities and towns and references from the appendices are not included in this index

Bureaus, Commissions, Legislation, and Unions

Bank and Improvement Act: 14, 15
Brotherhood of Sleeping Car Porters: 72
Chattanooga Terminal Authority: 45
General Improvement Law: 78
Interstate Commerce Act: 33
Interstate Commerce Commission: 33, 37, 127
Jim Crow Laws: 73
Northwestern Land Association: 191
Railroad and Public Utilities Commission of Tennessee: 137, 138
Railway Retirement Act: 55
Southern & Western Convention: 16
United States Railroad Administration (USRA): 37, 38, 118, 120
Western Weighing and Inspection Bureau: 127

Camps, Events, Hotels, and Institutions

Burns House Hotel (Chattanooga): 112
Camp Campbell Military Post: 41, 106
Camp Forrest Military Post: 41, 106, 155
Chattanooga Choo-Choo Hotel (Chattanooga): 113
Dutchman's Curve (Accident): 38, 74, 109
Gone with the Wind (1939 Movie): 116
Great Locomotive Chase: 39, 231, 233, 235, 238
Great Locomotive Chase (1962 Movie): 243
Panic of 1837: 14, 16, 227
Panic of 1893: 95
Vanderbilt University: 54

Companies; Express

Adams Express Company: 37

American Express Company: 37
American Railway Express: 37
Railway Express Agency: 37, 57, 127
Southern Express Company: 37, 124, 231
Wells Fargo and Express Company: 37

Companies; Railroad Equipment and Terminals

American Locomotive Company: 43
Baldwin Locomotive Works: 43
Budd Company: 46
Chattanooga Station Company: 113
Electro-motive Diesel (EMD): 43, 51, 53
Louisville & Nashville Terminal Company: 98
Memphis Railroad Terminal Company: 36, 123
Pullman Equipment and Service: 34, 37, 46, 97, 122, 232

Companies; Railroads, Railways, and Mining

Atlanta & West Point Railroad: 115, 229, 230
Atlanta, Birmingham & Coast Railroad: 118
Atlantic Coast Lines Railroad: 29, 118, 120
Bon Air Railway: 190, 193
Campbell Coal & Coke Company: 34
Caney Fork & Western Railroad: 194
Central of Georgia Railroad: 28, 38, 45, 113, 118, 120
Chicago & Eastern Illinois Railroad: 210
Chicago, Memphis & Gulf Railroad: 172
Chicago, Burlington & Quincy Railway: 39, 209
Cincinnati, Alabama & Atlantic Railroad: 197
Duck River Valley Narrow Gauge Railroad: 26, 194, 195
East Tennessee & Georgia Railroad: 19, 110, 111, 113, 230
East Tennessee & Virginia Railroad: 19
Edgefield & Kentucky Railroad: 90
Four Rivers Transportation: 210
Gulf, Mobile & Northern Railroad: 39

Gulf, Mobile & Ohio Railroad: 39

Hickman & Obion Railroad: 19, 78, 165, 166

Illinois Central Railroad: 1, 34, 39, 44, 54, 85, 122, 125, 165, 166, 167, 171, 172, 173, 180, 182, 208, 210, 220

Kansas City, Fort Scott & Memphis Railroad: 121, 122

Kansas City, Memphis, & Birmingham Railroad: 121, 122

Kentucky & West Tennessee Railroad: 173, 212

Macon & Western Railroad: 115, 227, 228, 230

McMinnville & Manchester Railroad: 19, 26, 78, 190, 193, 194

Memphis & Charleston Railroad: 8, 14, 54, 85, 111, 113, 121, 127, 130, 139, 149, 171, 189, 230

Memphis & Ohio Railroad: 20, 121, 165, 166, 171

Memphis Branch Railroad & Steamboat Company: 233

Middle Tennessee & Alabama Railway: 197, 198

Missouri Pacific Railroad: 123, 127

Nashville & Clarksville Railroad: 142

Nashville & Eastern Railroad: 147

Nashville & Knoxville Railroad: 34, 35, 150, 171

Nashville & Northwestern Railroad: 19, 23, 24, 25, 51, 72, 77, 78, 83, 84, 89, 159, 160, 162, 163, 164, 165, 166, 180

Nashville & Owensboro Railroad: 30

Needmore Coal Company: 34, 140

New Orleans & Ohio Railroad: 164

Paducah, Tennessee & Alabama Railroad: 31, 83, 165, 209

Pea Vine Railroad: 212

Seaboard Railroad: 1

Sewanee Mining Company: 135, 136, 137

South Central Tennessee Railroad: 176

Southern Railroad: 30, 37, 45, 113, 118, 123, 124, 231, 232

Southwestern Railroad: 190, 193

St. Louis Southwestern Railroad: 123

Tennessee Central Railway: 34, 35, 54, 150, 151, 171, 172, 173, 174, 176

Tennessee Coal & Railroad Company: 135, 136, 140

Tennessee Consolidation Coal Company: 136

Tennessee Midland Railroad: 16, 31, 84, 121, 122, 208, 209, 216, 217, 221, 224
United States Military Railroad: 21, 23, 24, 25, 72, 77, 163, 164, 189, 193, 223, 229
Walking Horse & Eastern Railroad: 133
Western Point Route Railroad: 118, 120
Winchester & Alabama Railroad: 19, 26, 78, 188, 189, 190, 193, 194, 195, 202

Individuals

Andrews, James: 233, 238
Arnold, William Ernest: 67
Barney, A. E.: 134, 135
Baxter, Jere: 34, 142, 143
Beckman, Benjamin: 116
Berg, Walter G.: 87
Bilbo, William N.: 134
Blodgett, Foster: 231
Bragg, Braxton: 21, 22, 193, 229
Brown, Joseph: 231
Brownlow, William G.: 78
Bruce, W. P.: 211
Bullock, Rufus: 231
Burns, Michael: 25, 170, 171
Butts, Joseph: 2
Butts, Samuel A.: 1, 2, 3
Calhoun, John C.: 16
Clark, M. P.: 171
Cole, Edmund W.: 27, 28, 29, 30, 54, 78, 232
Corput, Max: 117
Crabtree, F. E.: 55
Crawford, Alexander: 141, 142
Darden, Clarence M.: 43, 46, 47
Forrest, Nathan Bedford: 29, 76, 168, 170
Fuller, William A.: 231, 233, 238
Galvin, John A.: 124
Gardner, John A.: 166

Gibbs, George Washington: 165
Grant, Charles: 97
Grant, James H.: 75, 76
Hall, Fitzgerald: 41
Heiman, Adolphus: 90, 91
Hood, John Bell: 23, 170, 229, 230, 231
Jackson, Andrew: 13, 15, 206
Johnston, Joseph E.: 22, 229
Kennedy, Leslie: 134
LeHardy, Eugene: 111
Lewis, Eugene C.: 31, 34, 93, 94, 95, 99, 100, 101, 102, 103
Linck, W. T.: 90
Long, Stephen Harriman: 114
Lumpkin, Wilson: 226, 227
Mitchell, Samuel: 115, 116
Monfort, Richard: 99, 100, 103
Morgan, John Hunt: 29, 76, 168
Morrow, C. S.: 52
Overton, Dr. James: 17
Porter, James D.: 30
Richardson, Romanesque: 99, 112
Richardson, Henry Hobson: 87, 99
Scarbrough, J. F.: 62
Schley, William: 114, 226
Sherman, William T.: 23, 116, 117, 120, 229, 230
Smith, Milton: 102
Smith, William C.: 92, 95, 112, 189, 201
Spurlock, J. M.: 111
Stahlman, E. B.: 94
Stanton, Edwin M.: 168, 169
Stevens, Alexander: 231
Stevenson, Vernon K.: 8, 9, 18, 19, 29, 71, 75, 93, 97, 129, 133, 160, 161
Thomas, Sr., John W.: 31, 47, 95
Thomson J. Edgar: 129, 133

Tilford, John E.: 53
Tracy, Samuel F.: 134
Vanderbilt, Cornelius William H.: 87
Wright, Virgil: 62

Newspapers

Atlanta Constitution: 118
Nashville American: 103
Nashville Banner: 94
Nashville Tennessean: 53, 94

Railroad Operating Procedures and Tracks

Centralized Traffic Control (CTC): 43, 44, 60, 65, 68, 69, 133, 178, 232
Form 19: 67
Form 31: 67
Order Hoop: 67
Semaphore Signal: 68
"The Windy" (Nashville Division): 12, 165, 173
T-rail: 229, 230
U-rail: 230

Stations, Terminals, and Yards

Central Station (Memphis): 122, 125, 127
City Yards (Chattanooga): 36
Cowan Tunnel (Cowan): 71, 130, 134
Cravens Yard (Chattanooga): 36, 37, 45, 151, 154
Cummins Station (Nashville): 105, 106
Kayne Avenue Yards (Nashville): 53, 100, 104, 105, 106, 107
Mercury Statue (Nashville Union Station): 101, 102
Terminal Station (Atlanta): 38, 118, 120, 121
Terminal Station (Chattanooga): 45, 113
Terminal Station Tennessee Centennial (Nashville): 96
Union Station (Atlanta): 39, 60, 117, 118, 119, 120, 121
Union Station (Chattanooga): 35, 45, 111, 112, 113

Union Station (Memphis): 36, 60, 122, 123, 124, 125, 126, 127

Union Station (Nashville): 23, 33, 35, 41, 53, 60, 90, 92, 93, 94, 98, 99, 100, 101, 102, 103, 104, 105, 106, 107, 109, 145, 161, 167, 175, 242

Trains, Locomotives, and Cars

"576" Locomotive: 52, 92

Hopper Car: 41, 193

Jim Crow Car: 73, 74

"Marie" Locomotive: 47, 50

"Old Smoky" Train: 52

Powder Puff Special: 145

Pullman Sleeping Car Company: 48, 127

Railway Post Office (RPO): 212, 229

"Tennessee" Locomotive: 129

City of Memphis Train: 13, 46, 47, 50, 53, 60, 74, 88, 107, 125

Dixie Express Train: 118, 232

Dixie Flagler Train: 49, 88, 105, 107, 118

Dixie Flyer Train: 34, 37, 38, 40, 60, 88, 105, 118, 182, 232

Dixie Limited Train: 88, 105, 107, 118, 232

Dixie Mail Train: 105, 118

Dixieland Train: 118

Flamingo Train: 88, 118

Georgian Train: 60, 88, 89, 114

Hummingbird Train: 105

Lookout Train: 46, 88, 211

Pan American Train: 105

Quickstep Train: 46

Southland Train: 88, 118

Tennessean Train: 128

Volunteer Train: 88

"William R. Smith" Locomotive: 233

www.ingramcontent.com/pod-product-compliance
Lightning Source LLC
Chambersburg PA
CBHW081150290426
44108CB00018B/2497